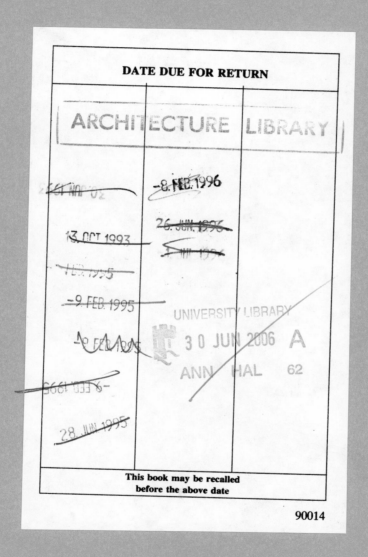

DATE DUE FOR RETURN

ARCHITECTURE LIBRARY

-8. FEB. 1996

13. OCT 1993   26. JUN. 1996

-9. FEB. 1995

UNIVERSITY LIBRARY

3 0 JUN 2006   A

ANN HAL   62

28. JUN 1995

**This book may be recalled
before the above date**

90014

New Zealand
Architecture

FROM POLYNESIAN BEGINNINGS TO 1990

FOREWORD

The Fletcher Construction Group is proud to provide sponsorship support for this book, which celebrates New Zealand's diverse architectural heritage.

Fletcher's long association with New Zealand's physical environment began just after the turn of the century, when my father, James Fletcher, stepped ashore in Dunedin as a 22-year-old Scottish immigrant. He had just £12 and a bag of tools but, most importantly, he had an operating philosophy — handed down through four generations of builders — of never building a job 'you have to run past'.

From small beginnings, Fletcher Construction has grown with this country's building industry and is proud to have been associated with a significant number of the buildings featured in this book. This has involved working with some colourful individuals within the architectural and engineering professions. One such character was Timaru architect Herbert Hall, designer of Chateau Tongariro, of whom my father had this to say:

> No architect organised more building with less drawings than he. Every morning he would arrive in our drawing office, immaculately dressed, with a flower in his button hole. With a few swift pencil sketches and an occasional word of criticism the plans quickly came together. Later when Hall was ill and additional details for the building were urgently required, he supplied them from his sick-bed carefully drawn on a roll of toilet paper. A note explained: 'They would not allow me to work, but this they could not remove.'

Nowadays architects are more likely to be found in front of CadCam machines carrying out wind and shadow tests or working on three-dimensional cross sections of a building. However, many of the requirements for a good architect remain unchanged: an intuitive feeling for what works in design, an ability to relate to people and work as part of a team and to deliver an end product that meets the client's needs.

The challenge for New Zealand architecture as it nears a new century will be to build on the successes of the past and to learn from the failures. This book plays a very important role in this regard. I hope it encourages us all to focus on structures that we can — again to paraphrase the words of my father — walk past with pride.

Sir James Fletcher

FLETCHER CONSTRUCTION

New Zealand
Architecture

FROM POLYNESIAN BEGINNINGS TO 1990

Peter Shaw

PHOTOGRAPHS BY
Robin Morrison

Every building tells a story, tells it plainly.
With what startling clearness it speaks to the attentive ear,
how palpable its visage to the open eye, it may take you some time to perceive.
But it is all there, waiting for you.

Louis Sullivan
Kindergarten Chats

Hodder & Stoughton

AUCKLAND LONDON SYDNEY TORONTO

The publishers gratefully acknowledge
the support of The Fletcher Construction Co. Ltd
in the production of this book.

Designed by Donna Hoyle
Typeset by Typocrafters Ltd, Auckland
Printed and bound by Everbest Printing Co. Ltd,
Hong Kong, for Hodder & Stoughton Ltd,
46 View Rd, Glenfield, Auckland, New Zealand

CONTENTS

ACKNOWLEDGEMENTS

To list the names of all the people who have allowed Robin Morrison and me to peer about in their gardens and houses would occupy many pages. We were continually delighted by the generous response they gave our requests to invade their privacy.

No less important was the contribution of librarians in public institutions throughout New Zealand. In particular I should like to thank Wendy Garvey, Bruce Howie and the staff of the University of Auckland School of Architecture Library for their support, interest and tireless efforts over a long period. Anyone who writes about New Zealand architecture owes a considerable debt to the work done by Dr Ian Lochhead at the School of Fine Arts, University of Canterbury, in teaching, writing, and encouraging students to produce theses on architectural subjects. I am most grateful for his help in unravelling difficult problems of chronology and fact. At the National Library of New Zealand, Wellington, both Walter Cook and Joan McCracken were generous with time and information. The New Zealand Historic Places Trust allowed me full access to its files on individual buildings and I am indebted to Michael Kelly for his help during my research trips to Wellington.

Many individuals have given me invaluable assistance. Cecil Badley, Dr Michael Bassett, Peter Beaven, Maru Bing, Roger Blackley, David Broad, Leslie Vernon Brown, Carol Bucknell, Revd Wesley A. Chambers, Pip Cheshire, Chris Cochran, Marshall Cook, Michael Findlay, James Hackshaw, Rodney Hamel, Elizabeth Hinds, Terry Hitchcock, Ivan Juriss, Johannes La Grouw, Martin Lodge, Lynne Logan, Clive Lucas, O.B.E., Owen McShane, Jonathan Mane-Wheoki, Bruce Petry, Gail Pittaway, Dr Nigel Prickett, Dr I. V. Porsolt, David Reynolds, John Stacpoole, Jeremy Salmond, Alice Strauss, Di Stewart, Linda Tyler, Sir Miles Warren, Richard White and Pam Wilson all deserve thanks. I am grateful to Arikinui Dame Te Atairangikaahu for permission to photograph at Turangawaewae, Ngaruawahia.

It has been a pleasure to collaborate with such an architectural enthusiast as Robin Morrison. Donna Hoyle, the book's designer, brought great experience and sensitivity to her difficult task. Tom Beran and Alison Dench at Hodder & Stoughton were always patient and encouraging; I have many reasons to be grateful for their expertise. Michael Christini made an intensive period of research in the summer of 1988/89 a very enjoyable rather than merely gruelling experience. Coral Shaw read the manuscript chapter by chapter and offered a great deal of valuable advice, all of it gratefully heeded. Andrew and Miriam Shaw were tolerant of interruptions to domestic routine and many car journeys made suddenly perilous at the sight of an unusual building.

AUTHOR'S NOTE

Vincent Scully wrote in *American Architecture and Urbanism* that 'since civilisation is based largely upon the capacity of human beings to remember, the architect builds visible history'. This book is a history which, perhaps unfashionably, selects significant buildings from the past and holds them up chronologically for evaluative comment.

I have resisted the temptation to make it appear that New Zealand's architectural history unfolded along a tidy continuum, when, in fact, events more often than not proceeded haphazardly and without logic. Early settlers, tipped on to beaches at New Plymouth in 1840, had to make do as best they could using leftover whalers' dwellings or raupo whare built by Maori; they were not supplied with some kind of Victorian kitset cottage, but had to adapt what little they knew about building to the materials at hand. Fortuitous, too, was the fact that Louis Hay of Napier owned a copy of the Wasmuth folios of the work of Frank Lloyd Wright or that later architects Sir Miles Warren and Terence Hitchcock chose to go to Scandinavia in the late 1950s in pursuit of contemporary buildings which might be adapted to New Zealand conditions. Similarly, state-sponsored housing in New Zealand might have been very different without the arrival of Modernist architects from Central Europe, who came here to get as far away as possible from the Nazis. Chance has played a significant role in determining the changing appearance of our buildings, and the process of recording such changes should reflect the fact.

That there is a need for some kind of exposition of the country's architectural history is evident from a number of popular misconceptions, such as the one which has it that only the very oldest buildings are worthy of preservation. The frequently stated conviction of the owners of Gummer & Ford's unique 1940 State Insurance Building that their former head office is of no historic importance and a suitable case for demolition is an example of this attitude. Mainzeal's stealthy demolition in June 1990 of Alva Bartley and Imi Porsolt's 1939 Broadcasting House in Auckland and Brierley's of the 1920 Edmonds Factory, Christchurch, are further evidence of the lack of informed respect for our architectural heritage.

As the composer Martin Lodge observed of our only recently documented musical history, 'tradition is another word for the usable past; it is the function of historical writing to make the past available and usable'. Very little of the old Maori architecture survives today — until comparatively recently it was hardly intended that it should — but historic marae buildings are now frequently the subject of careful restoration. New Zealand's European-derived architectural history may be short but it should be accorded the same respect we now give as a matter of course to our native forests, lakes, mountains and rivers.

INTRODUCTION
by Peter Beaven

Sixty years ago in the Canterbury Museum, but removed now, there was a model of a Maori pa. In the green glass water there were lines disappearing down to little wooden fish. The brilliantly coloured palisades were surmounted by bulging heads staring directly at you, their tongues touching your mind. What a statement of identity this was, a panoply of visual icons as powerful as Olivier's field at Agincourt. This book is about identity and the search for a full and creative architectural response to a benign and beautiful land. The search is as uneven and wayward as you would expect such natural beauty to demand.

New Zealand was not only a country for making new fortunes; there was always intense public debate about the form and shape of the new cities and informed discussion raged on the correct architectural styles for major new buildings. Always there was profound insight shown in the creation of *real places* in the cities: Hagley Park in Christchurch and the Botanic Gardens in Wellington amply illustrate a sensitivity to both cultural roots and the notion of real place.

The history of the Ministry of Works is the history of the creative and pragmatic concerns of this new country. The rapid development of rail transport and the increase in government administrative bureaucracy, which began in the 1880s and continued until the outbreak of the First World War, led to the designing of many important new buildings. The Ministry of Works gathered some of the most talented architects in the country to work in a studio atmosphere, there to produce architectural monuments that celebrated an emerging nation's confidence. Clayton's magnificently eclectic Gothic Parliament Buildings could have stood with calm certainty by the River Thames beside the Mother Parliament. Campbell's erudite mastery of styles still shows in the Auckland Chief Post Office, Dunedin's Supreme Court and the Wellington Public Trust.

The accession of the first Labour Government in 1935 created a monolith of the Ministry of Works, expanding its power as a method of directly controlling funds and building. For over forty years all planning had to march in file to the functional style. New Zealand's confidence rolled over and slept; the quickest minds left the country and the Ministry of Works became the patriarch. A nine-to-five mentality took over the old studio concept and repetition and standardisation took over architecture — all this in what had been a most individualistic country.

This post-war lack of style and minimal use of architectural history, this departure from the very idea of building as an art form, was encouraged by Vernon Brown, senior lecturer at the School of Architecture in Auckland, and the enthusiastic gathering of like-minded students called the Group. I knew Vernon in 1943, his first year lecturing at the school. He was a man in the best English tradition: eccentric and visually flamboyant, with a Bloomsbury-ish breadth of social and artistic erudition and a nimble mind for all occasions. Because he was wholly devoted to style, he did not need an architectural style. He cocooned the post-war search for an existential, abstract reality in fun and wit. The Group was the Modern Movement personified; their shed architecture was linked to an ordinary vernacular of Mondrian-like formal abstractions. If you don't have to exhaust yourself all day in a drawing office, such reduction of architecture to functional minimalism can be highly diverting.

Thatcher and Mountfort, trained Gothic architects, translated the great, northern, light-flooded cathedrals into works of local genius; they sensed that the truthfulness and optimism of the style were well suited to a new colonial society. Their church interiors are shaded against the bright light; they are sculptured with remarkable originality and almost casually made to suit the available skills. No less impressive are the geometric shapes of Parnell, the village atmosphere and romantic passages of the Christchurch Provincial Chambers, the stunning pure wooden sculpture at Old St Paul's in Wellington, and the extraordinary maturity of St Mary's Procathedral in Auckland.

This wooden procathedral originally settled down the hill slope in a geometry of descending mouldings and, at the eastern end, vertical apses rose in a cluster to form the perfect contrast to the sinking west end. I can recall no building in New Zealand resting more beautifully on its site. The ruthless shifting of this masterpiece to a flat site beside the banal new cathedral lost us a precious icon to our capacity for making real places, and licensed two decades of deliberate demolition of our colonial inheritance.

Travelling in about 1970 with the Civic Trust and the South Island Tourist Board to Mt Cook to try to stop the Ministry of Works from demolishing the Hermitage Hotel and shifting the old Mt Cook village to a position out of sight of the mountain, I stopped at the just-completed Aviemore Dam. The water was only just beginning to rise and there in front of us was the wall of the dam, a cathedral of concrete and metal excellence. Refined in the studios of the Ministry of Works, untrammelled by cost control or criticism, and about to be buried in a watery tomb, it was a testament to the skills of this remarkable country.

The Futuna Chapel of John Scott was the very first modern building in New Zealand to bring one's whole sensibility alive. One knew Ronchamp from pictures; one knew the gradual formal advance towards the Maori meeting-house; one knew to boring extinction the standard building details of the Ministry of Works; and of course one knew the colour-splashed interiors of Christchurch's Gothic buildings. Suddenly here was a building which in completely new form held all these understandings in transparent release.

I remember driving with Roger Walker past two of his partly built houses. The builders waved cheerily as we went by and then bent down immediately to run another brace over a window or insert another concrete drainpipe. Walker and Ian Athfield created a simple system by breaking a house into its separate elements, enabling many different assemblies of stairs, inglenooks, chimneys, and conical and geometric roofs on any site, to suit both pocket and, more importantly, available energy.

These fairytale assemblages of natural material, bright paint and astonishment arose on the dark green foothills of Wellington, cocking a snook at the commercial and authoritarian banalities below. They caused a state of shock among those architects who knew the past, because they were most truthful to classical history. The work of Walker and Athfield has resulted in a true people's architecture. It has led us directly to the hillsides and subdivisions of today, which are covered with kitset architecture endlessly reshuffled and flavoured with dashes of Post-modern classical history, Los Angeles Pop, L.A. Law or Miami Vice.

Miles Warren returned from England in 1958 with a brilliant collection of stylish methods suitable to fill the void he knew existed here. Whitewashed blockwork supporting fair-face concrete grids came from Brutalism; beautifully jointed artefacts of the richest kind, planes of mahogany, brass connectors and the best accessories came from Finn Juhl and the Danish school. Possibly the greatest contribution of all was the restatement of the exposed timber structures and Gothic roof spaces of early Christchurch. An architectural style for all seasons was created and supported by a vigorous office system of clever standardisation. The office grew to be the country's biggest but never departed from the primary concepts. From the almost ramshackle assembly of components at the Auckland Student Union to the taut collegiate square of Christchurch College, the judicious use of tradition, structure and the best materials provided a release from the functionalist grip and appealed immediately to those with the money and privilege to state their separateness from those around them.

Warren & Mahoney have maintained the big office characteristics of the Ministry of Works and placed architecture strongly in the field of disciplined pragmatism and business management. As a direct result, in the last few years their style has become international Post-modernist. I believe, however, that New Zealand is better served with smaller offices working in a creative regional context.

Where are the patrons who see the natural ornament of their success in fine architecture? The record of the great investment companies is dismal. Robert Jones has never produced a good building while Brierley's record of destruction of our urban heritage is disgraceful. All the buildings of real excellence in our history have come from enlightened individuals or from the humane institutions of education and religion. How differently things are done in successful small countries such as Finland and Switzerland. As an egalitarian culture we have succeeded brilliantly — nearly all our buildings, commercial or domestic, have been the work of engineers or draughtsmen! Their solutions are simple and can be seen in the ranks of banal office buildings standing alone in the accidental leftover bits of a once close-knit Victorian street.

In this pragmatic world we desperately need creative architecture — otherwise we reduce the pleasure in life. At the weekend in Christchurch the Arts Centre at the old University, the Victorian public gardens of Hagley Park, and Mountfort's Canterbury Museum, provide the best public architectural environment in New Zealand. It is usually crowded with people.

Architecture must again become concerned with the creation of art objects. The most creative, historically informed and dedicated architects must be the ones to design public buildings and public spaces. Our Institute of Architects must shake off its obsessive management role to concentrate on the promotion of the finest architecture; it must encourage criticism and debate and set standards of excellence. Creative architects have their own survival built in; they don't need to be taken by the hand. In New Zealand there are short periods of cheap money which produce cheap buildings, then nothing much happens until the next mini-boom. We don't need directive planning and we certainly don't need zoning and other restrictive ordinances. These simply make it easier to give up the possibility of real dialogue about the making of cities.

In old Christchurch the big factories had public gardens round them. They were placed in suburbs to be near the workers — how sensible, and what a saving on roading costs. We need to plan our cities in detail, using advisory committees of informed people, and we need display centres where the history of environmental debates can be viewed. Town planning in a slow-growth country should be a matter of urban design devoted to the creation of beautiful places by filling the gaps left by the old uncreative planning system, which could never preserve a good environment. Such procedures as we have today do almost nothing to encourage great architecture, becoming instead the perfect tool of the greedy speculator.

Dunedin is the best-preserved city in New Zealand, where the traditional buildings and colonial open spaces still dominate. I went there recently after ten years' absence and found that a brilliant, modern refinement and certainty exists in all the important new buildings. The old buildings have rich colours, some picking out the detail, others sweeping across the facades to create a bold geometry. Tim Heath's delicate Hi-Tec extension to Otago University's Psychology Department floats between colonial cottages. Lawson's Town Hall has been faithfully refurbished by the City Architect; messy alterations over the years have been removed and replaced with new spatial effects in which a ringing certainty obtains. Ashley Muir's Oncology Centre has splendid classical weight and mass with delicate, almost Lawson-like mouldings and a floating, tiled roof-light. The Works Consultancy architects of the shelters in the Octagon searched the world for suitable cast-iron litter bins and lamp standards; these are joined by perfect arched canopies like old trams yet never seen before.

Dunedin is a proud city weighted with the persistent memory of history. There, real places both old and new are held in that respect which is civilisation.

CHAPTER ONE
Raupo, Timber and Stone

Rangiatea
(page 22)

A history of the architecture of New Zealand must begin with the buildings of the tangata whenua, the people of the land. The indigenous Maori developed a distinctive architecture in communities centred on a variety of specialised buildings, some of them richly carved. These buildings were keenly observed by early explorers, and several left colourful and accurate written and visual accounts of what they saw.

The first inhabitants of Aotearoa were groups of Polynesian explorers who discovered and settled these islands in the period A.D. 800–1000. The new arrivals in an empty land probably did not take up a nomadic way of life, but recreated the communities they had just left. They established small, permanent settlements well suited to their familiar life of gardening and sea fishing. There is archaeological evidence of coastal and river-mouth settlements throughout New Zealand, particularly on the east coast of the Coromandel Peninsula, along the Hawke's Bay and Wairarapa coasts and down the east coast of the South Island.

Ethnographic evidence indicates that Maori architecture was extremely diverse, despite the limitations imposed by stone tools and available materials. There were many forms of buildings, including temporary lean-tos, dwellings and sheds both round and rectangular, cooking sheds, and rectangular buildings made of poles and thatch or carefully fashioned timbers.

Anthropologist Te Rangi Hiroa, also known as Sir Peter Buck, regarded the round structures as makeshift and of little interest except for the fact that they could be built quickly and without ceremony. The rectangular buildings, however, were quite another matter. Generically known as whare, these more permanent buildings were characterised by a very small door, an extension of roof and walls at the door end to form a porch, and an internal plan with one or more hearths down the centre and sleeping places down the sides. The whare was a repository of tapu which was indistinguishable from that of its owner. One such prehistoric whare was excavated in the Moikau Valley, Palliser Bay, in 1971–72.

The Moriori people of the Chatham Islands, who shared a common ancestry with the Maori, had evolved a culture of their own after being isolated from the mainland since the fourteenth century. They too used a form of lean-to dwelling during the summer months, but in winter they used the rectangular structure, sometimes with a sunken floor and earth piled up around exterior walls for warmth.

As the Polynesian settlers adapted to the resources available in their new country, to the cooler climate and the larger land area, a specifically Maori culture evolved. The built forms which were established then persisted without significant change, so that the twelfth-century Moikau house bears remarkable similarities in both use of materials and method of construction to those seen by the first European explorers. When they encountered the Maori in the eighteenth century they found a race of warlike people who lived either in kainga (villages) or in fortified pa, and cultivated the land and harvested the sea. Most of the pa were in the North Island, where there were in excess of 6000; in the South Island the number was much smaller. Some were used only once; others were reoccupied many times following attacks.

From 9 October 1769, when Captain James Cook's *Endeavour* anchored off Turanga, now the city of Gisborne, the Maori were the subject of ever-increasing written and pictorial analysis. The most important early descriptions of Maori architecture were made in April 1772 by Jean Roux, an ensign on board the French ship *Mascarin*, which sailed with the *Marquis de Castries* to the Bay of Islands under the command of Marc-Joseph Marion du Fresne. Unlike earlier explorers, du Fresne decided to establish camps on shore.

He was equipped with a Tahitian vocabulary, which made conversation with the Maori possible; as a confirmed believer in Rousseau's idea of the Noble Savage, he was undeterred by the sight of twenty fortified pa in the area. Nearby there were large trees suitable for refitting spars and masts before his two ships began their proposed exploration of the Pacific. Because of the leisurely pace, Ensign Roux had time to look around and to record his observations.

Among other things their houses prompted our admiration, so skilfully were they made. They were rectangular in shape and varied in size according to need. The sides were stakes set at a short distance from one another and strengthened by switches which were interlaced across them. They were coated on the outside with a layer of moss thick enough to prevent water and wind from getting in and this layer was held up by a well-constructed little lattice. The interior was woven with a matting of sword grass on which there were at intervals, by way of ornament as well as to support the roof, little poles or, more accurately, planks, two or three inches thick and rather well carved. In the middle of the house there was also a big carved pole which supported the weight of the roof (together with two others at the two ends). What surprised us still further was that the whole construction was mortised and very strongly bound together with their sword grass ropes. On the centre pole was a hideous figure, a sort of sea devil. As we have found this figure in all their houses and in the very same place, which seems consecrated to it, there is every reason to presume that it is their divinity that is represented under this form.

Each house had a sliding door, so low that we had virtually to lie down to enter. Above it there were two small windows and a very fine lattice. Running right around the outside was a little ditch for water to flow in. Their houses are roofed with reeds; in some of them was a rather poorly made cot and inside it some very dry straw that they sleep on. In front of each door three stones were to be seen, forming a sort of hearth where they would make a fire: there was another stone a little way off, which they would use to grind their red pigment. I had the post taken from one of these houses; it was very well carved . . .[1]

What Roux described was a Maori whare. Unlike the houses of earlier times, this one had distinctive side walls. In this type of whare, the pou tahu or ridgeposts and tahu or ridgepole were often made of totara, while the framework would be constructed of manuka saplings tied to the ridgepole with vines. Walls were raupo bundles sewn to the manuka framework; the roof thatching was also of overlapping bundles of raupo, laid so that rain would run off efficiently. The tiny doorway was designed to contain the warmth.

Roux's whare was unusually elaborate in having two windows and a carved tahu. There is a distinct possibility that he was shown a chief's whare, as neither carvings nor the provision of a bed were common in other whare. Whare were used for specific functions and took their names accordingly, for example, whare wananga (learning), whare pora (weaving) and whare taua (mourning).

If Roux was able to remain relatively objective in his description of Maori domestic architecture, his aristocratic countryman Lieutenant Théodore de Blois de la Calande had no qualms about recording very different reactions. In the journal he kept during the April 1824 visit to the Bay of Islands of the *Coquille* under the command of Louis-Isidore Duperrey, he wrote:

You cannot imagine anything dirtier and more revolting than the huts of these savages. A single room makes up the whole house and contains rotten fish, meat, dried and reeking, prepared fern roots and in the midst of all that some poor quality mats, on which the occupants of the house all sleep higgledy-piggledy. All the huts have weapons and paddles hung about on all sides. Dogs, fleas and the most disgusting vermin succeed in making these hovels unbearable for the European.[2]

The Maori also constructed larger whare puni, or sleeping-houses, which consisted not only of ridgepoles and ridgeposts of dressed timber but also a timber framework of poupou, or wall posts, and epa, or end posts. These houses often had a verandah at the front to which were attached maihi (bargeboards), which were carved or painted and surmounted by a carved human figure called a tekoteko, perhaps Roux's sea devil. The interior verandah walls of these more elaborate whare puni were often lined with panels of red-dyed kakaho. The interior walls of the whare itself were sometimes decorated with geometric patterns made from bracken and fern stems, flax, and kiekie, a climbing plant. These panels were known as tukutuku and were made by women.

The whare whakairo, a carved meeting-house, was a more elaborate version of the whare puni, distinguished from it in terms of function and decoration. The structure reflected tribal status and dignity, though early meeting-houses tended to be smaller than those built today. A whare

J. W. Giles (after) George French Angas (1822–86), House of Iwikau, brother of Te Heuheu, and Falls of Ko Waihi at Te Rapa, Taupo Lake, *1844. Hand-coloured lithograph.*
AUCKLAND CITY ART GALLERY COLLECTION.
The artist's caption: A red dwelling house, of Maori architecture, with a savage image adorning the summit of its gabled verandah, stands overlooking the broad expanse of the lake — now blue as the vault of heaven that overhangs it . . . the inner apartment consists of a spacious sleeping chamber, which has no orifice besides the door and window opening on to the verandah . . . where food is eaten in wet weather.

whakairo was built under the supervision of a tohunga (priest). The whole process was tapu and had to be abandoned if a woman or a slave entered the whare before it was complete. Building began with the placement of the pou tuarongo and pou tahu, the back and front ridgeposts. These were made from half tree-trunks, with the convex sides facing inwards so that they could be carved. A triangular tahu was placed on the ridgepoles, then the poupou were set in the ground and braced to act as vertical cantilevers. Heke (rafters) did not sit over the posts but were notched between the poupou and then lashed to them. Framing was completed with kaho (wooden battens) and papaka (skirting boards), which were fitted between the poupou. These were not fixed to the heke but were fastened together by ropes.

The thatching, tapatu, consisted of an internal lining of toetoe screens laid over the purlins and tied to them; this was covered with a layer of raupo and the layering process repeated until the desired thickness was reached. According to A. Hamilton, author of the earliest authoritative book on Maori art and architecture, each layer had a name, the last layer being known as the ara whiuwhiu, but in some cases there might have been only two such layers. Tukutuku lined the interior walls.

The structure projected from the front wall to form a porch (whakamahau), the sides of which were sometimes slightly narrower than the rest of the building. The front wall contained a single sliding door and a window; the maihi and their

supports, the amo, were often completely carved. The raparapa (the projecting portion of the bargeboard) often had pierced carving. Sometimes interior rafters were painted with pigments of yellow, red and black, mixed with shark oil.

Although these whare must have had dark interiors and been ill ventilated, they were the focal point of a tribe's life. About them the people's history was graphically represented in carvings. The whare itself quite literally represented an ancestor: the heke were the ribs, the tahu was the backbone, and the pou tahu was the heart. The tahu terminated at the front with a koruru (carved head). The carvings referred to specific people and events, serving a similar purpose to the writtten record of literate cultures. Early commentators always commented on the grotesqueness of the carvings; perhaps this was because the Maori had to find a way of representing the human figure on an architectural member, which was usually a plane surface, such as a poupou. The carvers solved the problem by taking the two side profiles and joining them to create a frontal view.

The role of the early pa is uncertain. From early descriptions it is clear that they were inhabited semi-permanently and were associated with outlying hamlets and camps designed for specific economic pursuits. There is evidence that the pa on Auckland's volcanic cones during the 1600s were heavily populated, but by 1750 had been deserted as the result of inter-tribal fighting. After European contact the unfortified kainga developed as centres for domestic activity and pa, with defences adapted for musket warfare, became refuges in times of emergency.

Ambroise-Bernard-Marie Le Jar du Clesmeur, a member of du Fresne's 1772 expedition, took over the captaincy of the *Marquis de Castries* after the idealistic du Fresne had been killed by Maori, probably as the result of an infringement of tapu. He commented in his journal on the siting of pa on steep headlands, observing:

> it is astonishing to see what measure of perfection they have achieved in their entrenchments and their fortifications. I have seen several villages where the approach was defended by twenty feet wide and ten feet deep, within which there were double and triple rows of palisades and in the space between them a form of raised platform from which spears can be thrown to considerable advantage. In each fortified village there is usually a storehouse of roots and potatoes.[3]

Inside the fortifications there was usually a

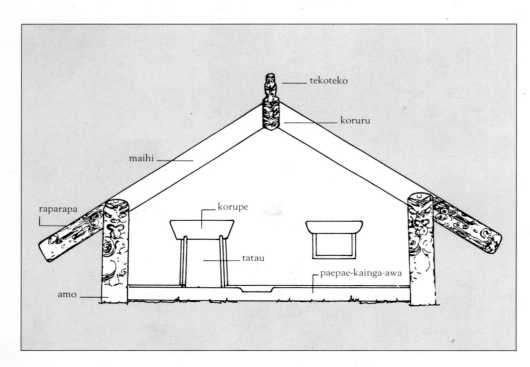

The parts of the whare whakairo.

tekoteko

koruru

maihi

korupe

raparapa

tatau

amo

paepae-kainga-awa

Raupo, Timber and Stone

TOP: *J. W. Giles (after) George French Angas (1822–86)*, Maketu House, Otawhao Pa, built by Puatia to commemorate the taking of Maketu, 1844. *Hand-coloured lithograph.*
AUCKLAND CITY ART GALLERY COLLECTION.

The artist's caption: This remarkable edifice was built by Puatia, the late chief of Otawhao Pa, to commemorate the taking of Maketu on the East Coast. The two principal figures with protruding tongues that are placed on each side of the verandah entrance are intended to represent Hikarea, a chief of Tauranga . . . and Tarea another chief . . . The lower figure supporting the central pole is Taipari, a chief of Tauranga and now a convert to Christianity. The two carved spaces further up the pole are also designed to represent warriors; the upper one is for Tara, who was slain at Taranaki. The figure ornamenting the central gable represents Puke, killed at Rotorua, and the one surmounting the top, Wakatau, who fell at Maketu. The figures surrounding the exterior of the house are all intended to represent various parties connected with the war.

BOTTOM: *Isidore-Laurent Deroy (after) Louis August de Sainson (1801–86)*, Interior view of Kahouwera Pa, New Zealand. *Hand-coloured lithograph.*
AUCKLAND CITY ART GALLERY COLLECTION.

cluster of whare. Internal fences were erected to keep dogs, to protect those who might sleep outside, or perhaps for privacy. As well as the fighting stages commented on by du Clesmeur, other buildings might also include high food stages, sheds for sheltering canoes, and pataka (food storage structures), sometimes carved, which were raised on piles to prevent rats entering. Cooking was done in the open or, during wet weather, in a lean-to made from manuka frames thatched with raupo; food was never consumed inside any whare, but in wet weather could be taken on the porch.

When the artist George French Angas (1822–86) spent three months in 1844 travelling through the North Island among 'native pas and stately chiefs', he recorded some unusual forms of buildings of which no trace remains today, unlike those traditional Maori structures which still form the basis of modern marae architecture. One of the strangest was the house called Urutomokia, at Raroera on the Waipa River. It

NEW ZEALAND ARCHITECTURE

J. W. Giles (after) George French Angas (1822–86), Entrance to a House at Raroera Pah, 1844. Hand-coloured lithograph.
AUCKLAND CITY ART GALLERY COLLECTION.
The entry on the long side of the house is most unusual.

J. W. Giles (after) George French Angas (1822–86), Monument to Te Wherowhero's favourite daughter at Raroera Pah, 1844. Hand-coloured lithograph.
AUCKLAND CITY ART GALLERY COLLECTION.
There are no surviving examples of such structures because they were deliberately left to decay.

belonged to Te Wherowhero, later to become the first Maori king. Particularly unusual was the side entrance and the exceptionally long frontal beam which served as a maihi above a wide but undecorated verandah. The amo were carved in the form of faces and had eyes of paua shell. The house was painted red, the tapu colour, and would have been highly decorated inside. According to Angas, 'its close affinity to the many temples of Egypt is at once obvious'.

Another structure that Angas included in his book *The New Zealanders Illustrated*, published in London in 1846, was the monument at Raroera to Te Wherowhero's daughter. Already in decay when Angas drew it, this richly carved mausoleum, in which the body was placed in an upright position, was not replaced. Its site, however, would have remained tapu and would probably have been marked with a wooden post called a pou rahui, which proclaimed the fact to all visitors.

The very first Pakeha to inhabit rather than merely to visit New Zealand were whalers and sealers. In 1792 a sealing gang from the ship *Britannia* had been landed at Dusky Sound, where its members were expected to survive for a full year until they were picked up again. They lived in a dwelling of which no record survives save its dimensions: 13 metres long, 5.5 metres wide and 4.5 metres high. Until the 1830s, when increasing numbers of shore stations were established around Cook Strait, on Banks Peninsula, on the coasts of Otago and Southland, and along the Hawke Bay/Poverty Bay coastline, temporarily stranded whalers and sealers had sheltered in framed tents or flax huts.

When members of this predominantly male European population began to live with Maori women and form friendly relationships with their families, the 'settlers' were provided with raupo whare. A sizable whaling settlement numbering some twenty whare was established at Te Awaiti in Queen Charlotte Sound. Some whare were constructed of raupo woven over a wooden frame, while others had walls of clay pressed onto a wooden frame and were topped with a thatched roof. Windows were shuttered, and at one end of the whare there was a large chimney stack. Bunks lined the walls. By 1840 this whaling station had become a respectable town, boasting wooden houses and a hotel.

On arrival in New Zealand, the earliest European settlers were entirely without familiar building materials, so they emulated the style and construction methods of Maori dwellings and adapted them according to European ideas of hygiene and comfort. On 31 March 1841 the *William Bryan* anchored off Moturoa Beach at New Plymouth. Some of the 141 steerage passengers were said to be reluctant to disembark, even after the exigencies of a five-month voyage. Their promised harbour did not exist at all and an initial survey party sent to the proposed settlement had achieved very little. Huddled on the beach was a row of empty raupo whare which had earlier been vacated by the whaler Dicky Barrett. It was hardly an inviting prospect to have to exchange the cramped conditions of shipboard life for a tent, which was what many of the new arrivals had to live in until the local Maori, in return for gifts, built more whare.

Before long, as at the whalers' shore stations, timber-walled houses replaced both the tent and the windowless raupo dwelling. In her recollections Kate Flight, whose family had arrived at New Plymouth on 23 February 1842, recorded:

After a time my father built a wooden house. All the family liked the idea of this firmer structure; they thought that the new residence would be a decided improvement on the tent. What was their disappointment to find it was very much colder; so much so in fact that my mother and Aunt when indoors wore shawls on their shoulders! The house was erected by emigrants some of whom were skilled workmen.[4]

In fact skilled builders were few and far between. The wealthier settlers brought prefabricated houses with them; sometimes they were complete in all details, but more often only the framework was shipped out. Charles Hursthouse Jnr's *An Account of the Settlement of New Plymouth* was just one of the many handbooks published in London for the enticement and guidance of intending emigrants. Hursthouse warned his readers that 'it is frequently charged of works descriptive of new countries that the "promised land" is painted in colours too glowing'. He advised the young emigrant farmer 'to devote a few months before leaving his English home to learn the use of common tools' and to take great care 'to select the best situation for the homestead; an excellent one is that on a gentle eminence backed by a few acres of timber . . . he should then employ a carpenter to build his house (this is a matter of

taste — a dwelling could be erected for much less)'. Elsewhere, in detailing the cost of a variety of building materials, he includes the cost of a 'Post Raupo Cottage in the native style, good for 3 or 4 years' at £10 to £15.[5]

The raupo whare could be very quickly built and was capable of being adapted to circumstances. Before long its traditional one-roomed structure was partitioned, walls were given greater height and earth floors were timber-lined. Imported doors were fitted, calico windows were glazed, verandahs appeared along the fronts of houses, and occasionally a dormer window was seen.

In various parts of the country, where timber was not so plentiful, settlers built one- or two-roomed cottages out of various combinations of earth and timber. In Canterbury, cob- and sod-walled structures appeared, and in Otago and Southland Scottish settlers made dwellings of cob, wattle-and-daub, or turf, as the crofters had done at home.

In a wattle-and-daub house, strong stakes formed the frame on which kareao (supplejack) was used to create a basket-weave structure, then wiwi (tussock grass) was mixed with clay to form a 'pug', which was then applied. Sometimes, in rainy areas, the exterior mud coating would be timber-lined to prevent the walls turning into a muddy sludge. On 5 June 1840, the 21-year-old Ensign Best described in his journal the wattle-and-daub Government House at Port Nicholson as 'about thirty-six feet long and fifteen wide and

Raupo whare (c. 1860), Rahotu Redoubt, Taranaki. Already such European features as door and window frames are visible, but the wall construction is of tied bundles of dried raupo, a technique which European settlers were taught by the Maori. The roof was probably a layer of raupo covered with totara bark and finally with dried grasses laid vertically so that rain would run off.
PARIHAKA ALBUM, ALEXANDER TURNBULL LIBRARY.

Interior of The Cuddy.
The interior walls of this
simple box-shaped house are
made from cob pugging.

divided into three rooms only one of which is
finished at present and serves for drawing, dining
and bedroom as well as the court house to hold
petty sessions in'.[6]

Walls could also be constructed out of turf cut
into blocks and laid on a stone base, or formed
out of cob, a mixture of clay, chopped straw and
cow dung. Another method, taking its name
from the tool called a pisoir, with which earth
was rammed into moulds, was pisé. In this
comparatively rarely used technique, clay was
mixed with small pebbles and a little water, then
rammed into the moulds in layers. Later the
moulds were removed and a very hard wall,
which could be plastered, revealed. Mud bricks
shaped in wooden moulds were dried in the sun
and used as a building material; these had the
advantage of being quicker to make than cob or
pisé. A group of mud-brick buildings still survives
at Oturehua in Otago.

The qualities of New Zealand native timbers
were readily appreciated by the first European
settlers, despite the fact that they were better
accustomed to stone buildings. At first, sawn
timber was infrequently used because its
production was labour intensive, so ponga was
tied together and laid horizontally within a
timber frame. More common were slab houses
made from split logs of totara, rimu or kauri;
sometimes they were roofed with shingles or bark

instead of a thatch of grass. But sawn timber was
the ideal wooden building material and by the
early 1840s timber mills were being set up to
provide weatherboarding. The best-known
surviving slab cottage is that built at the Levels,
near Timaru, by George Rhodes. With his
brothers, Rhodes had been in 1851 the first to
graze sheep in South Canterbury. A slightly later
development was board-and-batten construction,
where wide boards were fixed vertically and the
point where they joined covered with a narrow
batten. Jeremy Salmond has pointed out that 'by
1860 the small timber house had become
established as the New Zealand vernacular
dwelling, and from this little wooden cottage the
forms of other ordinary New Zealand houses
developed'.[7]

The Cuddy (1854),
Te Waimate Station. This
tiny cottage with its steeply
pitched, hipped roof,
symmetrically placed
windows and entry porch
was built from vertically
laid totara slabs. The roof
is now thatched with corn
straw.

Although there were stonemasons among the country's early European settlers, the majority of buildings were wooden. Stone, expensive as a material for housing and therefore only available to the relatively wealthy immigrant, was usually more popular for large public buildings. Only in Central Otago, where there were abundant deposits of schist, were stone cottages a common sight.

New Zealand's first substantial buildings were those associated with missionary activity in the Bay of Islands after 1814, when Samuel Marsden had set up the Anglican Church Missionary Society at Rangihoua. The mission later moved to Kerikeri and then in 1830 to Waimate North. The Wesleyan Missionary Society established a mission at Mangungu; and in 1838 Bishop Pompallier founded a Roman Catholic mission at Hokianga, which was later moved to the trading centre of Kororareka, now known as Russell.

Marsden recommended that the Church Missionary Society's emissaries be artisans who could converse with the Maori about sin and salvation while engaged in building and farming. When he moved the mission settlement from Rangihoua to Kerikeri in search of better agricultural prospects, he marked out land for a public store. At first the chief Hongi Hika supplied temporary buildings, then the store was passed over in favour of the Kemp House, which was begun in August 1818. Work proceeded slowly; two of the mission carpenters had to be reprimanded for idleness. In 1820 William Hall arrived from England and was appointed Supervisor of Public Buildings, but he proved a disappointment, although the plans were said to be partly his work. Most of the building was done by the Reverend John Butler, his son and gangs of Maori sawyers, who transported logs by raft to Kerikeri from Waikare and Kawakawa and then turned them into planks. Occupied in 1821, the

Kemp House is the first example of what architectural historian John Stacpoole has called 'the persistent Georgian tradition' which was to characterise the earliest colonial buildings. In their stripped-back simplicity the early buildings are quite free of the stylistic elaborations of the English Georgian style.

Part of the problem that arose between Butler and Hall, the building supervisor, had been a disagreement over whether the Kemp House was to be provided with such typically Georgian refinements as pilasters, fanlights, six-panel doors and framed shutters. The only concession to such notions of elegance is the front doorway, which has sidelights and a fanlight; everything else is pared back. The house is a wood-framed, two-storeyed building in the shape of a rectangular box. Its ground floor is enclosed by a verandah on three sides, the roof is hipped, and the upper storey has three symmetrically placed double-hung sash windows across its facade. In the 1830s more rooms were added, with the building of a skillion or lean-to, joining the now extended side verandahs at the rear of the house.

The Stone Store next door, built in 1832, is Georgian too, though unlike its white-painted wooden neighbour, it was constructed from surface basalt lava from the banks of the Kerikeri River, shaped on site. Sydney sandstone was used to form arches, quoins and keystones. It was received from New South Wales in rough form and was also shaped on site, to the designs of George Clarke, a lay missionary who had had

Raupo, Timber and Stone

LEFT: *Schist cottage (c. 1900), Central Otago. The characteristic box form with a lean-to at the back. Such cottages were quickly built by gold miners who took advantage of the tendency of Otago stone to split into slabs suitable for working by untrained stonemasons.*

Rear of Kemp House (1818–21), Kerikeri. A skillion roof built in the 1830s to enable the addition of more rooms at the back of the house did not disturb its Georgian simplicity.

LEFT: *Stone Store (1832–36), Kerikeri. New Zealand's oldest stone building is a well-proportioned rectangular structure with walls of local basalt rubble, although its arch stones, quoins and sills are of imported Sydney sandstone. The three hipped dormer windows are further evidence of the persistent Georgianism of the country's earliest builders.*

TOP RIGHT: *Waimate Mission House (1830), Waimate North. Built by Maori carpenters to plans by the missionary George Clarke who had been trained as a carpenter at an early age, the Mission House was in 1842 the home of George Augustus Selwyn, New Zealand's first Anglican bishop.*

BOTTOM RIGHT: *The Elms (1847), Tauranga. Clarke is said to have designed this distinctively Georgian house for the Church Missionary Society's station at Te Papa. Here there is no verandah, shuttered French windows leading directly on to the garden.*

building experience. Missionaries James Kemp and Charles Baker supervised construction and a stonemason named William Parrot trained Maori workmen, one of whom, Parore, became a competent stonemason himself. The original plan is said to have been the work of Kemp, although Methodist missionary John Hobbs drew another and calculated the kauri timber required for upper-level floors, internal partitions and roof bracing. In 1834 the Stone Store was given a rather grand bell tower which was denounced as an extravagance by some of the missionaries and which did not survive beyond 1858. Three symmetrically arranged dormer windows were damaged by a storm in 1856 and were replaced with skylights, but in 1980 the New Zealand Historic Places Trust restored them at the same time as it replaced the corrugated-iron roof with the kauri shingles of the original conception.

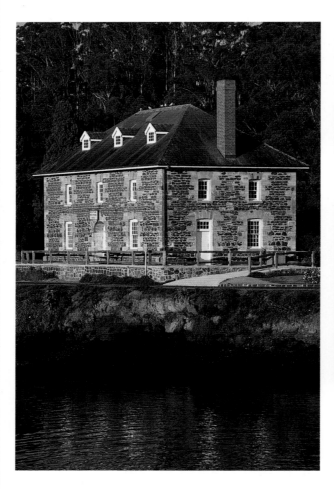

Meanwhile, in 1830 at Waimate North another mission had been set up, on land bought from descendants of Hongi Hika. Planned as an agricultural settlement for the training of Maori farmers, it was built by Maori labourers under the supervision of George Clarke, its first occupant. The Waimate Mission House was built according

to Clarke's plans, as was The Elms Mission House at Tauranga (1847), believed to have been built from plans supplied by Clarke to the Reverend A. N. Brown of the Church Missionary Society. They have similar roofs and overall proportions, although The Elms has no verandah to shade the front rooms, which through shuttered windows give directly onto a spacious garden. The Elms has an elegant spiral staircase, Waimate a curving one; both are more sophisticated than the Kemp House's simple dog-leg stair. At Waimate, the skill of Clarke's Maori carpenters can be seen in the adzed kauri linings, moulded architraves to doors and windows, and six-panel doors.

Although the Waitangi Treaty House of 1833 has a secular origin, it shares the Georgian stylistic features of the missions. It was prefabricated in Sydney to a design by the architect John Verge (1782–1861), who 'between 1830 and 1837 conducted the most influential and fashionable practice in New South Wales',[8] and who had been engaged by James Busby, the British Resident in New Zealand. At first, the house consisted only of three rooms connected by a hall, in a revision by Ambrose Hallen, for reasons of economy, of Verge's original plan. The kitchen, storeroom and servants' quarters were built at the rear using local materials. Parts shipped to the Bay of Islands included framing timbers with studs and plates, mortised and tenoned and carefully numbered in Roman numerals, as well as weatherboards, laths for interior linings, roof shingles, chimney bricks and Sydney sandstone verandah paving. There were also solid six-panelled doors, French casements with matching shutters and eight turned columns for the verandah front. The rest of the windows were small-paned, double-hung sashes.

There were various enlargements of the house after 1841. A skillion was added at the back and a plan dated 1848 shows both north and south wings. In the early 1900s the original lath-and-plaster interior linings were replaced with timber, scrim and paper. In 1933 architects W. H. Gummer and William Page replaced much of the original building when they tidied up the whole structure, making its original Georgian features more uniform, though the plan and front elevation of the house remained much as they were originally.

In 1989 conservation architects removed the unauthentic material in an attempt to restore the Treaty House to something approximating its state at the time of the signing of New Zealand's

founding document, the Treaty of Waitangi, on 6 February 1840.

There is evidence that the Langlois-Etévenaux House (1841) at Akaroa was prefabricated in France. Its wooden mouldings, inward-opening casement windows and exterior weatherboard cladding show no signs of having been pit-sawn. Built by the storekeeper to the Nanto-Bordelaise Company in what has been described variously as Louis Philippe or French Empire style, the house has an absolutely symmetrical facade with shuttered windows, pilasters, cornice, flat entablature over the doors and windows, and a steeply pitched, scalloped, shingled roof. Under its eaves there are ingenious vents which allow air to circulate inside.

At Russell in 1841 French Roman Catholic missionaries built a large printing house and store known since 1913 as Pompallier House, after the first Catholic bishop of the south-west Pacific. Most of the Marist brothers had come from the Lyons district in France, where pisé construction was common. A Lyons architect and lay missionary, Louis Perret, supervised work for the first eight months of construction. Pompallier House, although it is the oldest building associated with the Roman Catholic Church in New Zealand, was never a bishop's residence. In its early years it did not have the now familiar diagonally braced verandah; this attractive feature was added in the 1870s when the owner, James Greenway, transformed the building into a home. Nor was there an upper verandah, although the brothers did project the roof line, supporting it on posts as protection for the thick pisé walls. During the late 1980s, the deteriorating building was subjected to thorough analysis by conservation architects in the interests of restoring it to its original form. The process of removing all traces of what one of them has called Pompallier House's 'bizarre transformation into an historic monument' is under way.[9]

Raupo, Timber and Stone

TOP LEFT: *Treaty House (1833), Waitangi. Plans for this house were revised by Ambrose Hallen from originals by Sydney architect, John Verge. A prefabricated house, its numbered parts were shipped from Sydney to become the home for James Busby, British Resident in New Zealand. The Treaty House takes its name from the signing of the Treaty of Waitangi, which took place on the lawn in front on 6 February 1840.*

LEFT: *Langlois-Etévenaux House (1841), Akaroa. Prefabricated in France, the house shares design features with the Church Missionary Society's Georgian buildings in the north, but it has a greater number of decorative features, including pilasters, projecting cornice and flat entablature.*

RIGHT: *Pompallier House (1841), Russell. French Marist brothers, under the supervision of architect and lay missionary Louis Perret, built this large house with outer walls of pisé de terre (rammed earth). The upper cross-braced verandah decoration is a much later addition which is to be removed as conservation architects continue the restoration of the house.*

NEW ZEALAND ARCHITECTURE

TOP: *Esk Head Homestead (1863), North Canterbury. The verandah is original, projecting from the main roof line as much to protect the low cob walls from rain as to provide shade.*

BOTTOM: *Hulme Court (1843), Parnell, Auckland. A simple box with a surrounding verandah, the house was constructed out of bluestone (now plastered) rather than timber. The paired verandah posts connected by trellis work are peculiar to this house.*

The homestead at Esk Head in North Canterbury is a remarkable survivor. It was built by Christoper Edward Dampier in 1863 with thick cob exterior walls and interior walls of wattle-and-daub, which is less bulky than cob or pisé. In places the snowgrass thatch can still be seen, although the roof has been covered with corrugated iron for many years. The squat appearance of the L-shaped house is due to a long roof line, which projects directly down to form a wide verandah held up with posts.

Some of the wealthier European settlers were able to afford rather more substantial dwellings, often built of stone. Hulme Court at Parnell, Auckland, was built in 1843 by the lawyer Frederick Whitaker, 'a land speculator on the grand scale',[10] who in the 1860s encouraged the takeover of Maori land in the Waikato and was later twice Prime Minister. The house was occupied by Bishop Selwyn between 1844 and 1846, but takes its name from Colonel Hulme, who lived there before it became a temporary Government House for the Governor, Sir Thomas Gore Browne. It was constructed of bluestone which was later plastered, and has a hipped slate roof and a surrounding verandah, notable for the fine detail of its trellis work, on paired supporting posts. Again the familiar Georgian symmetry gives the house an elegant facade even if, today, it looks slightly incongruous now that its once expansive garden has been taken for much later buildings.

Robert Rhodes held a dinner on 28 December 1853 at Purau on Banks Peninsula, to celebrate the laying of the foundation stone of his substantial homestead, which was probably designed by Samuel Farr (1827–1918), Canterbury's first architect, although no drawings or documentary evidence exist today to prove the matter beyond dispute. In March 1850 Farr had arrived at Akaroa on the *Monarch* after an unusually perilous voyage. Having intended to go to Auckland, he decided to stay at Akaroa, where he remained for twelve years. He later moved to Christchurch, where he established a flourishing practice.

Farr was not as talented an architect as Benjamin Mountfort, who arrived in Canterbury only eight months after him: he was reliable and competent rather than outstanding. The bulk of his work was domestic, and many of his later houses were designed for wealthy people who were keen to have their homes reflect their status. Like the work of the early missionary builders and indeed many later New Zealand architects, Farr's houses were frequently scaled-down versions of English models. He was able to design in both Gothic and Italianate styles, but his houses tended to be similarly planned, with a central front door on either side of which was a drawing room and a dining room. Purau is said to be one of his earliest houses, although Farr went on to build many 'prestigious gentlemen's residences'[11] throughout the 1860s.

The multi-gabled Purau was built in local reddish brown stone by William Chaney. French windows open onto a verandah which wraps around three sides of the house. In 1858 the original wooden verandah was replaced by a much more ornate one embellished with cast-iron 'lace', the work of architect George Mallinson. The two main gables on the front facade have also been enlivened with Carpenter Gothic heavy white pierced bargeboards with a pendant at each gable point. A smaller central gable carries the Rhodes monogram on shield. Inside there are other indications that this was the house of a man of means: the drawing and dining rooms are connected by folding doors arranged in sets of three, which slide into recessed jambs and can be completely hidden by a moulded hinged flap. These rooms also have the original grey marble fireplaces and Italian gilt pelmets above the doors and windows. The servants' quarters, a common feature of Farr's domestic work, are reached by a separate staircase with a rope handrail, which opens out of a cupboard and is separated from the main stair by a wall.

Richmond Cottage (1853), New Plymouth. Although just a little box with a lean-to at the back, this stone cottage has paired French windows instead of the more usual central front door with a window on either side of it.

Purau (1853–54), Banks Peninsula. Possibly designed by Samuel Farr. Like many early New Zealand houses for wealthy landowners Purau is a scaled-down version of the kind of English Gothic mansion which was popular 'at home'. The elaborate bargeboards are an early example of the Carpenter Gothic style which was already very popular in the United States.

The Richmond Cottage (1853) at New Plymouth is a more modest stone house. C. W. Richmond, with his partners the Atkinson brothers, had already built the wooden cottage Hurworth ten kilometres from New Plymouth but he found that there was demand for his legal services in the new colony and so commissioned a local stonemason to begin work on a town house as well.

Richmond Cottage (originally known as Beach Cottage) resembles many of the early cottages in that it is built on a simple rectangular box plan, topped with a shingled saddleback roof with a lean-to at the back and a verandah at the front. Instead of the usual central front door with a window either side, it has three pairs of French windows which originally gave access to a sea view, but since 1961, when it was moved to a central city location to avoid demolition, they have faced a pleasant rose-planted lawn.

It is unfortunate that while significant examples of the domestic architecture of this period survive, there are none of the original churches or chapels associated with the earliest missionary activity. John Stacpoole has described chapels in the north which were

rectangular in plan without any proper chancel and had hipped roofs; but window heads made obeisance to the newly received Gothic fashion by being pointed, and slight Gothic influences seem to have been allowed in decorating the interior fittings. A similar building, Christ Church, Russell was put up in 1834 . . . a later generation saw fit to give this a gabled roof.[12]

After 1871 the Russell church also gained a porch, buttresses and a belfry, as well as being greatly altered inside to the point where its original Protestant, chapel-like architectural character was modified. An early raupo chapel sufficed until a chapel was built at Te Papa, Tauranga, but today only The Elms Mission House and its little library remain. Most of New Zealand's significant church buildings were the work of architects engaged by Bishop Selwyn when the early period of tentative and often unsuccessful missionary activity had given way to something more securely established; these will be discussed in the next chapter. However, there remains at Otaki a unique church which was the first to blend Maori and European building traditions.

Built between 1848 and 1851, Rangiatea was inspired by Octavius Hadfield of the Church Missionary Society and the great Maori chief, Te Rauparaha, and its construction was supervised by Hadfield's assistant, the Reverend Samuel Williams. Its name, Rangiatea or the Abode of the Absolute, derives from the name of an island at Hawaiki; it is sited at the foot of a hill named Mutikotiko, where sacred soil was deposited from an altar at Tapu-tapu-atea in Hawaiki. Such was the mana of Te Rauparaha that he was able to draw a large force of workers from local tribes to help in the construction of the church. Although he never consented to baptism, Te Rauparaha was, in the words of Patricia Burns, 'one of the many chiefs who were interested in Christianity in so far as it did not conflict with, and at times complemented, the people's traditional beliefs'.[13]

The totara ridgepole of Rangiatea is supported by three 12-metre-high pillars, which were lifted into place by tripods and pulleys. The ridgepole symbolises not an ancestor but the new faith, and the pillars, which were adzed out of individual trees, symbolise the Trinity. The forty-two poupou and epa also bear the marks of stone tools; between them are tukutuku panels twelve metres high. It is said that the pattern, the purapura whetu (star dust), was chosen by Te Rauparaha to signify his hope that the followers of the new religion would number the stars. On the rafters a kowhaiwhai pattern displays the hammerhead shark design, the mangopare; the beams are all dovetailed and inlaid in traditional style, without nails. Every feature of the church has some carefully thought-out significance. The weatherboard exterior was once roofed with shingles and incorporates a number of pointed lancet windows, but many later renovations, particularly one in 1949, have given it a dull appearance which quite belies its inner splendour. Te Rauparaha died in 1849 before it was finished. In 1886, when the church was reopened following buttressing and reroofing, a memorial to him was unveiled outside the church gates.

In these first years of settlement there had been little or no work for trained architects but this situation was to change as provincial councils and legal officials came to require more substantial buildings. The raupo whare and chapels that had served the early settlers as homes and places of worship were clearly not built to last and were quickly replaced with more solid structures. Although the Maori continued to live much as they always had, the introduction of European tools and methods of construction meant that their traditional structures were also subject to modification, particularly as timber began gradually to replace raupo as a building material. In the following decades the architecture of the colonists increasingly reflected a more settled relationship with their new environment.

CHAPTER TWO
The Birth of Antipodean Gothic

Old St Paul's
(page 28)

It was in buildings associated with the Anglican church that the first significant expression of the desire for a more settled architecture was made. The Selwyn Gothic style takes its name from the work of the first Anglican Bishop of New Zealand, George Augustus Selwyn (1809–78), who was its moving spirit. His 26-year episcopacy began in 1842 when he arrived in New Zealand to take on the formidable task of organising a system of church government in a colony where missionary activity had earlier been largely confined to work with the Maori people. The growth of European settlement now made the erection of substantial church buildings a priority. In 1844, following a protracted period of difficulties with the missionaries, Selwyn shifted his headquarters from the Church Missionary Society's property at Waimate to Auckland, where he established St John's College at Tamaki. It was here that the Selwyn Gothic style had its beginnings.

Before he left England, Selwyn had made extensive inquiries as to how best to provide churches in the new country. Naturally he had turned to those who, like himself, were associated with archaeological and antiquarian research into the medieval buildings which were the basis of England's Gothic Revival. Selwyn himself had been a member of the Cambridge Camden Society, later known as the Ecclesiological Society.

Ecclesiological principles of church building were based upon the belief of some churchmen that in reviving medieval forms of architecture the church could be spiritually renewed. The built structure and the faith were perceived as indivisible, hence the dogmatic way in which the Camden Society laid down its principles of church building and decoration. A church had to have a chancel, that is, a portion set aside for the clergy and the choir; it had to have open seats instead of closed pews; exterior towers and projecting transept could be omitted for reasons of economy, but a steeply pitched roof was obligatory.

The Gothic architecture of the fourteenth century, known as Decorated Gothic, was the preferred style, although its complex roof vaulting and ornate window tracery were to prove beyond the resources of New Zealand's early church builders. The Italian- and Greek-derived Neo-classical styles of seventeenth- and eighteenth-century English church architecture were condemned as pagan.

In the very first volume of the Cambridge Camden Society's journal Selwyn placed a request for plans which might be suitable for building in New Zealand, stating that 'as the work will be chiefly done by native artists, it seems natural to teach them first that style which first prevailed in our own country'.[1]

From the beginning there was no doubt in Selwyn's mind that Gothic was the only suitable style for the young colony's churches. He received advice that simpler Norman or Early English styles of Gothic would be the most suitable, and the ecclesiologists produced some designs based on the church of St Etienne at Than, near Caen in Normandy, France. The Oxford Architectural Society gave him casts of the types of details, from a church at Iffley near Oxford, which they thought Maori carvers might be capable of imitating.

When he arrived at Auckland, Bishop Selwyn was not impressed with William Mason's brick St Paul's Church, which was then being built. As the architectural historian Jonathan Mané pointed out, 'Selwyn was determined to erect archaeologically "correct" churches, preferably in stone, although he realised that the ideal might have to be approached through piecemeal building.'[2]

The first attempts at building were in fact disastrous. Selwyn commissioned Sampson Kempthorne (1809–73) to design two small stone churches, St Stephen's (1848) at Judges Bay, Parnell, and St Thomas's (1847) at Tamaki. Although he was satisfied that the designs of both buildings conformed with true Gothic principles, Selwyn must have been dismayed when the scoria rock structure of St Stephen's began to disintegrate the day after its consecration. St Thomas's did the same shortly afterwards. Both churches were condemned, although the remains of St Thomas's can still be seen today. Selwyn hesitated before employing Kempthorne again and was no doubt relieved when he was able to replace him with the much abler and more experienced Frederick Thatcher (1814–90).

Selwyn had asked Kempthorne to design St John's College, having first provided him with an ambitious sketch of what he intended. The sketch shows just how indebted the bishop was to the works of the great Gothic Revival theorist, A. W. N. Pugin, copies of whose work were held in the St John's College library. By the middle of 1845 Selwyn's plan to erect these stone buildings at St John's had also to be abandoned because of the poor quality of the local materials.

After such a shaky start with stone buildings, it was quite apparent that church architecture

The Birth of
Antipodean Gothic

*St Mary's Church
(1845–46), New Plymouth,
by Frederick Thatcher. The
ecclesiologically correct first
section of the church was
designed by Thatcher, who
was also responsible for
extensions in 1862 and
1866. The sanctuary, a
five-sided apse, was the
work of Benjamin
Mountfort in 1893.*

would have in future to be wooden. While the
Gothic Revivalists were initially devoted to the
great stone churches of Europe, after 1840 they
began to examine the less prominent vernacular
timber buildings which had survived from the
medieval period. It was these buildings which
were to provide architectural models in the new
British colonies, where buildings often had to be
put up quickly using local materials. The bishop
had to resign himself to a more temporary
architecture of timber.

Frederick Thatcher, a London-trained
architect, had become a member of the Institute
of British Architects within a year of its
foundation. He arrived at New Plymouth in 1843
and remained there for a year, until he came to
the attention of Selwyn. First, he was given the
task of adapting Kempthorne's drawings of the ill-
fated St Stephen's so that they could be used as
the design for the chancel of St Mary's Church
(1845–46), New Plymouth. His small chapel at Te
Henui, out of New Plymouth, built of slabs of
rimu with a thatched roof and a rammed earth
floor, no longer survives, but a portion of the
stone parsonage nearby does. This design, as
Mané pointed out, was clearly indebted to Peter
Robinson's Design No 8: The Parsonage House,
published in his book *Village Architecture* in 1830.
A copy of the 1837 fourth edition was held in the
St John's College library.

Thatcher's New Plymouth Colonial Hospital
(1846), now known as The Gables, was designed
after he had left New Plymouth for Auckland,
where he was at first obliged to supplement his
meagre architectural income by becoming acting
clerk to the Executive Council of New Ulster
and assistant secretary to the Governor, Sir
George Grey. The New Plymouth hospital was
the first of Thatcher's buildings to have the
exposed timber frame which was to become a
distinctive feature of his buildings. Such detailing
was approved of in architectural circles because

*The Gables (1846), New
Plymouth, by Frederick
Thatcher. Designed as a
hospital, the building shows
the architect's preference for
steeply pitched Gothic roofs
even on secular buildings.*

*Chapel of St John the
Evangelist (1847), St John's
College, Auckland, by
Frederick Thatcher. The
architect exposed the
building's structural frame
using arched bracing.*

*All Saints' Church (1847),
Howick, Auckland, by
Frederick Thatcher and
Reader Wood. The church
was prefabricated at the St
John's College workshops
and shipped to Howick.
The external timber frame
is not arched, having
instead diagonal cross
braces.*

its 'revealed construction' was truthful to the materials used.

When Thatcher came to Auckland he first superintended the completion of a stone house and kitchen at St John's, begun earlier under Kempthorne. Following the expensive failure of the two stone churches, Selwyn decided to build the college chapel of St John the Evangelist in wood. Although designed to be temporary, it is still in use today and is one of New Zealand's most admired colonial buildings. Although Selwyn was a more than usually interested client who enjoyed producing architectural sketches himself, there can be no doubt that the chapel was built to Thatcher's design. Thatcher was, however, willing to listen to the bishop's suggestions. Another architect, Reader Wood (1821–95), who had arrived in New Zealand in 1844 and was later to rise to positions of considerable eminence, was also paid a salary for superintending buildings constructed in the college workshops by students and lay personnel.

In her reminiscences, Mrs Selwyn observed that the St John's College chapel (1847) was based 'on a plan which George found in a book of beautiful sketches chiefly of French churches by Mr Petit of Lichfield'.[3] R. M. Ross pointed out that the two apsidal ends of the chapel may owe something to Petit's interest in French Gothic architecture. The chapel's single-skin wooden structure sits on a stone base. Like the Colonial Hospital at New

Plymouth, it has an exterior of vertical board sheathing with very distinctive exposed arched framing. Thatcher was later to abandon this style in favour of internal framing, clad with board-and-batten to prevent water being trapped in the angles of the cross bracing. The windows are small and quite narrow, square-headed with diamond-shaped glazed panels, except for those in the transept, which are paired and pointed in the manner of the Early English Gothic. The shingle roof's steep pitch has a central belfry, a feature much approved by ecclesiologists.

All Saints' Church at Howick, also designed by Thatcher, probably assisted by Reader Wood, in 1847, is the only one surviving of the eight churches prefabricated in the St John's College workshops. Here the external structural frame has been simplified and consists of diagonal cross

braces that are painted black and stand out against the white vertical boards. There is no belfry, but rather a square tower placed on the steeply pitched gabled roof. The plan is that of the traditional Latin cross; nave, chancel and transept were originally all of equal span but in 1862 it was necessary to add a second aisle to accommodate the growing congregation. The interior boards, including those of the ceiling, have been painted white, so that the roof timbers are obscured. The St John's College chapel, in contrast, retains its dark-stained timber and magnificent timber roof trusses.

In 1848 Thatcher himself entered St John's College, and he was ordained a priest in 1853. After he returned from a visit to England in 1856 he produced a design for a replacement for Kempthorne's collapsed St Stephen's Chapel at Judges Bay. This tiny building has a Greek cross plan and consists of five 3-metre by 3-metre units, one for each arm of the cross, and one at the centre crossing, which is capped by a belfry. It was at this central point that a group of churchmen gathered on 13 June 1857 to sign the Constitution of the Anglican Church in New Zealand. The exterior cladding of St Stephen's consists of simple vertical boards with no expression of structure; instead all interior structural details are exposed. There are lancet windows with latticed glass panels and a rose window over the door.

These early churches designed by Thatcher and others under the watchful eye of Bishop Selwyn form the basis of the Selwyn Gothic style. In 1848 the now much-altered church of St Peter at Onehunga was designed and built by the St John's construction department. Dr Arthur Purchas (1821–1906), its first vicar, was a redoubtable figure: a doctor, missionary and inventor who, it is said, was associated with Thatcher in the church's design and who supervised its construction. It was Purchas who designed St James's, Mangere, in 1857 and the frontier church of St Bride's at Mauku in 1860, very much in the Selwyn Gothic style. The 1859 Church of St Mary, Parnell, a Selwyn Gothic church said to be Thatcher's work, was replaced in 1888 with Mountfort's magnificent St Mary's Procathedral.

Thatcher's other major work for Selwyn was the creation of the residence for Selwyn and his successors, begun in 1863 and now known as Selwyn Court. The complex included a library, complete with adjoining baptistry and bell tower, built in 1861; it is now called the Selwyn Library. Placed around a central courtyard, the buildings plainly exhibit Thatcher's stylistic hallmarks: the vertical board-and-batten walls; shingle roofing on sharply pitched, but this time broken, gables, which flatten towards the eaves line; the groups of square-headed windows, sometimes varied by trefoils or quatrefoils. The library is a large timber-lined room with a trussed rafter roof and two rows of supporting columns; outside, tall, narrow groups of windows with fanlights form an elegant facade.

In the late 1850s Thatcher designed three stone

LEFT: *Interior of All Saints' Church. Light floods into the crossing from a lantern above.*

Selwyn Court (1863), Parnell, Auckland, by Frederick Thatcher. This was built as a residence for Bishop Selwyn.

buildings, the best known of which is the Headmaster's House, now known as the Kinder House after its first occupant, the Reverend John Kinder, who was headmaster of the Church of England Grammar School, as well as a watercolourist and photographer. Kinder had been a committee member of the Cambridge Camden Society, so it is not surprising that an enthusiasm for the Gothic can be detected in the two-storeyed house which Thatcher designed for him in 1856. For its walls the stonemason Benjamin Strange used basalt lava collected from the foreshore of Rangitoto Island, disposed as random rubble and held together with mortar, although facings around corners, doors and windows were made from large, squared blocks.

laid under its foundations, so the dining room remained damp unless a fire was lit even in summer. This no doubt contributed to the illness and death of so many of the students and thus resulted in the closure of St Andrew's College as early as 1867.

Thatcher's last building, St Paul's at Wellington, is his most important. Although he was appointed vicar to the parish and began designing the church in 1861, St Paul's was not consecrated until 1866, by which time Thatcher had left his clerical and architectural position because of ill health to again become Sir George Grey's secretary. In 1867 Bishop Selwyn left New Zealand at the insistence of both Queen Victoria and the Archbishop of Canterbury, to become Bishop of Lichfield, Staffordshire, and in 1868 Thatcher joined him as his secretary.

LEFT: *Kinder House (1856), Parnell, Auckland, by Frederick Thatcher.*

RIGHT: *Old St Paul's (1861–66), Wellington, by Frederick Thatcher. This was Thatcher's last and largest building.*

In 1858 Strange built similar walls for the Melanesian Mission (formerly St Andrew's College) at Mission Bay, to a design by Reader Wood. The only part of the building that still remains is the dining room and kitchen. The college, where youths from the Loyalty Islands were trained to become priests, was partly financed by the literary efforts of English writer Charlotte Mary Yonge; the proceeds from her novel *The Daisy Chain* were donated to Bishop Selwyn for the purpose. No damp course was ever

Old St Paul's, as it is now known, has been subjected to many additions since 1866 but in its original form, as Margaret Alington has pointed out, 'there was little in the plan and siting of the church that the ecclesiologists would have found fault with'.[4] Its apsidal chancel, although a continental feature, was clearly distinguishable in the interior; its engaged porch was entirely liturgically suitable for the services of baptism and marriage, which traditionally took place at least partly here; its square tower at the west end and its octagonally planned detached vestry, reminiscent of the chapter houses of the great English cathedrals, were both beyond reproach. The chief glory of St Paul's is its wooden interior. Alington observes that the absence of tie beams in the roof's scissor trusses would also have pleased Thatcher's intellectual mentors, who wished that nothing should detract from the appearance of height. 'The fact that Thatcher exposed all his framing and did not cover it with plaster work was very much to his credit, for the ecclesiologists condemned such "pretence" most forthrightly.'[5]

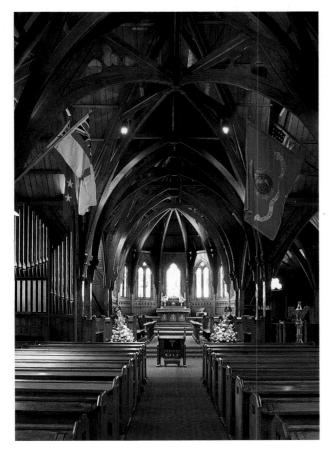

Thatcher used wood and so did not have to resort to arcading in the nave; straight horizontal beams placed between the columns were sufficent to support the clerestory. Where the beams and columns join he used moulded knee braces, decorated with trefoils. This motif is also to be found at the apex of windows in the church, which are provided with a variety of hood mouldings. The architect spent many patient hours working on such details, particularly those of the great west window. He was prepared to combine Early English Gothic features with more elaborate ones from the transitional period between the Early English and Decorated Gothic

periods. Later additions include a transept and a choir vestry, but the church retains its original character. In 1966 it was purchased by the Government and it has since been fully restored.

New Zealand's other great architect in the Gothic style was Benjamin Woolfield Mountfort (1825–98). Although Mountfort and Thatcher are often paired for purposes of discussion, their interests and careers were, apart from a shared High Church intellectual background, markedly different. Unlikely though it may appear, there is no evidence that they even met. Mountfort arrived at Lyttelton in December 1850 on board the *Charlotte Jane*. The architectural historian and Mountfort specialist, Ian Lochhead, calls him 'the pre-eminent exponent of the Gothic Revival in nineteenth century New Zealand',[6] and points out that Mountfort's earliest church designs show his awareness of ecclesiological ideas about timber church buildings as well as his familiarity with medieval and contemporary sources.

Mountfort had been a pupil of R. C. Carpenter, designer of an unbuilt colonial wooden church for the island of Tristan da Cunha which had an exterior cladding of vertical boards and battens and, inside, a timber roof. The design was published by the Ecclesiological Society in 1851 and again in the influential *Instrumenta Ecclesiastica* in 1856. Mountfort's earliest New Zealand church at Hemingford (1852) has not survived and may not even have been built, but the design is known to have a steeply pitched roof, vertical log construction and dormer windows in the manner of the medieval church of St Andrew's, Greenstead, in England. The timber tracery indicates that, like Thatcher at Old St Paul's, Mountfort inclined more to

St Bartholomew's Church (1854), Kaiapoi, by B. W. Mountfort. Vertical boards are cross braced and roof trusses extend beyond the walls to ground level in order to counteract the effect of strong winds.

The wooden interior of Old St Paul's is notable for the sense of spaciousness achieved by the roof's open scissor trusses.

Canterbury Provincial Government Buildings (1859), Christchurch, by B. W. Mountfort. The central stone tower has alternating courses of red scoria and limestone, creating a polychromatic effect.

Decorated than Early English Gothic at this stage of his career.

In 1853 Mountfort had the misfortune to be the architect for the larger Holy Trinity Church at Lyttelton, which had to be demolished in 1857 when its brick noggings were weakened by wind forces. In 1854, however, he employed similar wind-resisting techniques to those used in St John's College Chapel and All Saints', Howick, in his design for St Bartholomew's Church at Kaiapoi. It is highly likely that Mountfort had the opportunity of discussing the problems associated with colonial church architecture with Selwyn, who was at Lyttelton at the time of the architect's arrival in New Zealand. Mountfort remembered Selwyn's solution to the problem of battering winds and for St Bartholomew's designed a structure based on a series of equilateral triangles formed by the roof trusses. He extended the roof trusses beyond the walls to ground level, where they were bolted to the bottom plate.

In 1856 Mountfort lost a round in a colonial version of the 'battle of the styles' when he was invited to submit a Gothic alternative to William Mason's Neo-classical design for Government House, which Governor Gore Browne had objected to. Mountfort's design was returned to him, and Mason's used instead (see page 34). In 1859 Mountfort designed the first church of St John the Baptist at Rangiora and in 1861 he built a free-standing belfry for St Michael's Church, Christchurch, in a manner that derives from medieval examples.

In 1859 Benjamin Mountfort, in partnership with Isaac Luck, designed the wooden portion of the Canterbury Provincial Government Buildings. In 1865, this time in partnership with Maxwell Bury, he was to add the magnificent Provincial Council Chamber, but the earlier part of the building, with its long, stone-paved corridor, is more restrained.

The entrance archway of the council chamber rises to the full height of the building, while to the left three stepped windows mark the stairway. Precise Gothic detailing is everywhere apparent, as it is on Pugin and Barry's Houses of Parliament, London, the prime exemplar of this type of government buildings. John Stacpoole has described the stone council chamber itself as having 'the finest High Victorian interior in New Zealand'.[7] Geometrically laid coloured tiles line the lower walls, the upper walls are banded with differently coloured stone, and engaged columns resting on corbels create vertical emphases. The ridge-and-furrow arched ceiling was painted in multi-coloured chevrons designed by Mountfort and executed from stencils by J. C. St Quentin, a French decorative artist who came out from Australia. There is a world of difference between the pared-back Gothic restraint of Thatcher's

LEFT: *Interior of the
Provincial Council
Chamber (1865),
Christchurch, by
B. W. Mountfort.*

RIGHT: *Christchurch
Cathedral (1860), by
Sir George Gilbert Scott. In
1873 B. W. Mountfort
supervised construction,
which was not finally
complete until 1904.*

correct little churches and the flamboyantly
secular High Victorian Gothic of Mountfort's
Provincial Council Chamber. The early
prosperity of the province of Canterbury was
obvious to all contemporaries.

Later in his career Mountfort was to design the
Canterbury Museum (1876) and opposite it, the
clocktower and entrance to Canterbury College
(1877–79) in a free Gothic style in which he
allowed himself to vary such details as window
heads and arches using basalt from the Port Hills
with Oamaru stone facings. The museum facade
on Rolleston Avenue incorporates such
ecclesiastical features as a rose window in the
gable above its entrance portico and the
inevitable pointed windows set into taller recessed
arches.

In 1873 Mountfort supervised the building of
English architect Sir George Gilbert Scott's
Christchurch Cathedral. In the early 1850s Scott,
another enthusiast for medieval timber buildings,
had designed a parish church with a timber nave
and stone chancel, which Ian Lochhead and
Jonathan Mané argue was probably intended for
the Anglican settlement of Canterbury. It was
never built, but the colonists, this time
determined to get nothing less than a cathedral,
later approached Scott again. He suggested a

stone building in the Early French style, but for
its interior 'proposed a lofty timber arcade and
clerestory that is without parallel in the history of
the Gothic Revival'.[8] But the discovery of sound
building stone in Canterbury forestalled the
construction of Scott's timber design and he
consequently produced an alternative plan for a
stone arcade and clerestory.

Work on building this version of the cathedral
began in 1864 but had to be abandoned through
lack of funds. Work began again, under
Mountfort's supervision, in 1873. The nave and
tower were consecrated in 1881, the transept and
chancel remaining incomplete until 1904.
Mountfort made changes to Scott's very plain
design: he added towers to the north and south
porches and designed balconies, tabernacles and
pinnacles for the tower. The patterned design for
the slate roof was also his idea, as was the use of
Oamaru stone for quoins and facings. All these
features add variety to what might otherwise have
been a rather stolid exterior.

Mountfort also redesigned the bases of the
engaged columns, which in Scott's design
extended only as far as the capitals of the piers of
the nave arcade, thus unifying the whole
elevation. He was also responsible for introducing
polychromic tile panels similar to those in the

*Interior of St Mary's
Procathedral. The architect
has eliminated all
suggestion of the horizontal;
the angled roof trusses
project upwards to meet
king posts which rise to the
ridge.*

Provincial Council Chamber, and designed the stained glass for the west end rose window of the original architect's semi-circular apse, with its three lancet windows.

Mountfort himself was responsible for more than forty churches. These culminated in 1888 with St Mary's Procathedral in Auckland, which replaced the 1859 church, thought to be Thatcher's work. Until 1898 the old church served as a temporary nave while Mountfort's east end and three bays of the nave were built, then it was entirely demolished and Mountfort's new cathedral completed.

The timber walls of St Mary's are of the familiar board-and-batten construction, but their surfaces are enlivened with a string course which runs around the whole building, rising and falling with the different window levels. Side gables at right angles to the main roof create a jagged effect against the patterned slate roof of the nave. The apse exterior, which once faced the street, is unusual in that its windows break the main roof line and are capped with their own small, sharp gables.

*St Mary's Procathedral
(1888), Parnell, Auckland,
by B. W. Mountfort. Side
gables break the patterned
slate roof line.*

The interior exhibits none of the massiveness or flamboyance of detailing that marks some of Mountfort's earlier Christchurch buildings. The central focus of the church is, rightly, its chancel, which is lit by three windows; in accordance with ecclesiological principles the choir and altar are raised up above the level of the nave so that the congregation can see every aspect of the service. Mountfort also designed the church furnishings, including a pulpit with exposed timber and rich

Gothic detailing. Mountfort died in 1898 and thus never saw the completed St Mary's Procathedral.

Thatcher and Mountfort were the most significant figures in the chapter of the history of the Gothic Revival to which Ian Lochhead has given the title Antipodean Gothic. Other colonial architects also favoured the Gothic, notably Edward Rumsey (1824–1909), a former pupil of Sir George Gilbert Scott who emigrated first to Melbourne and then settled in Dunedin. His most notable building is the 1865 Supreme Court at Auckland, now known as the High Court. Rumsey had the good fortune to obtain work in the city during a public building boom, which resulted from increased prosperity after the population was swelled by the arrival of members of the armed forces brought in to quell the Maori in the Land Wars of the 1860s.

In 1864 Sampson Kempthorne, by now secretary of the newly formed Public Buildings Commission, had drawn up a plan for a city centre comprising sixteen buildings, one of which was to be a baronial Gothic Government House, sited on a hill in the Domain. When the Prime Minister, Frederick Weld, refused permission for the building to proceed, Rumsey was asked to

accept the courthouse commission instead. It was built much as he designed it, except for the omission of steep tower roofs, something which gives the building a squat appearance not entirely alleviated by the vertical emphasis of the central square castellated tower and two octagonal ones on the east and south elevations. The courthouse was built in brick with facings in lighter coloured stone, reflecting not only the tendency after 1860 for Gothic Revival architects to look more favourably on this material, but also an unexpected shortage of funds which caused the provincial government to abandon the intended scoria construction. A number of picturesque Gothic features give the building added character: the central tower's oriel window complete with gargoyles; the richly carved and panelled main courtroom and the heads carved in stone by Anton Teutenberg, a young German engraver.

Ecclesiological principles had infiltrated English educational design since 1840, and in the Anglican settlement of Canterbury it was appropriate that in 1874 S. C. Farr chose the Gothic style for his Normal School (now Cranmer Court apartments). The L-shaped, two-storeyed building had two wings, one each for girls and boys, with separate entrances; a low octagonal tower at the corner formed the junction of the wings. Pam Wilson has mentioned a number of similarities with English collegiate

Cranmer Court apartments (1874), Christchurch, by S. C. Farr. Formerly the Normal School. Canterbury's predominantly Anglican settlement determined that Gothic Revival principles would dominate the city's educational buildings as well as its churches.

buildings by A. W. N. Pugin, William Butterfield and Richard Carpenter, although it is worth noting that the Normal School displays little of the High Victorian eclecticism popular in the 1870s in England.

The main influence on Maxwell Bury's 1878 Otago University buildings was Sir George Scott's Glasgow University of 1870. Built in the local grey basalt with Oamaru stone facings, Bury's design is more restrained in its detail than Mountfort's Canterbury College, although the

Otago University (1878), Dunedin, by Maxwell Bury. The university was built in appropriately Scottish Baronial Gothic style.

Old Government House (1856), Auckland, by William Mason. Classical details are here executed in wood rather than stone, a practice frowned on by those who insisted on truth to materials.

magnificent tower with its tourelles gives it an impressive scale. Another feature of the Otago building is the faceted rustication of the string course which divides the foundations from the wall surface. The asymmetrical exterior facade gives expression to the building's interior, particularly at the north end, where a single gable with an oriel window indicates the presence of the hall inside.

William Armson (1834–83), another English-born architect, had come from Melbourne to Dunedin but settled in Christchurch. In 1870 he designed Christchurch Boys' High School for a site near Mountfort's Canterbury College. Now, like the College, part of the Arts Centre, its picturesque details blended well with the surrounding Gothic and gave further expression to the conviction that this was the most suitable

style for educational buildings.

Despite the pre-eminence of the Gothic, a number of fine Classical Revival buildings were erected during the early colonial period. Government House, now part of the University of Auckland, was built in the Classical style by William Mason in 1856. Unlike the Gothic Revivalists, who were all for truth to materials, Mason was quite prepared to treat the timber front as if it were stone, providing imitation stone quoins and keystones around lower windows. Its end elevations are, however, clad in plain weatherboards. Originally the symmetrical garden facade's roof balustrade was decorated with a row of urns. A central segmental pediment was later replaced with a triangular one; the proportions of the upper Palladian window were disturbed by a canopy, and a porte cochère was added to the main entrance. John Stacpoole, in his study of Mason, wrote of a 'strong resemblance between the centre block and the north front of Inigo Jones's Queen's House at Greenwich', and a similarity 'in scale and general feeling to some of the London clubhouses of Pall Mall and St James'.[9] Its plan Stacpoole describes as straightforward, although he refers particularly to the fine proportions of the dining room, drawing room and central hall, linked by a wide gallery behind.

An Australian, Leonard Terry (1825–84), was responsible for the Bank of New Zealand (1865) in Queen Street, Auckland, now merely a facade. There were protests from local practitioners when this distinguished Melbourne architect was selected to design Auckland's 1856 Union Bank (demolished) and the Bank of New Zealand; a competition was hastily organised but the B.N.Z.'s directors adhered to their original decision to use Terry, although the building was supervised by the second prizewinner, Richard Keals. A Greek Revival building faced with Tasmanian sandstone, the facade has a rusticated ground floor with attached fluted Doric columns supporting an entablature and cornice. The tall first-floor windows have their verticality enhanced by the segmental pediments high above them and each is provided with a cast-iron balcony. The small upper windows are framed by pilasters, the capitals of which are extended to form a continuous band below the bracketed cornice. A framing band of rustication rises from ground to cornice level at each side. In the following years many banks were to be built in the Classical style; it seemed generally accepted that this was appropriate for commercial buildings.

The Birth of
Antipodean Gothic

Bank of New Zealand
facade (1865), Queen
Street, Auckland, by
Leonard Terry. The Greek
Revival style was considered
fitting for banks. An
Australian architect
provided the design, using
Tasmanian sandstone as the
facing material.

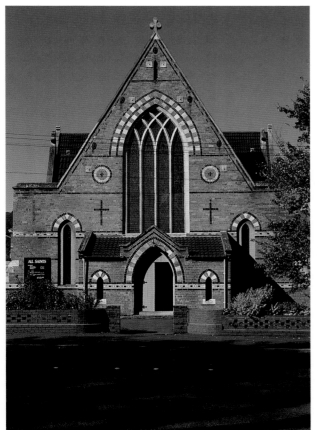

All Saints' Church (1865), North Dunedin, by William Clayton and William Mason. Bricks in contrasting colours enliven the surface of a simple facade.

In Wellington, the Tasmanian-born but London-trained William Henry Clayton (1823–77) designed the Government Buildings in 1876. In 1863 he had become the partner of William Mason in Dunedin, where in 1865 they daringly gave their basically Early English All Saints' Church, North Dunedin, a significant number of High Victorian details in emulation of William Butterfield's All Saints' Church (1849–59), Margaret Street, London. Their use of black and white glazed bricks against a plain brick surface, and bands of differently shaped slates for the roof, shows an experimental approach which neither was to repeat. They did, however, stop short of painting the ceiling in blue and gold as originally planned.

Clayton's preference was for Italianate Classicism and he used this style for Government Buildings, a four-storeyed structure which occupies almost an entire city block. Like Mason's Government House, Auckland (see page 34), this building faithfully reproduced Classical stone details in wood. The weatherboards at ground-floor level suggest rustication and the corners are defined with wood. As with the Bank of New Zealand there are marked distinctions between window details on each ascending floor. A string course gives added definition to the separation between floors, bracketed projecting eaves replace a cornice line, and unfluted Doric

Government Buildings (1876), Wellington, by William Clayton. Built in wood in Italianate style to house the country's civil service.

Ivey Hall facade (1878), Lincoln College, Christchurch, by Frederick Strouts.

columns support elegant porticos. Clayton had been appointed Colonial Architect in 1869. He had built an Italianate Government House in Wellington on the site now occupied by the Beehive; his later Gothic Parliament House burned down in 1907. In 1877 he designed the Christchurch Chief Post Office, in an Italianate style, and it has much in common with his Government Buildings, Wellington, despite being built in brick and stone rather than wood. He followed it in 1879 with the Classical Supreme Court in Wellington.

More unusual were two buildings in Elizabethan style; one, Maxwell Bury's Nelson Provincial Building (1859–61), was demolished but the facade of the other, Frederick Strouts's Ivey Hall, remains. Having trained in London where he had been a member of the Royal Institute of British Architects (R.I.B.A.) Strouts (1835–1919) had arrived in New Zealand in 1859. A confusing start to a career as architect, surveyor and ironmonger brought him to bankruptcy but Strouts was able, in 1871, to found the Canterbury Association of Architects with Mountfort, Armson and Alexander Lean. It was the first society of its kind in New Zealand.

During a trip to England in 1868 Strouts became aware of a number of neo-Elizabethan country houses being built using the architectural vocabulary of Flemish craftsmen: the distinctive curved and stepped gables, bay windows, strapwork and cresting of buildings erected during the reigns of Elizabeth I and James I. When Strouts entered the competition to design a School of Agriculture at Lincoln in 1878 he enthusiastically employed such features to create a building which fully justifies John Stacpoole's description of his work as 'oddly eclectic'. The gables are Dutch, the windows of the English mullioned variety, the bell tower and porte cochère French Renaissance. The emphasis is on variety. Even the disposition of rooms built to house the school's director, Dr Ivey, his family and twenty students, was irregular within its L-shaped plan, although today only the facade remains.

In his later years Strouts was to return to the Gothic idiom as other architects, especially those involved in domestic work, were increasingly drawn to the kind of experimental outlook Strouts had adopted at Ivey Hall. In the years after 1880, as colonists prospered and wished to display the fact, architects were encouraged to adopt a freer approach. In England the ideology of the Arts and Crafts movement, like the Gothic Revival based largely on English vernacular traditions, attracted many architects and their clients. There was to be a considerable delay before such ideas filtered to the South Pacific. Although New Zealand architects had not yet finished with either the Gothic or the Classical, they were to continue the tradition of the first colonial architects in adapting their European heritage to circumstances here.

CHAPTER THREE
Cottages, Villas and Country Houses

Threave
(page 51)

In the years between 1850 and 1880 New Zealand's European population increased from 26,000 to nearly 490,000. New settlers continued to arrive, encouraged mainly by immigration schemes, developments in pastoral farming and the promise of gold. 1874 was the record-breaking year: 38,106 new migrants arrived in New Zealand. To fill the need for housing, huge numbers of trees were felled for processing by an increasingly mechanised timber industry. By 1880 the days when simple cottages were laboriously constructed from timber shaped by hand were long past.

Robert Furneaux Jordan asked readers of his *Victorian Architecture* to remember that 'all Victorians lived in the shadow of the idea that "ornamented building" was a definition of architecture'.[1] This was particularly the case for those powerful people who were able to afford large country homes for themselves as early as the 1860s. Later, it was no less true for the increasingly wealthy middle-class New Zealand home buyer who could now study catalogues illustrating plans of villas and detailed drawings of a vast array of mass-produced doors, windows, ornamental balusters, bargeboards and mouldings. Thousands of these richly decorated wooden houses were built out of sturdy timbers

and can be seen in most New Zealand towns to this day.

For those who found colonial life less prosperous, the small wooden cottage of two to four rooms with a central door and a window on each side remained the basic form of house design. Sometimes these cottages consisted merely of a single-gabled roof with one or two rooms beneath; others might add a lean-to on the back or a verandah on the front. Cottages could be extended by adding floors above or by combining the basic box structure in various ways to produce an L-shaped house or, more rarely, something as complex as an H-plan. Today such cottages are visible mainly in early settled towns

such as Thames or Oamaru, where workers were housed close to their places of employment. In 1981 the Nelson City Council took the enlightened step of ensuring the preservation of a collection of wooden colonial cottages, originally part of the city's Town Acre 456, later to become South Street. The houses are situated close together and close to the narrow street itself, and helped to establish the character of this settlement as early as 1867.

Cottages could be aggrandised if owners wished for something displaying a greater sense of style. Roof overhangs could be increased. Verandah posts and balustrades could be more or less elaborately turned or cut out, and verandah roofs could be either convex or concave in shape. Guttering might be concealed by boxing. A higher stud could reduce the pokiness of the cottage interior, or the edge of the roof could be supported on elaborately moulded brackets which were Classical in origin. The hipped roof associated with a Georgian sense of proportion gradually became more popular than the more rudimentary single-gabled roof.

Throughout New Zealand there were a number of mostly large houses displaying ornamental features that clearly showed the influence of the Gothic Revival in domestic architecture. Some of the most notable of these were built for Nelson's wealthier settlers by the architect William Beatson (1807–70), whose house Woodstock (c. 1854) shows his fondness for steep gables elaborately decorated with patterned bargeboards, which derived from Pugin's studies of Gothic tracery.

Another significant influence on domestic architecture was the work of the American architect Andrew Jackson Downing. His Carpenter Gothic style, which reproduced Gothic stone tracery in wood, became popular in the U.S.A. during the 1850s and 1860s. It

achieved popularity here too in the period when builders and their clients wished to move beyond the simple unadorned forms of the earliest colonial housing. When the large cob house called Broadgreen at Stoke, outside Nelson, was built for the wealthy merchant Edmund Buxton in 1857, its gables were adorned with scalloped wooden bargeboards in much the same way as the 1853 Purau on Banks Peninsula had been (see page 20). Finely carved Carpenter Gothic fretwork appears on the bargeboards of the tiny Plimmer House, which was built in Wellington's Boulcott Street in 1870, but the style was to reach its zenith at Highwic at Epsom, Auckland, which was built in 1862 for the stock and station agent Alfred Buckland.

Highwic was constructed in stages, but it bears few signs of a lack of unity. It is largely decorated with Gothic motifs which feature in Andrew Jackson Downing's book, *The Architecture of Country Houses* (1850). It has always been thought

TOP: *Broadgreen (1857), Nelson. This large cob house has been decorated by such elegant features as a oriel window above the porch, hood moulds over dormer windows and scalloped bargeboards. The bay windows are a much later addition.*

BOTTOM LEFT: *Square-planned, hip-roofed cottage (c. 1870) at Northcote, Auckland, with convex curved verandah.*

BOTTOM RIGHT: *Plimmer House (1870), Wellington. This gentleman's residence was built in picturesque Gothic style.*

Highwic (1862 with later additions), Epsom, Auckland. At Highwic American Carpenter Gothic came to the antipodes. The bargeboards of roof and door gables are decorated with patterns carved in wood, reminiscent of Gothic stone tracery. Above the latticed windows are hood mouldings, complete with dripstones.

strange that the architect of Highwic should not be known, yet there is a probable explanation for the fact. The *New Zealander* for 1 January 1862 contained an advertisement in which architect Reader Wood and his partner invited tenders 'for additions to Mr Buckland's house at Newmarket' Beyond this notice, nothing exists to connect Wood with Highwic. In view of the fact that the house's Carpenter Gothic style clearly derives from Downing's book, it is unlikely that the full services of an architect were necessary.

All the characteristics of the Carpenter Gothic style are present at Highwic. The walls are of vertical board-and-batten construction, while the bargeboards of the roof and door gables are decorated with patterns reminiscent of Gothic stone tracery, carved in wood and frequently capped with high finials. Above the latticed casement windows there are sharply defined hood mouldings, which terminate in dripstones carved in wood. The extravagant parapets make a feature of the quatrefoil and the steep roofs above are of slate. One of the early additions was to the south side, where a large ballroom was built on the ground floor with a wood-panelled dormitory above to house Buckland's seven boys. The windows in the addition are of the sash variety and four-panel doors are used instead of the pointed Gothic ones of the original part of the house.

Despite superficial similarities between the Gothic-inspired Selwyn style and the Carpenter Gothic of Highwic, there is a clear difference of approach between the two. Ecclesiologically inspired buildings displayed their allegiance to the Gothic in much more modest fashion than Highwic, where the intention of the builders was rather to appropriate the extravagant qualities of the Gothic for purposes of secular display. In building his home, Alfred Buckland was able to command greater financial resources than a clerical community struggling not only to build churches and create a network of parishes but to maintain a precarious collegiate educational system as well.

In 1869 the architect Frederick George Allen (active in Wanganui 1863–86) used many Carpenter Gothic features in designing the house Oneida at Fordell, outside Wanganui. His English-born client, Joseph Burnett, had lived in various parts of the U.S.A. before emigrating to New Zealand in 1856, where he set up business as a confectioner and baker in Victoria Street, Wanganui. In 1860 he became a landowner, but it was not until 1867 that he gave his architect some sketch plans of the kind of house he wished to build on his newly cleared land. The house was inspired by what he had seen in the U.S.A. and, like Highwic, was to be a translation of the Gothic style into domestic building.

*Oneida (1869), Fordell,
near Wanganui, by F. G.
Allen. This building shares
many Carpenter Gothic
features with Highwic.*

Oneida saw many additions, most of which
were done by its original architect. It is built
mostly of totara and is clad with vertically laid
boards. The original totara shingle roof was
eventually replaced by corrugated iron, but its
steep gables remain as they were intended,
decorated with deeply cut fretwork bargeboards.
Pointed windows predominate, most of them
outlined with mouldings and dripstones. In 1880
a curving, latticed verandah was added so that
guests in the dining room could step out onto it
through French windows. Inside the front door
one is confronted with a remarkable panelled hall
which rises to the full height of the two-storeyed
house; it is broken by a gallery which runs
around three sides of the upper floor and gives
entry to the bedrooms. An organ once occupied a
loft halfway up the staircase.

A number of New Zealand's most magnificent
houses were built during this period for business
or political figures, who lavished their wealth on
homes which far outstripped anything the rest of
the country could afford. In some cases these
houses were 'grandified' early colonial homesteads
which never quite managed to disguise their
humbler origins. Other houses were wholly
designed by architects who were eager to show
that none of the currently fashionable revivalist
styles were beyond their professional capabilities.

The Auckland house, Alberton, had been built

*Alberton (1862),
Mt Albert, Auckland. In
1870 the architect Matthew
Henderson added verandahs
and corner turrets to the
two-storeyed farm-house.*

on the slopes of Mount Albert in 1862 as a two-
storeyed gabled farm-house. As Allan Kerr
Taylor prospered, extra bedrooms, a conservatory
and a ballroom were added. Most spectacular of
all were the elaborate verandahs which were
wrapped around the house on three sides by the
architect Matthew Henderson (active in
Auckland 1866–86) in 1870. For three corners he
designed towers with ogee tops, which John
Stacpoole perhaps fancifully regarded as giving
the whole house an oriental appearance. This he
explained by the architect's being influenced by
the fact that his client had been born at
Seringapatam, India.

In 1874 the architect Charles Tringham (active in Wellington 1869–95) designed a two-storeyed wooden house to be built outside the town of Marton for Sir William Fox. Its most notable feature is a square tower which owes something to those on Queen Victoria's Italianate house at Osborne, built in 1854. The Italianate appearance of Westoe derives from the paired arched windows of the upper storey and from the modillions that support the cornices on the main roof and tower. The tower is beautifully detailed, with timber quoins, an arched entry on the ground floor and a pedimented roof. A projecting string course forms a sharp defining line between the two storeys.

Thomas Mahoney (1854–1923) was responsible

in 1877 for another even larger Italianate mansion, known originally as The Pah, at Hillsborough, Auckland. Situated on what was formerly Whataroa Pa, the house was designed for the prominent Auckland businessman James Williamson, a man who had invested heavily in Waikato land holdings following the land confiscations of the 1860s. Deliberately planned on the most extravagant lines, the house took two years to build and was constructed on stone foundations with plastered brick walls. The building boasts an impressive porte cochère supported on groups of Ionic columns, but great attention was also given to the garden front, which was originally approached by a sweeping carriageway. A long, curving verandah supported by paired wooden columns follows the curves of the generously proportioned rooms within.

As at Westoe, the hallmarks of the fashionable Italianate style are evident, although on a much grander scale. Window groupings are more elaborate and some are provided with balconies; a heavily modillioned eaves line rises to form a low gable above the windows of upstairs rooms. No expense was spared with inside furnishings; inlaid floors, Italian marble fireplaces and decorative plasterwork distinguish the principal rooms. Within a decade of building The Pah, its owner, who had risen to be chairman of the Bank of New Zealand, was to see his fortune evaporate and his house sold. Today it is called Monte Cecilia and is owned by the Sisters of Mercy, who use it for emergency housing.

It is said that James Williamson had envied the 43-roomed Larnach Castle, which William Larnach began building for himself in 1871 on the Otago Peninsula. The building was designed by the eminent Dunedin architect R. A. Lawson (1833–1902), and first-rate craftsmen were employed to work on the materials which Larnach, as a wealthy importer, had at his disposal. While undeniably impressive in its scale and the extravagance of its appointments, Larnach Castle has been criticised for its ill-matched features: for example, the Scottish baronial crenellated parapets and the tower conflict with the horizontal emphasis of the enormously wide, colonial, cast-iron and glass verandahs. Its planning is confused, although there is much to admire in the exquisite woodcarving and plaster work by overseas craftsmen. The stone work, including the lions and eagles on the entrance steps, and also some of the carved woodwork in the dining room, are by the sculptor Louis Godfrey. William Larnach achieved great wealth and eminence, but he lost a

great deal of money in the 1898 collapse of the Colonial Bank, and committed suicide in his office at Parliament Buildings, bringing an end to a distinguished parliamentary career.

Two particularly impressive examples of domestic architecture in stone were built in Dunedin, where supplies of good building stone were plentiful. The house at 521 George Street was built in 1881 for the brewer Robert Wilson to plans by Joseph L. Shaw (1818–1906), while the architect and exact date for 111 Highgate, called Renfrew House, are unknown. Both houses have elaborate cast-iron lace work verandahs of a type infrequently seen in New Zealand outside Dunedin, although they are common in both Sydney and Melbourne.

Professors' Houses at Otago University were built in 1879 in a bright-red brick which worried local inhabitants. It was later plastered over with a finish of Moeraki gravel, which enhanced the original design. Bury again emulated his former partner Mountfort in the Gothic verandah detailing he gave each house, although it is perhaps their extraordinary cross-braced gables which excite most admiration today.

Wychwood, at Andersons Bay, Dunedin, was built of local phonolite (so called because of the distinctive ring it gives when struck). Dating from the late 1870s and attributed to R. A. Lawson, it was originally called Pomphrey Court and was built for the wines and spirits merchant C. R. Howden. The exterior stone work is squared rubble and is faced with contrasting Oamaru stone, while the interior is of finest kauri, Oregon pine and mahogany.

Maxwell Bury's two stately semi-detached

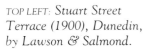

TOP LEFT: *Stuart Street Terrace (1900), Dunedin, by Lawson & Salmond.*

TOP RIGHT: *Dundas Street Terrace, Dunedin.*

BOTTOM RIGHT: *Chapman's Terrace (1882), Dunedin.*

RIGHT: *Dilworth Terrace (1900), Parnell, Auckland, by Thomas Mahoney. Half-timbered gables, oriel windows and verandahs are cleverly positioned to create an impression of architectural variety.*

In Dunedin there are also some fine examples of terrace housing. This is a rare phenomenon in New Zealand: settlers who had escaped crowded English cities were hardly likely to want to recreate their domestic circumstances here. Those that were built are small-scale, like Dunedin's two brick Dundas Street terraces, which have thirteen and six houses respectively. Chapman's Terrace in Stuart Street (1882), whose architect is unknown, has three Greek Revival portico entrances, while the other Stuart Street terrace (1900), by Lawson & Salmond, opposite Edmund

Sedding's 1916 St Paul's Anglican Cathedral, has six.

Most of Dunedin's terrace houses are repeats of one basic design unit and its mirror image. Later, in Auckland, Thomas Mahoney's 1899 Dilworth Terrace, built as a rental investment by the Dilworth Trust, was given a quite different

treatment. It consists of eight houses, each one having a distinctive verandah and shingled gable; the four larger gables correspond with three-storey houses and four smaller ones with two-storey houses. The deliberate asymmetry of these gables not only provides visual interest but also disguises the fact that the main ridge of the tiled roof steps down towards Augustus Terrace. The rear of each house was far less elaborate than the front elevation, each one having a small fenced yard with an out-house. Originally, in a way reminiscent of English seaside terraces, the Dilworth Terrace houses overlooked St Georges Bay. When the bay was reclaimed after 1914, the street, still known as The Strand, gave access to the railway yards instead of the shore.

By the 1870s the basic forms of the simple symmetrical cottage had been elaborated. Successful European settlers were no longer satisfied with a cramped life inside small, four-roomed, passageless houses. Architects and builders began to think of ways to satisfy clients' needs for more space. A central hall giving access to more generously proportioned rooms became common; the lean-to verandah became almost an obligatory feature. When one of the front rooms was pushed out under a gable to form a bay window, the bay villa was born. The bay villa caught the imagination of home owners and examples sprang up all over New Zealand. They are still to be seen in great profusion today. Frequently the brackets and bargeboards of the villa's projecting gables were decorated with turned wood or fretwork designs which could be chosen from a bewildering array of patterns available in builders' catalogues. On corner sites it was appropriate to have two projecting bays connected by a verandah, which would invariably be decorated with cut or turned balusters.

Jeremy Salmond has pointed out that between 1860 and 1910 'there were few changes in the way wooden houses were put together in New Zealand'.[2] Although more and more factory-made materials became available, the basic building procedures remained the same. Houses were supported on piles set out in rows; bearers and joists were laid to form the grid on which floorboards would be laid once the roof was on. Outer wall frames were made on the ground and then propped into place; load-bearing interior walls were braced, but partitions that did not support the roof were often put up after the floor had been laid.

The old board-and-batten construction died out and walls were generally weatherboarded, by

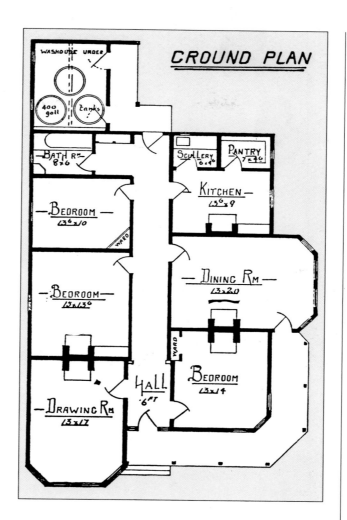

CROUND PLAN

Cottages, Villas and Country Houses

Design No. 44 from James Christie's catalogue of New Zealand Homes (c. 1910). The plan illustrates the way in which clearly separated rooms were entered from a central corridor. Kitchens were always at the back of the house but by the 1890s the dining room had become a common feature and was frequently given a bay of its own. Improvements in sanitation allowed the bathroom to be brought inside the house, although the lavatory remained outside or in the back verandah.

a method which involved a system of overlapping the boards. By the 1870s the points at which weatherboards joined at corners were boxed with scribers, battens cut to the required shape. Interior walls were often lined with horizontally laid boards, which proved draughty, so those who could afford it lined their walls either with a lath and plaster covering or with tongue-and-groove boards. Another common method of wall lining, called matchlining, was achieved by joining boards with a thin bead.

As the size of villas grew, the simple gable-type roof was no longer adequate and a U-shaped roof plan around a central gutter became a common solution to drainage problems. Roofs were clad with slates or corrugated iron, but after 1900 the distinctive orange Marseilles tile was much favoured. All houses had fireplaces, which for reasons of economy were usually placed back to back; chimneys sported elaborately corbelled tops and combinations of different coloured bricks.

Those responsible for producing the catalogues of decorative exterior ornaments had no interest in the rival academic claims for the precedence of either Gothic or Classical motifs. The battle of

FROM TOP RIGHT:

Villa (1909) at Broad Bay, Otago Peninsula. This was the first structure built by James Fletcher, founder of New Zealand's largest construction firm. The gable of its modest flattened bay was ornamented with an unusual pressed metal design and its return verandah decorated with Art Nouveau-derived balustrading.
FLETCHER CHALLENGE ARCHIVES.

A corner-bay villa (c. 1910) at Thames, with return verandah, turned balusters and fan-shaped bracketing joining wall to roof.

A single-bay villa (1904) in Manukau Road, Auckland, built on a brick base then clad with stucco pointed to resemble brick. Its timber ornament is characteristic of the Eastlake spindle style imported from the U.S.A.

the styles was an irrelevance to house builders, who simply chose elements from both. No one worried that fretwork designs deriving from Gothic tracery might be incompatible with a roof supported on Classical modillions, or that Italianate arched windows and Gothic pointed ones ought not to be found on the same house.

Other ornamental influences were enthusiastically taken up: the profusion of turned knobs and knockers to be found on eaves brackets or at the tops of verandah posts had its origin in the Eastlake style, which was imported from the U.S.A.; after 1900 plain stick patterning was sometimes combined with turned balusters to create a kind of antipodean chinoiserie.

The builders of New Zealand's villas repudiated historical ornament in favour of something much more exotic. Inside, the same decorative profusion was also evident. Textured and highly patterned wallpapers were regarded as suitable backgrounds for pictures of all kinds; mantelpieces groaned under the weight of pendulous ornaments, photographs and arrangments of feathers and flowers; ceilings, often the only visible surface, were plastered or, after 1900, made of pressed-metal sheeting no less highly patterned.

This single-bay villa (c. 1900) at Herne Bay, Auckland has typical sash windows, an arched pediment with a finial, fretwork bracketing and a diamond-paned stained-glass window at the end of its verandah. The bay is faceted rather than flat. The square side bay incorporates a dining room.

A double-bay villa (c. 1900) at Somme Parade, Wanganui. The enlarged central porch incorporating the bay is a regional characteristic.

*The design of the Bayly
House (1906), Wanganui,
a corner-bay villa, is
unusual in bringing the
gable forward to treat it as
part of the verandah.
Timber fretwork decoration
for this house was imported
from France.*

*This house in Northcote,
Auckland, has a
conventional villa plan.
Although its sash windows
remain, the hipped roof
now has exposed rafters
instead of rows of
modillions, and the
simplified verandah
decoration is characteristic
of the bungalow.*

*The Sarjeant House (1909), next door to the Bayly
House in Bell Street, Wanganui, is Italianate in design
and is said to have been based on a sketch done by Mrs
Sarjeant during a visit to Italy. This two-storeyed villa
has a low-pitched roof, wide projecting cornice and
quoins of timber to resemble stone. The arcaded
verandah with balustraded balcony above has views of
Mt Ruapehu in the distance.*

By 1910 the impact of the Californian
bungalow was being felt and many architects,
while continuing to design houses according to
the traditional villa plan, began to incorporate
bungalow features into house facades. Roof angles
were flattened, fretted and turned verandah
decorations were simplified, and double-hung
sash windows were replaced with casement-and-
fanlights. The transition between villa and
bungalow lasted some ten years; Jeremy Salmond
has noted that 'after 1918 no speculative builder
with any commercial sense would have bothered
to advertise a new house in the villa style'.[3]

*In Wellington tall 'up-and-
down' town houses were the
natural response to the
city's hilly topography.
These houses on Tinakori
Road were designed by
Robert Roy Macgregor and
built in 1902.*

*'Domus' at 22 Patrick
Street, Petone, Wellington,
designed by Joshua
Charlesworth as part of the
1905 State Housing
Scheme.*

Two further aspects of domestic design closely
related to villa architecture remain to be
considered: the state housing scheme of 1905 and
the Railways Department's provision of houses
for its workers after 1885. In the late 1890s the
Prime Minister of New Zealand, Richard Seddon,
observed new workers' houses built by local
councils in London and Glasgow. He returned
home determined to do something similar here
and, in 1905, the Workers' Dwellings Act came
into force. Under it the Minister of Labour could
make use of Crown land to build workers'
dwellings which could be rented, leased or sold
conditionally to any person who at the time of
his or her application did not earn more than
£156 per annum and was landless. An applicant
had to appear before the Land Board to furnish
proof of these facts and that he or she was a
moral and deserving person. In fact the whole
scheme has been described as 'profiteering and
patronising'.[4] Officials discouraged all applications
by women for fear that the houses might be used
as brothels and made it very difficult for a tenant
to attain the freehold title to his house,
apparently out of fear that he might become a
capitalist landlord.

The architectural character of the Seddon state
houses was determined by a competition held in
1906 which attracted 150 entries, from which
thirty-four designs were selected. Wellington's
houses included two-storeyed designs, while
Auckland's were all one-storeyed with verandahs.
The South Island houses were to be more solidly
constructed and were provided with covered-in
entrances. All had five major rooms: living room,
combined kitchen/dining room and three
bedrooms. Three bedrooms were required so that
children of different sexes need not sleep in the
same room and a small separate bathroom was
regarded as essential. In this way the moral tone
of the country would be improved.

The architect Joshua Charlesworth (1861–1925)
designed the two-storeyed house called 'Domus',
a fine example of which can still be seen at
22 Patrick Street, in the historic precinct at
Petone, Wellington. 'Domus' was clad in plain
weatherboards on the ground floor but was half-
timbered on the upper storey. The shallow
hipped roof had eaves supported on large ornate
brackets and an ornamental band of scalloped
tiles marked the division between floors. Smaller
brackets supported the window hood in the living
room, and to one side there was an indented
porch. There were understandable complaints
from tenants who were not used to having an
earth closet within the confines of the house.

The two-storeyed 'Kia Ora' by Jack Hoggard at
14 Patrick Street was notable for some fine but
restrained detailing, including leadlight windows.
An example of William Gray Young's 'Young
New Zealand', a single-storeyed structure, can still
be seen at 24 Patrick Street. Like Samuel Hurst
Seager's and Cecil Wood's Design No. 3, it
incorporates some bungalow features, although
Gray Young kept to the sash window instead of
using casements. Seager was no doubt responsible
for the attractive rimu panelling and coved ceiling
used in Design No. 3, a reminder of his houses at
Clifton Hill, Sumner (see page 85).

*Design No. 3 at 19 Patrick
Street, Petone, by
Christchurch architects
Samuel Hurst Seager and
Cecil Wood.*

Seven of the chosen designs were eventually built at the Heretaunga Settlement, Petone. To avoid monotony they were dispersed at random along the street, single-storey dwellings alternating with double-storey ones. All were built of wood on concrete foundations. Ever-increasing building costs meant that only 657 houses were built by 1919, so Seddon's figure of 5000 remained a dream. The Heretaunga houses were not well received. 'Are they homes?' asked the *Evening Post* of 26 July 1906, deriding them as workers' 'dwellings', and headlining them as 'a bizarre spectacle'. The five houses built on the bungalow plan were described as 'squat things that look as though they have not yet decided to stand up or sit down'.

Another foray into workers' housing was carried out by the Railways Department, which had been in the business of providing accommodation since the early 1880s, when tents had sufficed to shelter construction workers building a railway through remote parts of the country. By the turn of the century a shortage of housing for Railways staff was already apparent, but little was done to alleviate the problem until as late as 1919, when the Railways Architectural Branch was formed under the direction of George Troup (1863–1941). In 1920 the Railways Department established a housing factory at Frankton Junction, where timber was to be cut to

size for a standard form of house which could them be transported by rail to all parts of the country. Troup visited American housing factories which specialised in cut-to-fit continuous house-building operations and it was on these that the Frankton factory was modelled.

Railways houses dating from 1909 had been built on a very simple square cottage plan, which was to remain in use with only very slight alteration for the next forty years. Troup's American trip produced little or no modification to this basic villa plan, beyond the provision of porches which hint at some influence from the Californian bungalow. Typical examples can still be seen at Ngaio, Wellington, where, as late as 1927, construction of twenty-two prefabricated houses from the Frankton factory began in Tarikaka Street. All have the villa floor plan but front porches and roof types were varied. Railways houses were finished in horizontal weatherboarding; gable ends of the houses were clad in a new building material — asbestos panels — with battens covering the joints. The walls and ceilings of utility rooms were lined with tongue-and-groove boards; other rooms had wallpaper pasted on to scrim, which was tacked to rough timber wall linings. Other finishings were minimal. Roofing, including window hoods, was galvanised corrugated iron; porches were decorated with trellis work in specified patterns.

Railways houses at Tarikaka Street, Ngaio, Wellington. Designed in 1927 and prefabricated at the Railways Housing Factory at Frankton Junction, Hamilton, they differ only superficially from the small villas produced for Railways employees as early as 1907.

*Marshall House (1877),
Thames. The original
owner made a fortune in
the gold boom and moved
into town. He added the
verandahs at the turn of the
century.*

*Holmeslee, Rakaia,
originally a four-roomed
farm cottage, was greatly
enlarged in 1900.*

The Railways houses from the Frankton factory
were old-fashioned from the day they were first
produced. The plan created spatial relationships
which only frustrated the increasingly informal
lifestyles of their occupants; their 285-centimetre
stud height and sash windows marked them out
as being conceived in an earlier era. Always
carefully oriented towards the street frontage, the
siting took little cognisance of sunlight, wind or
privacy. Their advantage was ease of transport
and speed of erection; there was considerable
advantage, too, in their similarity in that workers
and their families on transfer need not worry
about their furniture fitting in their new house.
Many such houses were built and can be seen
today in the central North Island towns of
Taihape, Taumarunui, Te Kuiti, Huntly and
Frankton, but the Ngaio houses were among the
last to be prefabricated at the Frankton factory,
which was closed in 1929 and its plant sold off.

Housing for employees of New Zealand
Railways was to be taken up by the state after the
election of the first Labour Government in 1935.
Although they were much despised in their day,
the Railways houses were always solidly
constructed and served the purpose for which
they were built. They are now eagerly sought at a
time when former New Zealand Railways
properties are being sold to the public.

The villa and its derivatives dominated
domestic housing in New Zealand from 1860 to
1910. Qualities associated with villa decoration
can also be seen on much larger houses which
were built or altered during the same period,
particularly around 1900. Although the Marshall
House at Parawai, Thames, dates from 1877 it
shows considerable similarities of plan and
decoration to Holmeslee at Rakaia. Neither house
was to reach its final form until as late as 1900,
when expansive double-storeyed verandahs were
added.

The Thames house was originally built for John
Marshall, a landowner at Puriri who was later
successful during the investment boom in gold
mining between 1895 and 1897. Although the
boom was short-lived, Marshall was not
disadvantaged and went on to set up a drapery
business in Thames. The grounds of his house
have long been subdivided, but the magnificent
verandahs continue to express its first owner's
confidence. Holmeslee was a four-roomed cottage,
greatly enlarged in 1900, when the original
cottage was swallowed up in what later became a
billiard room. Both houses have central halls
which run the full length of the ground floor,
with stairs at the far end.

*Leslie Hills (1900),
Culverden, by R. W.
England.*

The homesteads Greenhill, outside Hastings,
and Leslie Hills, at Culverden in Canterbury,
were both built in 1900 and are sprawling single-
storeyed houses with facades distinguished by
deep verandahs and a central highly ornamented
turret with entry portico beneath. Leslie Hills was
the work of the Christchurch architect R. W.
England, while Greenhill was designed by George
Sollitt of Hastings. Villa-style verandah
decoration reached a pinnacle of elaboration on
the enormous house originally called Threave, in
High Street, Dunedin, which is attributed to
R. A. Lawson. Its building was supervised by
J. L. Salmond in 1903, the year after Lawson
died.

*Greenhill (1900), Hastings,
by George Sollitt.*

*Threave (1903), High Street, Dunedin, is attributed to
R. A. Lawson and now called the Watson Shennan
House. Its turned wood verandahs are particularly
elaborate.*

TOP LEFT: *Coverdale (1907), Christchurch. The Christchurch photographer Steffano Webb made a unique record of this now demolished two-storeyed bay villa.*
STEFFANO WEBB COLLECTION, ALEXANDER TURNBULL LIBRARY.

TOP RIGHT: *Coverdale. The hall ceiling has Jacobean detailing and the carpet has an Art Nouveau design.*
STEFFANO WEBB COLLECTION, ALEXANDER TURNBULL LIBRARY.

BOTTOM: *Coverdale. The drawing room displays the taste for clutter. The wallpaper frieze is a conventional Edwardian feature and the bay window divider and the stained glass are Art Nouveau. Turned wood furniture is everywhere and the room is dominated by a large ebonised fireplace. It was fashionable at the time to fill rooms with bamboos, palms and other spindly plants.*
STEFFANO WEBB COLLECTION, ALEXANDER TURNBULL LIBRARY.

*McLean's Mansion (1899),
Manchester Street,
Christchurch, by R. W.
England. New Zealand
architects seldom had the
opportunity to build on such
a scale. Constructed entirely
of kauri, Holly Lea, as it
was originally known, is
indebted to the English
mansion Mentmore Towers
(1852), built in stone for
Baron Rothschild in the
Jacobean style.*

The now demolished Coverdale (1907) at Christchurch is a typical example of the enormous two-storeyed bay villas built particularly in Canterbury and Otago after 1900. Despite their size such houses were often built from American catalogues. Architects, if engaged at all, were employed to exercise their ingenuity in designing the elaborate decorative trim.

The Lyttelton-born architect R. W. England (1863–1908) was also responsible for the remarkable Christchurch mansion called Holly Lea (now McLean's Mansion), which he designed in 1899 for one of Canterbury's wealthiest men, the run-holder Allan McLean. Robert England had been educated in Christchurch but studied architecture in England; in 1906 he was to take his younger brother, Edward, into partnership with him and this practice was responsible for many of the city's notable homes and commercial buildings. Because of its enormous size, McLean's Mansion is not typical of their work; clients as wealthy as Allan McLean were extremely rare.

The design of McLean's Mansion utilises traditional Jacobean features in a manner which clearly derives from Sir Joseph Paxton's Mentmore Towers (1852–54), built for Baron Rothschild in Buckinghamshire. Like Mentmore, McLean's Mansion is of massive proportions; altogether there are fifty-three rooms, occupying a floor area of 2140 m². It has a high concrete base, tall towers at each corner and a symmetrical, U-shaped plan. The imposing front facade is recessed and the towers extend outwards; their swooping cyma reversa, lead-covered domes are topped with cast-iron crestings. The roof and balcony are fringed with balustrading. Part of the appeal of the Jacobean style to the High Victorian architect was that it permitted the exhibition of such widely contrasting features as a Flemish gable in the centre front, wide Italianate eaves lines with heavy modillions, and not only Ionic but also Corinthian columns on the entrance portico.

Inside McLean's Mansion, a spacious arcaded gallery with a glass skylight reinforces the connection with Mentmore. The major difference between these two characteristically Victorian mansions is that while Mentmore is made of stone, McLean's Mansion is a kauri structure. In 1907 Allan McLean died and his will stipulated that the house should become a home for women of refinement and education in reduced or straitened circumstances. It was used as a hostel for many years; its present owners are gradually reinstating the elaborate, late Victorian interior decoration.

*Antrim House (1904–07),
Boulcott Street, Wellington,
by Thomas Turnbull. Now
the headquarters of the
New Zealand Historic
Places Trust.*

Interior of Antrim House.

In 1904 the wealthy Dunedin businessman D. E. Theomin had similar thoughts about spending his money on a magnificent house but, instead of choosing a New Zealand architect, he obtained a design from the prominent English architect Sir Ernest George. As at McLean's Mansion, some Jacobean influence can be seen in the Dutch gables and mullioned bay windows of Olveston; exterior walls are rendered with a pebble surface and Oamaru stone dressings are employed. The main entrance is beneath a tower to one side of the facade, and it leads into the most novel and successful space in the house: a galleried living hall, the social centre of the house. At one end of it a stairway, shipped from England, leads to a gallery which gives access to rooms on the first floor. As at McLean's Mansion, the upper floors were mostly sleeping accommodation while the ground floor was reserved for dining and drawing rooms, library, study and the many service rooms necessary in a home as large as this.

In Wellington's Boulcott Street, Thomas Turnbull and his son William designed in 1904 an eighteen-roomed Italianate house for the wealthy merchant Robert Hannah. Like McLean's Mansion, Antrim House was built on a concrete base with a timber frame clad in weatherboard and roofed with corrugated iron. The house is enclosed on three sides by an elegant verandah supported by paired columns and with turned balustrading. Like many Italianate houses of the period built in New Zealand, the architects treated wood as if it was stone, introducing keystones over windows and false quoins at corners. The juxtaposition of extensive classical detailing, Colonial verandahs and a crested High Victorian central turret indicates that Antrim House is more an expression of the wealth and aspirations of its owner than any particular style of architecture. Since 1978 Antrim House has been the national headquarters of the New Zealand Historic Places Trust.

*Te Tokanganui-a-Noho
(1872), Te Kuiti. This large
whare whakairo was built
by followers of the prophet
Te Kooti Rikirangi.*

Some of the important Maori meeting-houses
built during this period stand in excellent states
of preservation today. One of the finest, situated
at Te Kuiti, is the whare whakairo called Te
Tokanganui-a-Noho, built in 1872 by followers of
Te Kooti Rikirangi and photographed by the
Burton Brothers in 1878. It was presented to
Ngati Maniapoto tribal leaders in recognition of
the hospitality they had extended to Te Kooti
while he eluded capture by government forces
from 1872 to 1876. Originally roofed with
bundles of manuka held down by a framework of
manuka stakes, this large house has been
dismantled four times and moved twice,
according to W. J. Phillipps.[5]

Phillipps records that the base of the pou
tokomanawa represents the celebrated
Mahinarangi, for whom the great whare
whakairo at Ngaruawahia was to be named in
1927 (see page 126). Her husband, the Tainui
ancestor Turongo, is at the base of the third
ridgepole. Inside are the figures of other
ancestors, including Hoturoa, commander of the
Tainui canoe, and his wife Whakaotirangi, holding
the basket in which she brought the kumara to
Aotearoa. Maui, Kupe, Tuwharetoa, Ruawharo
and many others were also there. The carving
was done by skilled artisans from the East Coast
and the King Country, whose work on the porch
was particularly significant. Two poupou

represent marakihau, an ocean taniwha capable
of drawing food as well as people and canoes from
the sea through a long, tubular tongue. Phillipps
described it as a relatively rare feature, though
one which appears in unexpected and widely
separated places.[6]

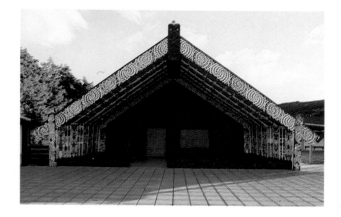

*Rongopai (1883), Waituhi,
Poverty Bay. This is a
painted house and
represented Maori
architecture in transition.*

The very large house Rongopai is also
associated with Te Kooti. It was built in 1883 at
Waituhi, Poverty Bay, in anticipation of Te
Kooti's return to his people after he was
pardoned by the Government. Te Kooti planned
such a visit in 1887 to open the house but was
rearrested and imprisoned in Mt Eden Gaol by
the Government when it was feared that his
reappearance at Waituhi would lead to further

Rongopai. Detail of porch painting which depicts ancestors naturalistically and in modern dress.

Awhakaueroa (1911), Kai Iwi, near Wanganui. Fret-worked bargeboards are used instead of the carved maihi. Such appropriation of European architectural detail was not uncommon during a period when the survival of the traditional arts of the Maori was in doubt.

in which members could sleep during the monthly three-day hui called Tekaumarua. After his freedom was granted, the warrior-prophet Te Kooti travelled widely throughout the North Island, instructing adherents to the Ringatu faith how to build such houses, a number of which survive in excellent condition today. Rongopai is by far the largest.

Built by the Whanau-a-Kai of Gisborne under the direction of the master carver and Ringatu priest Pa Ruru, Rongopai is characterised by the use of bright colours and the naturalistic depiction of ancestors in modern dress, flourishing weapons. The rafters and some tukutuku panels use traditional kowhaiwhai patterns in the usual red, white and black colours, but elsewhere both subject matter and colour are strongly influenced by European notions of pictorial representation. There are brightly flowering trees, vases of flowers, a man posed at the foot of a tree holding an axe, a hunting scene. Among the many painted portraits are those of Kahungunu, his daughter Tauhei, and Wi Pere and his mother, Riria Mauranui. Rongopai was the subject of extensive restoration by the Wi Pere Trust in 1977.

A small house called Awhakaueroa at Kai Iwi, near Wanganui, built in a period when the traditional arts of the Maori were in danger of being lost, also displays European influences. Constructed in 1911, the house is clad in horizontally laid weatherboard with a corrugated-iron roof. Instead of carved or unadorned maihi, it has fretwork bargeboards; there are two sash windows on either side of a glass-paned door and another above it. Many such houses, of modest size and blending both Maori and Pakeha influences, were built in the early years of the century, but it was not until the work initiated by the spiritual and political leaders Te Puea Herangi and T. W. Ratana in the 1920s that there was a return to major building programmes.

It was largely as the result of adaptation to local conditions that New Zealand's wooden villas proliferated. The earlier, smaller cottages had been welcome havens for the European settlers, but were clearly no longer adequate. It was inevitable that by the 1860s a rapidly growing population should lead to a demand for more substantial housing. Construction companies took advantage of plentiful supplies of wood and flooded the eager market with a multitude of plans which were to remain the basis of New Zealand's housing until the outbreak of the First World War, when other styles of housing had begun to displace the villa.

violence. Because the house was never officially opened a tapu was invoked on it; a corrugated-iron casing was placed around its walls and it was not used until 1926, when some limited functions were allowed to be carried out inside. It was not until 1964 that the original tapu was fully lifted.

Rongopai is a painted rather than carved house and thus represents Maori art and architecture in a transitional phase. According to the Ringatu faith established by Te Kooti, the whare whakairo should be able to function as a church

CHAPTER FOUR
The Architecture of Prosperity

Cathedral of the Blessed Sacrament
(page 75)

The two decades on either side of the turn of the century were highly significant in New Zealand's European-derived architectural history. No longer was it possible to speak of colonists or settlers, despite the fact that most New Zealanders still felt close to 'Mother' England. The feeling that New Zealand was a part of a mighty empire was expressed by the wave of patriotism which greeted the outbreak of the Boer War in 1899. The diamond jubilee of Queen Victoria in 1897 was celebrated enthusiastically in a country by now recovering from a long depression which had since 1879 brought about a serious loss of confidence in all types of colonial investment.

This was a time when governments, churches, banking organisations and commercial corporations were prepared to release large amounts of money for architectural purposes. Some of New Zealand's more notable architects were able to build up a consistent body of work in particularly favoured styles; their buildings can therefore be considered in groups rather than as isolated examples. Among the principal figures were William Armson, designer of Renaissance Classical banks; John Campbell, responsible more than anyone else for the proliferation of buildings in the Edwardian Baroque manner; and F. W. Petre, architect of great Roman Catholic basilicas in the South Island.

For the Maori, however, the years 1880 to 1914 involved considerable frustration as successive governments failed to take seriously their frequently expressed grievances about the alienation of Maori land. Economic depression was to remain a fact of Maori life for many years to come. Naturally, architectural trends reflected these factors. While Pakeha architecture tended to be English-derived, particularly during the upsurge in government building after the accession in 1901 of Edward VII, the often unscrupulous confiscation of their land hardly encouraged the Maori to maintain their architectural traditions.

Not unexpectedly, banks and large firms continued to prosper, even during the years when serious unemployment afflicted the country. One of the beneficiaries of this state of affairs was William Armson (1834–83), an architect who had arrived at Dunedin in 1862 from Melbourne, where he had served a lengthy apprenticeship in surveying, civil engineering and architecture. After two years in the Engineer's Department of the Otago Provincial Government, followed by periods in Oamaru and Hokitika, which he helped transform into classically dressed towns,

he set up a lucrative practice in Christchurch. From 1870 until his death, Armson concentrated on designing commercial buildings in the Classical and Venetian Gothic styles familiar to him from English architectural journals. Other influences included Sir Charles Barry's Renaissance palazzo-style clubs in Pall Mall, London, and the writings of John Ruskin, particularly *The Stones of Venice*, which was published in 1851.

Armson's extensive contribution to the appearance of Christchurch has been little respected and today few of his buildings remain. Of the twelve substantial structures he designed for Hereford Street, only the wedge-shaped Venetian Gothic Fisher Building (1880) still stands. In 1881 he designed Anderson's Building in Cashel Street, adding a distinctly Venetian touch to the Gothic detailing of the brick building by using round-headed windows and window surrounds on the facade. His modest but distinctive Public Library (1875) in Christchurch, restored in the early 1980s, is distinguished by groups of pointed windows with striped voussoirs and bands of black glazed brick alternating with red brick.

Fisher Building (1880), Hereford Street, Christchurch, by William Armson.

Anderson's Building (1881), Cashel Street, Christchurch, by William Armson.

BANK OF NEW ZEALAND

*Bank of New Zealand
(1879–83), Dunedin, by
William Armson. Each
floor is differently but
harmoniously detailed,
according to the procedure
followed by architects who
used a Renaissance
Classical style.*

At the time of his death in 1883, Armson was
engaged in building seven banks in various parts
of the country. His career as a designer of banks
dated back to his Melbourne years and included
timber structures, one of which still survives at
Rakaia (1875). Its architectural ancestry is
Renaissance Classical, the style which Armson
was to favour for all his banks, including the
magnificent Bank of New Zealand (1879–83), on
the corner of Rattray and Princes Streets,
Dunedin. Armson, conscious of failing health,
intended this costly bank to be his memorial and
let it be known that he would not tolerate any
economies in its construction. As it turned out,
at £30,000, the final cost was £4000 over the
contract price.

The Dunedin Bank of New Zealand exhibits
both a characteristic respect for High Renaissance
proportion and a love of embellishment. As such
it is a typically Victorian structure and proves
that Armson was in no way disadvantaged by the
geographical distance between London and his
Christchurch office. Above its rusticated
basement of bluestone are two floors of Oamaru
stone. On the ground floor, grey granite Ionic
columns flank round-headed windows and, on
the upper floor, pilasters frame the windows,
which are square-headed and capped with
segmental arched pediments. These windows are
tied together by a string course at pediment level,

*Interior of Bank of New
Zealand. Detail of coffered
ceiling in main banking
chamber.*

over which Corinthian columns are imposed.
There are five bays on each facade, each end bay
neatly concluding with paired columns. Above
these a large entablature is supported by consoles
and surmounted with a balustrade. Inside the
banking chamber an ornate coffered ceiling is
carved in high relief.

NEW ZEALAND ARCHITECTURE

First Presbyterian Church (1861–73), Dunedin, by R. A. Lawson. One of the New Zealand's finest churches, its Decorated Gothic manner seemed extravagant to many members of the Presbyterian congregation for whom it was built.

George O'Brien's watercolour of Lawson's original conception of First Presbyterian Church shows that the architect intended the church to have a clerestory above the aisle roofs. Walls already built had to be dismantled when, in 1871, it was decided to abandon the clerestory and give the building a single roof.
EARLY SETTLERS MUSEUM, DUNEDIN.

Another major figure who, like Armson, was attracted to prosperous Dunedin from Melbourne was R. A. Lawson (1833–1903). Born in Fifeshire, Scotland, he had served an architectural apprenticeship in Perth and Edinburgh before making his way to Australia in 1854, aged twenty-one. After a career as a gold miner and journalist he eventually set up a Melbourne office and it was from here in 1861 that he sent six finely executed drawings as his submission in the competition to design First Presbyterian Church, Dunedin. Lawson arrived in 1862 only to become embroiled in the dispute raging with members of the church who regarded the planned building as a worldly extravagance, a contradiction of all that their faith stood for. Bell Hill, on which the new church was to be built, required levelling, a process which took four years. It was not until September 1867 that work began.

First Presbyterian Church, complete by 1873, is a soaring Decorated Gothic edifice constructed in brick and faced with Oamaru limestone, its surface richly carved by Louis Godfrey, who had worked at Larnach Castle. Lawson's original design incorporated a clerestory above the aisle roofs, as shown in George O'Brien's watercolour, but this, to the architect's great disappointment, was never built. The church was given a single roof; the aisle walls were raised and the internal columns which would have supported the clerestory were omitted. The 56-metre-high spire is the church's chief glory and the clusters of turrets, pinnacles, gables and carved mouldings fully justify John Stacpoole's description of it as 'the most impressive of all nineteenth century New Zealand churches'.[1] Inside, timber roof trusses rise from hammer beams supported on corbels. Lawson went on to complete East Taieri Presbyterian Church in 1870 and Knox Church, Dunedin in 1876. His abiding fondness for Gothic gables, turrets, finials and pierced parapets can again be seen on the Otago Boys' High School (1885) which, like these two churches, is given further elaboration with the use of Oamaru stone quoins and window surrounds.

In 1871 Lawson designed the impressive Bank of Otago (now National Bank) at Oamaru. The extraordinarily rapid growth of this town between 1870 and 1895 was the result of the development of the port of Oamaru to serve the rich grain-growing and sheep-rearing hinterland of North Otago. Lawson's Bank of Otago was the first of many Classical or Renaissance buildings which were spectacularly to transform a pioneer village into a major provincial centre. All were

The 1871 Bank of Otago
(now National Bank) and
1883 Bank of New South
Wales (now Forrester
Gallery) at Oamaru, both
designed by R. A. Lawson.
The architect's expert
manipulation of Classical
vocabulary no doubt owes
much to his Edinburgh
training.

built in the pure white granular limestone to
which the town gave its name. Because Oamaru
stone was easily cut by hand and was readily
available locally, clients could commission
architects to build in this permanent material,
which was not only uniform in colour and
texture, but also cheap. The stone was popular
with architects because its softness made it
suitable for the highly ornamental carving so
fashionable in Victorian architecture.

Lawson designed his bank in the form of a
Classical temple. Its Corinthian portico forms a
front to a rectangular banking chamber which
has giant order Corinthian pilasters linking both
floors. The capitals were carved by Louis Godfrey
and the construction was supervised by Thomas
Forrester, who the following year became the
town's Inspector of Works, largely as the result of
a glowing testimonial from Lawson. In 1883
Lawson designed the Bank of New South Wales
(now Forrester Gallery) next door, creating a fine
hexastyle colonnade using the Corinthian order,
although this time the portico has no pediment
but rather an elaborate balustrade above the
cornice.

Like Lawson, Thomas Forrester (1838–1907)
was a Scot, born in Glasgow. He became a
plasterer with his father, then trained as a
draughtsman at the Glasgow School of Art. He
too was familiar with the fashion for Greek

Revival buildings in Scotland. He owned a copy
of Stuart and Revett's *Antiquities of Athens and the
Monuments of Greece* (1762), a book designed as
an 'archaeological record and architectural
treatise'[2] and the bible of all Greek Revivalists. In
1861 Forrester arrived in Dunedin and he spent
the years before his move to Oamaru working
first as a plasterer, and then as a draughtsman in
the office of Mason & Wales. Connal McCarthy
pointed out that Forrester, 'while receiving no
formal training as an architect, was a versatile,
skilled amateur from a related trade background
who promoted himself into the role of "architect"
as the result of the opportunities of the day'.[3] In
1872 he formed a partnership with John Lemon
(1828–90) whose contribution to the busy practice
was largely administrative; together they were to
transform the face of Oamaru. Between 1872 and
1885 they completed more than forty buildings;
thereafter the pace slackened somewhat.

The Harbour Board Office (1876), Oamaru,
built in the Venetian Renaissance idiom, is
typical of the highly decorated style of Forrester
& Lemon, with its vermiculated voussoirs and
quoins, carved consoles supporting the cornice,
and composite pilasters. They also designed
hotels and commercial premises, all richly
detailed — sometimes to the point of ostentation
— in an attempt to satisfy their client's desire for
a building which would out-do the other

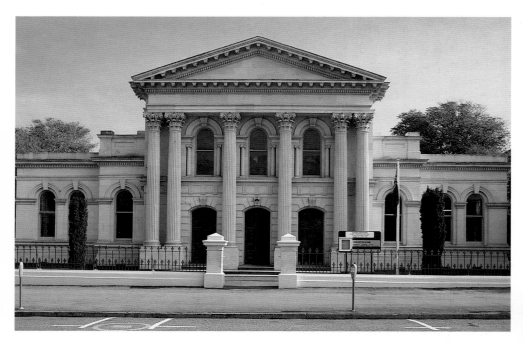

at the sides; but still the severity of the fluted Doric portico is impressive, also recalling Scottish Greek Revivalism.

Similarly impressive is the Classical portico and steeple which Matthew Henderson, embellisher of Alberton, placed on the 1847 St Andrew's Church, Auckland. It was the city's first Presbyterian church, originally known as Scotch Church and built as a simple, well-lit, rectangular meeting-house. Henderson's steeple, with its correctly superimposed Doric, Ionic and Corinthian orders, is less restrained than the portico, being provided with Wren-like balustrading, pinnacles and a variety of elaborate cornice lines.

TOP LEFT: Courthouse (1883), Oamaru, by Forrester & Lemon, many of whose buildings illustrate the fascination of Classicism for Scottish architects who emigrated to New Zealand.

BOTTOM LEFT: Otago Museum (1877), Dunedin, by David Ross. The architect was another Scottish-born Greek Revivalist.

St Andrew's Church (1847–50), Auckland, by Walter Robertson. It was a simple, box-like, bluestone church until Matthew Henderson embellished it in 1882 with a Doric portico and an elaborate steeple.

commercial buildings in the town. Their most accomplished design was the Oamaru Courthouse, completed in 1883. There are similarities between the 1882 Athenaeum (now North Otago Museum) further down Thames Street, and the Courthouse, which has a centrally placed temple-front portico with Corinthian columns. Unlike the portico on the earlier building, it extends through two stories and frames segmentally arched doorways and round-headed windows. Mouldings, architraves and pediment are all immaculately carved and correct. McCarthy wrote of its 'overall restraint and sober dignity appropriate to its social function'.[4]

Among the other notable Classical buildings built during the later Victorian period was the Otago Museum of 1877, designed by Dunedin architect David Ross (1827–1908). The interior has been significantly altered; the frieze intended for the blind panels beneath the cornice line was never put in place; the two wings were not added

Buildings like the 1869 Clyde Town Hall (now Lodge Dunstan) and its next-door neighbour the 1874 Athenaeum library show that use of the Classical vocabulary was not restricted to large buildings. As Clyde was the administrative centre for the prosperous Dunstan goldfield, it was

*Clyde Town Hall (1869)
(now Lodge Dunstan) and
the Athenaeum Library
(1874) indicate that the
Classical style was also
considered appropriate for
small public buildings.*

appropriate for these public buildings to be
Classical in style, despite their small size.

The wholesale borrowing of Classical motifs
was to continue for many years because they were
associated with permanence and stability,
qualities considered desirable in the precarious
economic climate of New Zealand's small
provincial towns. The trend was to continue well
into the next century. In 1905 a grant from the
American philanthropist Andrew Carnegie
enabled the citizens of Thames to be provided
with a new library designed by John Currie; its
facade borrows heavily from the Classical.

Given the great age of their sovereign, the
people of New Zealand must have been aware
that the 'Victorian' age was rapidly coming to a
close; it is not surprising that they should hark
back to the great British architects such as Wren,
Hawksmoor, Vanbrugh and Gibbs when seeking
to glorify their *imperium*. Late Victorian and
Edwardian architecture in New Zealand tended
to be backward-looking precisely because
architects wanted to give expression to that
British imperialism of which this country was an
essential, if far-flung, part. Among the exceptions
are two of Auckland's most remarkable buildings,
the Auckland City Art Gallery in Wellesley
Street and the Old Synagogue (now National
Bank) in Princes Street.

The synagogue was completed in 1885 to a

design by Edward Bartley (1839–1919), one of the
city's most prominent architects. Faced with what
must have been one of his more challenging
briefs, Bartley borrowed features from Christian
churches and also discreetly alluded to Judaism's
middle-eastern origins. Fortunately he had to
hand a copy of the *Builder* of March 1881, in
which was illustrated a new Glasgow synagogue,
complete with barrel-vaulted ceiling, Romanesque

*Old Synagogue (1885),
Auckland, by Edward
Bartley.*

NEW ZEALAND ARCHITECTURE

semi-circular arches, and an interior arcade composed of Gothic arches that ended in Byzantine fashion with an inward curve instead of the Gothic point. The plaster work over what used to be the Ark of the Covenant but is now the bank's main entrance is an exuberant blend of Classical and Moorish motifs.

The City Art Gallery (1887), the work of Melbourne architects Grainger & D'Ebro, originally housed the Auckland Public Library, which was entered from beneath the corner tower. Its sharply pitched roofs have finials and are lit by pedimented dormer windows; where the building turns on its corner axis a fanciful Moorish dome announces the fact; beneath it the curved turret wall forms an unexpected contrast with the patterned projections and recessions of the facade. There are other ornamental details, notably broken pediments and Corinthian pilasters but, because of the architects' interesting solution to the problem of a sloping corner site, the City Gallery reads very differently from the detail-encrusted Customhouse, built in the same year by Thomas Mahoney. Although it shares many decorative features with the gallery, its flatter surface is much more highly detailed, in the manner fashionable at the time. Similarly, F. de J. Clere's Wellington Harbour Board Offices (1891) looks back to the French Renaissance for some of its details, but is much more simply decorated.

When Samuel Hurst Seager (1854–1933) designed the Christchurch City Council Chambers in 1887 he gave New Zealand its first example of the fashionable Queen Anne style. The London-born Seager had trained in Mountfort's office but in 1882 returned to England for further study, remaining there for two years. When he came back to New Zealand he opened a Christchurch office, and the Council Chambers was his first major commission. The term Queen Anne, strictly speaking, refers to English Renaissance domestic architecture of Queen Anne's reign (1702–14), but a revival of the style took place in the 1870s and 1880s, led by English architect Richard Norman Shaw. The Christchurch City Council Chambers introduced the style as an alternative to the prevailing Gothic and Renaissance. John Cattell described

Old Christchurch City Council Chambers (1887) by Samuel Hurst Seager. The use of polychromic brickwork window surrounds is typical of Victorian Gothic but the newly fashionable Queen Anne style marked a significant departure from Gothic precedents in Christchurch.

the building as 'a clever amalgam of Dutch, Elizabethan and Gothic motifs meshed together and enriched by patterned and cut moulded brickwork'.[5] Its emphasis on picturesque details shows just how carefully Seager had observed London's Queen Anne buildings during his two years in the city. The pediment Dutch gable with its large windows is a typical feature of the Victorian Queen Anne style, while the corner tower is more Gothic in origin. An oriel window, fashioned in stone to contrast with the prevailing brick, is placed over the entry porch with an Elizabethan gable above it.

The very different Oxford Terrace and Worcester Street facades are composed with deliberate asymmetry, as much in response to the building's functional requirements as any need to provide a picturesque-looking building. The different types of window may seem randomly juxtaposed but are closely related to function: the large window on the Worcester Street facade lights the main council chamber; in the afternoons this window is shaded, so Seager designed an oriel window on the building's north west corner to allow sunlight into the chamber. Functional too is the small tower which runs up two storeys on the Worcester Street facade: the architect here gives external expression to an internal spiral staircase. The fine workmanship involved in the patterned brickwork and

terracotta tiling, and sculpted figures of Industry and Concord by George Frampton A.R.A. are characteristic features of a building which Cattell described as an important precursor of Seager's Arts and Crafts-influenced designs after 1900.

Another notable Queen Anne building, Dunedin's Central Police Station (1895), also demonstrates the free combination of motifs drawn from different architectural periods while giving equal importance to both picturesque and functional considerations. Designed by John Campbell (1857–1942) with William Crichton (1861–1928), it refers unashamedly to Richard Norman Shaw's New Scotland Yard (1887), which also has a symmetrical composition, corner tourelles and a brick construction interspersed with white horizontal bands.

Campbell was another Scot, Glasgow-born, who grew up familiar with both Gothic and Classical idioms. In 1882 he came to Dunedin, where he settled, having found employment as a draughtsman in the office of Mason & Wales. One of his first jobs was the detailing of Sargood, Son & Ewen's offices (1883–84) in Victoria Street West, Auckland, now known as Scott's Building, of which only the facade remains. The use of capitals, pediment, cornice and balustrade, and corbelling under its oriel windows is typical of the Edwardian Baroque detailing which was to characterise so much of Campbell's work as

Government Architect from 1909 to 1922. He
was rarely to use the Gothic style, although he
was called in to provide a revised design for the
roof, gables and parapet on Thomas Turnbull's
1898 General Assembly Library. The original
architect had withdrawn in protest at the
Government's announcement that cost-cutting
would reduce his Gothic building from three
storeys to two. Campbell's Law Courts (1902) at
Dunedin displays his enthusiasm for the Scottish
Baronial manner, its tower recalling Bury's Otago
University but its picturesque roof line indicating
a similarity of treatment to his reworking of
Turnbull's General Assembly Library.

Among Campbell's best-known buildings is the
Public Trust (1905–09), Wellington, designed in
florid Edwardian Baroque with the assistance of
Llewelyn Richards (1865–1945). Like the earlier
Queen Anne style, Edwardian Baroque offered
English architects the opportunity of escaping the
Gothic/Classical dichotomy by looking back at
English seventeenth- and eighteenth-century
architecture. During this so-called 'Wrenaissance'
many important government offices were built in
London, among them Edward Mountford's
1900–06 Old Bailey, William Young's War
Office (1898–1906) in Whitehall and John
Brydon's Government Buildings (1898–1912),
Parliament Square. The New Zealand
Government's resources did not allow such huge

*Public Trust (1905–09), Wellington, by John Campbell.
This is one of the most florid Edwardian Baroque
buildings in New Zealand.*

structures, so Campbell's buildings are pared back. Nonetheless, the Public Trust stands out as one of the most exuberant buildings designed during this period. This is largely due to its rusticated base and the rusticated columns which frame the entrance and continue to frame windows on two upper floors. The enormous aedicules which soar up on either side of the tower are no doubt influenced by John Belcher's Colchester Town Hall (1897–1902) and beyond that by a number of buildings by Hawksmoor.

pavilions at each end of the facade with the cupolas he had already used on so many of his larger post offices, and he articulated the first and second storeys with half columns with Ionic capitals. Baroque detailing such as cartouches, scroll-shaped keystones on arches and a parapet with an open-bed pediment were by now familar features of his style for public buildings.

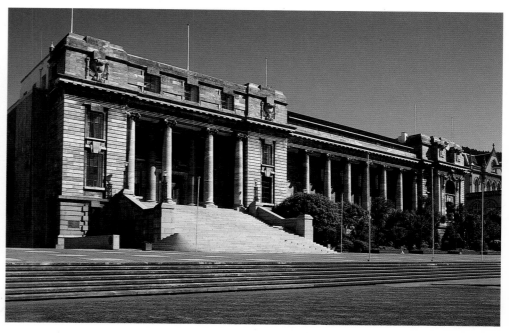

Campbell's Auckland Chief Post Office (1911) is the largest of many designed by the Government Architect's office under his direction. Although a number survive today they have been too little respected during the 1980s when, for example, despite vociferous protest the much admired Bulls Post Office (1905) was demolished. The spectacularly sited Ponsonby Post Office (1912) remains, as does another fine one at Cambridge (1907–08). The Auckland Chief Post Office owes a great deal to Sir Henry Tanner's 1907–10 General Post Office in King Edward Street, London, as the Prime Minister, Richard Seddon, pointed out at its opening in 1912. Both have four-storey blocks flanked by ornamental arches. Campbell topped the

With Claude Paton (1881–1953), a member of his staff fully committed to the Edwardian Baroque style for public buildings, Campbell in 1911 produced the winning entry in the competition to design Parliament Buildings, Wellington. Among the many submissions were notable ones from W. H. Gummer and Edmund Anscombe and another by Campbell in association with Charles Lawrence. Naturally Campbell and Paton returned to the English Baroque to invoke the British origins of New Zealand's parliamentary system. In fact only half of the designed structure was ever built; the colonnaded wing to the right of the entrance was to have been repeated on the left-hand side where the Beehive now stands, and its erection would have resulted in a very imposing, symmetrical building.

Both before his appointment as Government Architect and after it, John Campbell was accustomed to close working relationships with his staff. An affectionate memoir written by W. F. C. Vine, who worked with him from 1917, describes a genial personality who, although strict, was prepared to pretend not to see in the street members of his staff who sneaked out

RIGHT: *Parliament Buildings (1911), Wellington, by John Campbell and Claude Paton. Only half of the designed structure has ever been built.*

TOP LEFT: *Chief Post Office (1911), Auckland, by John Campbell. The Government Architect was committed to the Edwardian Baroque style for New Zealand's major public buildings.*

BOTTOM LEFT: *Ponsonby Post Office (1912), Auckland, by John Campbell.*

Dunedin Railway Station (1904–07), by Sir George Troup. Its flamboyant Edwardian Baroque manner reflects the confidence in rail as the twentieth century's major mode of transport.

during working hours. The patter of the feet of a small fox terrier that accompanied him everywhere was the signal for staff who might be smoking quickly to extinguish their cigarettes. A deaf draughtsman was the only person ever caught. Vine believed that the prizewinning design for Parliament Buildings was in fact by Paton and A. Stevenson, but regulations determined that the competition entry be ascribed to Campbell and Paton. Vine also believed Parliament Buildings was built to the plan of Campbell and Lawrence's entry and the elevations of the first prize entry.

Oamaru stone and dark granite, particularly on the porte cochère. Troup used classically derived architectural forms with an almost irreverent freedom: the pilasters on the porte cochère terminate not with capitals but with paired volutes; the line of dormer windows is framed by Ionic pilasters and capped with triangular pediments. Other windows with arched tops and elongated and pointed voussoirs add considerably to the overall impression of busyness. Only the high square tower at the southern end of the building provides respite from the jagged rhythms of the rest of the street elevation. Inside the foyer a mosaic floor of porcelain tiles and fine stained-glass windows feature railway motifs.

Dunedin Railway Station. Detail of lobby.

Dunedin Railway Station. Detail of mosaic tile work.

The building most commonly regarded as the pinnacle of the Edwardian Baroque style in New Zealand is Sir George Troup's Dunedin Railway Station of 1904–07. Interestingly, John Campbell had already designed a replacement for the old timber Dunedin station in 1883. A surviving drawing bears that date and Peter Richardson observes that if it is accurate then Campbell's 'must rank as the first work designed in New Zealand in the restrained English Baroque style'.[6]

There is nothing restrained about Troup's station; its restless facades are a perfect architectural reflection of the Railways Department's confident belief in rail as the major mode of transport for the twentieth century. The use of materials in contrasting colours is an important feature of Troup's design: long arcades on each side of the central ticket hall are supported on rusticated columns of pink polished stone, with square blocks of dark granite; elsewhere there is a sharp contrast between light

*Invercargill Town Hall
(1906) by E. R. Wilson.
This building reflects the
prosperity of New
Zealand's southernmost
city.*

Although none was quite as unrestrained as
Troup's Dunedin station, a number of other
buildings of the time clearly show that Edwardian
architectural taste favoured a highly decorated
surface.

Invercargill's more symmetrically composed
Town Hall by E. R. Wilson (1837–1925) was
opened in 1906. Its huge central rounded
pediment above the entrance is flanked by
pointed ones at each end; all the familiar
decorative devices of the Edwardian Baroque are
brought into play, just as they are on the much
smaller but no less elaborate 1909 premises for
A. E. Kitchen, Chemist, of Victoria Avenue,
Wanganui. In Auckland, too, many suburban
shopping blocks were provided with elaborately
detailed Edwardian facades above verandah level;
Portland Buildings (1914), sprouting decorative
urns and triangular pediments, is a particularly
fine example still surviving in the suburb of
Kingsland, close to one of Campbell's two-
storeyed post offices. The Leys Institute in St
Marys Bay Road, built in 1905 to a design by
Robert Martin Watt (1860–1907), forms a
remarkable Edwardian Baroque pair with
Campbell's Ponsonby Post Office (see page 67).

The Auckland Town Hall (1911) was the work
of Melbourne architect J. J. Clark (1838–1915)
and his brother E. J. Clark, who won a
competition for its design in 1907. The hall was

constructed on a triangular site between Queen
Street and Greys Avenue. At the apex of the
triangle a segmental colonnade is surmounted by
a square tower. Inside there is a finely decorated
elliptical concert hall and a semi-circular council
chamber. Alexander Wiseman's Ferry Building of
1912 employs a great number of classical motifs
which derive from the English Baroque of Wren.
Here again are the giant aedicules, the paired
Ionic columns and the tower, all of them

*A. E. Kitchen, Chemist
(1909), Victoria Avenue,
Wanganui. During the
1980s many of these smaller
Edwardian Baroque
buildings in New Zealand's
cities were demolished.
Wanganui has a
particularly rich Edwardian
architectural heritage.*

Rotorua Bath House (1908), by W. J. Trigg and B. S. Corlett, based on an idea by Dr A. S. Wohlmann. Although its half-timbered gables, strapwork wood panelling and towers are Elizabethan, that did not prevent the building of a verandah along its front so that patrons could promenade after taking the waters.

Ferry Building (1912), Auckland, by Alexander Wiseman. It was built of brick and sandstone on a base of Coromandel granite.

Ferry Building. Detail showing a semicircular, multi-paned window and a bull's eye window decorated with a sculpted swag. Many of the building's decorative features demonstrate the architect's familiarity with the English Baroque architecture of Sir Christopher Wren.

arranged to give a sense of height and the building, seen in profile from the eastern end of Quay Street, still dominates the landscape despite its modern surroundings.

But not all architects were to be tempted by the Edwardian Baroque. The notable Christchurch figure, J. C. Maddison (1850–1923), designed Government Buildings (1911) for the Square, in a return to the High Renaissance palazzo style associated with Armson. Why John Campbell as Government Architect did not design this building is not known, neither is the reason for the choice of Maddison, except for the obvious fact that he was local and already had great experience as a designer of large public buildings, including the 1902 Clarendon Hotel (see page 191), now merely a facade. The most interesting feature of Government Buildings is its unusual portico *in antis*, which rises above a heavily rusticated stone base. Inside, a fine staircase with cast-iron balusters rises through the full height of the building and spacious corridors are distinguished by carefully restrained Classical detailing including tall timber door surrounds capped with triangular pediments.

Even more unusual, given the prevailing architectural fashion for public buildings of the day, is the Rotorua Bath House, built in 1908. The plan was conceived in 1902 by the first Government Balneologist, Dr A. S. Wohlmann, although the building's foundation stone and the original plans are inscribed with the names of Trigg and Corlett. Although he would have preferred a stone building, Wohlmann realised that the expense of importing such materials made the use of wood obligatory. It was at his insistence that the model of an old English half-timbered house be favoured instead of a building in which wood masqueraded as stone. Wohlmann, who had made an extensive study of European spa buildings, was also influenced by a timber bath house he had seen at Nauheim, near Frankfurt, which he greatly preferred to 'the cold glory of marble palaces'.[7] His ideas were worked into architectural form by the draughtsman W. J. Trigg, with assistance from Rotorua architect J. W. Wrigley. John Campbell's only contribution was to provide some modifications to the finished designs.

Although the building certainly gives ample expression to the Government's desire to create an international resort at Rotorua, there was some conflict between B. S. Corlett, the Inspector of Works for the Department of Tourist and Health Resorts, and Dr Wohlmann, whose plans were on the grandest scale. There were problems with the capacity of the bath house foundations to cope with the top weight of the building and, as a result, the central tower had to be considerably reduced in height. Corlett objected to the building of a verandah along the front of an Elizabethan-styled building, but Dr Wohlmann was determined that visitors should be able to promenade having taken the waters. Wohlmann is said also to have regretted the fact that a casino was not built as an added attraction. The plush foyer with its marble sculptures by an Australian, Charles Summers, and magnificent wooden staircase, was intended to function as a focus of social activity in much the same way as the pump-room or *Kursaal* of an English or German spa.

In Christchurch, the Gothic splendour of Collins & Harman's Press Building (1909), with its carefully detailed and varied fenestration, indicated an increasing desire among builders of commercial properties to allow their employees much more natural light. Even more distinguished in this respect was the work of Alfred Luttrell (1865–1924) and Sydney Luttrell (1872–1932), who were influential in introducing modern American commercial building trends to a city whose architecture had been almost exclusively based on English models. In 1902 their Lyttelton Times Building, while still highly decorated in the manner of the time, showed that the Luttrells were aware of the work in Chicago of Louis Sullivan and John Wellborn Root, who designed buildings which not only let in much more natural light but also, by careful manipulation of facade detailing, gave the appearance of much greater height than their neighbours.

The Luttrells' seven-storeyed New Zealand Express Company (1905–06), on the corner of Hereford and Manchester Streets, was in its day the tallest commercial building in Christchurch. The influence of Louis Sullivan's great Chicago Auditorium Building (1887–89) is unmistakable. Its foundations and first two storeys are of reinforced concrete given the appearance of rusticated masonry. The upper brick structure, strengthened with steel ties, is dominated by brick piers which rise up to the cornice line and form a grid with recessed cement-rendered spandrels which emphasise the verticality of the piers. Ann McEwan regards the elegant corner tourelle as a feature that compromises the building's Chicago origin.

If, as McEwan believes, the New Zealand Express Company is 'stylistically and technically a compromise between English Edwardian architecture and the Chicago skyscraper style',[8] the Luttrells' 1908 building for the company's

head office (now called the Mutual Fund Building) in Bond Street, Dunedin, fully deserves its reputation as New Zealand's first skyscraper. It was constructed of pre-cast concrete slabs with a reinforced-concrete raft foundation, and because of an internal steel frame its external walls bear no load. The Sullivanesque division of base, shaft and cornice can clearly be seen in the treatment of its facade; slim columns in groups of four rise through three storeys to culminate in a defining arch which emphasises the verticality of the structure. This time only the slightly fussy insistence on Corinthian capitals to top each column indicates the Luttrells' unwillingness entirely to forego Edwardian Baroque precedents.

The building was visited by many architects intrigued to observe at first hand its application of modern principles. News of architectural innovation had taken a long time to filter down as far as New Zealand and architects usually had to rely on infrequent trips overseas for information. By the turn of the century a number of journals from Great Britain, the U.S.A. and Australia were carrying information about the work of the Chicago School, and in 1906 the publication of *New Zealand Building Progress* gave architects a national magazine which was to have a significant influence on building techniques and styles. Such a magazine specifically addressed to the New Zealand architectural profession was long overdue. Although most practitioners continued to receive the notable overseas periodicals, *Progress* was a success from the start, as can be seen from the number of architects who placed advertisements. Initially it was the field of domestic architecture that was most affected by this increase in the flow of information. Given the Luttrells' innovative work in Christchurch it is not quite so surprising as it might at first appear that New Zealand's first Californian bungalow should have been built in the Christchurch suburb of Fendalton as early as 1910 (see page 97).

It is said that Sir George Troup's penchant for the florid gestures of the Edwardian Baroque earned him the name 'Gingerbread George'. The work of Francis William Petre (1847–1918), one of New Zealand's architectural innovators, attracted for him the title 'Lord Concrete'. This refers not only to Petre's fondness for that material but probably also to the fact that his grandfather was Lord Petre, a director of the New Zealand Company when it was formed in 1839. Petre's father arrived at Port Nicholson (Wellington) in 1840 and his son was born at Lower Hutt, where he spent his first eight years before returning to England for a Jesuit education, followed by further study in France. Petre was articled to a firm of naval architects and engineers in 1864, later working for the North London Sewerage Company before returning to New Zealand in 1872. Following a period with a firm of English railway contractors, he set up his own practice as

architect and engineer in Dunedin in 1875. Petre is best known for his many fine churches for which his Roman Catholic education, extensive travel in France and Italy, and a large personal library, rather than any formal training as an ecclesiastical architect, were to be the most important sources.

Petre's early Dunedin house for Judge Chapman, originally called Woodside but now known as Castlamore (1875–76), was constructed of poured concrete, a material he was thoroughly familiar with from his English experience. The crow-stepped gables were in part determined by the flat surfaces of the concrete moulds used. Petre's nickname is misleading, for from 1878, when he built the Gothic St Joseph's Roman Catholic Cathedral at Dunedin, to 1911, when he designed the now-demolished Church of the Assumption at Nightcaps, concrete was not visible at all on his buildings. Philippe Hamilton has pointed out that it was Petre's practice to use concrete only for foundations and as a 'hearting' for walls, covered both sides with stone.

The 1876–77 St Dominic's Priory was given pared-backed Gothic triangular-headed lancet windows, which not only were appropriate for a monastic building but were also dictated by the exigencies of concrete moulds. The building's

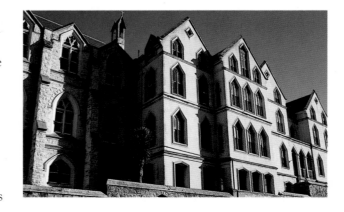

simple massing is kept from dullness by the projection and recession of bays within its symmetrical facade. The interior of the building is remarkably well-lit for its time and its purpose as the home of a closed order; the construction of a concrete hanging-staircase was a considerable technical feat and underlines the fact that the St Dominic's Priory was years ahead of its time.

nineteenth century as a means of emphasising the Roman connection and distinguishing the buildings from Anglican churches built predominantly in the Gothic style. New Zealand's Roman Catholic congregation was largely Irish in origin and its clergy, like Petre's patron Bishop Moran, Irish and Marist; Irish Catholicism traditionally placed great emphasis on its Roman connections.

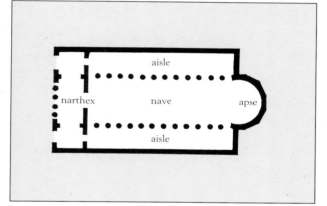

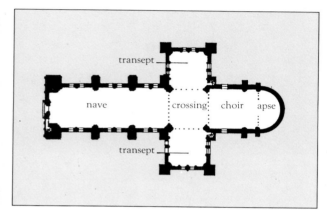

Gothic church plan.

Basilica plan.

St Joseph's Cathedral. The richly carved interior was not completed until 1905.

The next-door St Joseph's Cathedral (1878–86), although less than half complete, is just as unusual in that Petre, instead of using English Gothic models, referred to the highly elaborate French cathedrals of Rheims and Amiens. Diane Wynn-Williams attributed Petre's use of Gothic for the Dunedin Catholic Cathedral partly to the fact that 'he must have been particularly susceptible to the influence of Pugin'.[9] The Petre family had contributed money towards several of Pugin's churches and engaged him to build a chapel in the grounds of Thorndon Hall, their Essex family seat. Wynn-Williams pointed out that St Joseph's Cathedral is Petre's only Puginesque church; in his other work he favoured either simplified treatment of the Gothic or the basilican style. Basilicas had become popular for Catholic churches in the second half of the

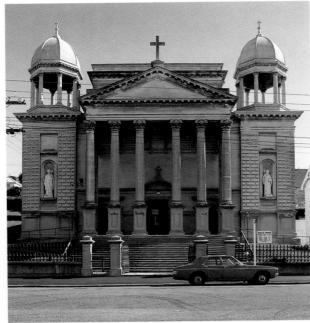

Petre's next Dunedin church — St Patrick's (1879–94), in South Dunedin — was a basilica. According to the Sacred Congregation of Rites, the Roman Catholic guide for the design of church interiors, high altars were not to be placed too far from the nave; screens of any kind or a choir between sanctuary and nave were discouraged because they distanced the priest from his congregation; devotional chapels were to be erected either at the sides of the altar or in a very short transept. Petre, in abjuring the Gothic cruciform in favour of the basilican oblong plan, was not only adopting an appropriately Roman precedent but also acknowledging that Gothic buildings were both financially and liturgically unsuitable. If Catholic congregations were to be seated as close to the altar as possible, a wider rather than longer nave was preferable. If the cost of increasing the width of a Gothic nave was prohibitive, a basilican plan in which width was not so dependent on height was essential.

St Patrick's, South Dunedin, was built on a floating concrete pad because of its swampy site. Its concrete walls are faced with Port Chalmers bluestone, and inside, moulded plaster work and a Wunderlich ceiling of prefabricated, mass-produced zinc panels replace the Louis Godfrey carving used in St Joseph's Cathedral. Unfortunately, the intended dome above the nave crossing was never built. All Petre's later basilicas had domes; in this they were influenced by the 1878 competition designs for London's Brompton Oratory, a building which was to have a great influence on Catholic architects all over the world.

Petre's next basilica was St Patrick's (1893–94), Oamaru. With its imposing towers, cupola and central dome over the sanctuary rather than the crossing, it was designed to cater for the spiritual needs of an increasingly wealthy Irish congregation whose numbers were swelled by a large group of Italian assisted-immigrants. For this building the architect used ashlar blocks of the local Oamaru stone to cover reinforced-concrete walls. While the entrance facade with its Corinthian portico is most impressive, the attic storey is too high and the side towers reduce rather than enhance the overall impact. Inside there are no such problems in resolving disparate elements. Corinthian colonnades supporting an entablature replace the heavy arcades of the South Dunedin basilica; light floods in from the clerestory above; on the ceiling, plaster cornices frame richly ornamented pressed-zinc panels.

It was on the strength of this church that Petre was selected to design a basilica to replace C. J. Toxward's 1851 St Mary's Cathedral, Wellington, a wooden Gothic structure which had burned down in 1898. The high cost of transporting Oamaru stone to Wellington meant that the Basilica (now Cathedral) of the Sacred Heart (1899–1901) was built in both polychromic brick and Oamaru stone. Like the Oamaru basilica it had a pedimented portico and flanking towers (since removed), but there was no sanctuary dome. Inside, Petre used arcading rather than colonnades, but with much greater refinement than in South Dunedin. The sanctuary is framed by a Palladian window motif, while the altar painting stands in a small barrel vault supported by Ionic columns. Another arch further forward in the chancel cleverly creates an illusion of depth. At the same time as he was working on this church, Petre was producing plans for a Wellington Roman Catholic Cathedral of St Mary strongly influenced by London's Byzantine basilica, Westminster Cathedral (1895–1903) by J. F. Bentley. In 1911 the architect J. S. Swan produced another set of plans heavily influenced by Petre's Christchurch Cathedral of the Blessed Sacrament, but neither structure was ever built and in 1984 Cardinal Williams declared that Petre's Basilica of the Sacred Heart would become his Cathedral.

George Bernard Shaw's remarks about Petre's next basilica, the Cathedral of the Blessed Sacrament, Christchurch (1901–04), are probably the best known about any piece of architecture in New Zealand. In the volume entitled *What I Said in New Zealand* Shaw is reported to have compared Petre's basilica to the work of Brunelleschi while dismissing Sir George Gilbert Scott's Anglican cathedral (see page 31) as 'a mere copy' and 'absolutely academic'. He added that in expressing such an opinion he had not been bribed by the architect, whose name he did not know, but supposed that 'he must be having an awful time probably expending his energies making little villas and wasting his time'.[10]

Although the enormous structure was built rapidly, its construction was marred by crises brought about because Petre was often absent and Bishop Grimes was an irascible employer. The bishop was to claim that Petre had deliberately misled him about the price of the Wunderlich ceiling, and there was a scandal when the two eastern piers of the nave subsided after rainwater entered the unroofed building. In 1904 the Prime Minister, R. J. Seddon, had to push a special Bill through Parliament to enable Bishop Grimes to borrow money so that the cathedral could be finished. Petre's professional reputation was harmed by the many battles, particularly one in 1901 in which the Christchurch City Surveyor questioned his concrete formula. Eventually the architect's specifications were upheld and the threat to halt work on the site was not carried out.

No doubt his use of what were perceived as new-fangled modern methods of construction was part of the problem. Such a large structure necessitated the importing of two steam cranes with jibs 23 metres long and capable of lifting weights of up to four tonnes. Among mass-produced components were the curved arches, which were made in a special moulding machine developed by the patient contractors, J. & W. Jamieson of Christchurch. Despite Grimes's 'perpetual and uninformed supervision',[11] Jamieson's extended him so much credit that their own bank threatened to foreclose their overdraft. Petre was able to save some time and

Cathedral of the Blessed Sacrament (1901–04), Christchurch, by F. W. Petre. This massive basilica, designed to rival the city's Gothic Anglican Cathedral, uses the full battery of Italian and French Classical influences.

Interior of the Cathedral of the Blessed Sacrament. The arches and pendentives that rise from the supporting piers of the sanctuary, and the colonnades that rise up three floors into the interior of the dome, create an effect of enormous grandeur.

Church of the Sacred Heart (1910), Timaru, by F. W. Petre. The basilica exploits the contrast between red brick work and cream Oamaru stone. Petre was probably influenced by J. F. Bentley's Byzantine Westminster Cathedral (1895-1903), London.

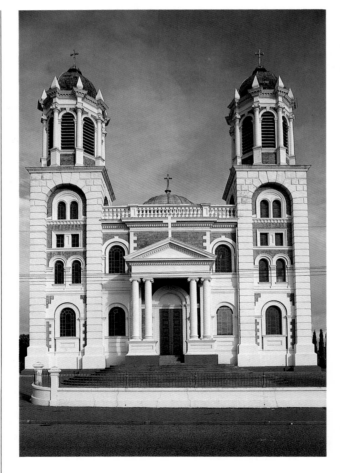

importance, too, was the fact that this Roman Catholic cathedral had to be seen as a worthy rival in both style and size to the Gothic Anglican Cathedral, which already dominated the city's centre. The grandeur of its exterior is unmistakable; nothing could have been more distinct from the Gothic than the French and Italian Classical influences drawn upon by the architect.

Inside, because of the need to accommodate large numbers of clergy at diocesan ceremonies, the domed sanctuary is much longer in proportion to the nave than in any of Petre's other basilicas. The sanctuary does not finish with a blank wall but with a semi-circular colonnade inspired by Hittorf's Parisian Church of St Vincent de Paul. Subsidiary chapels around the outer walls do not disturb the flow of movement in the ambulatories for the processions which are an essential part of the Catholic liturgy. Hittorf's church, like Petre's cathedral, also has an upper colonnaded gallery and its nave is similarly divided from the side aisles by colonnades. As in the Oamaru basilica, the sanctuary of the Christchurch basilica is dramatically lit by the main dome, which is supported by four huge piers at each corner. John Stacpoole commented that the rear view of the cathedral 'transports the onlooker direct to Rome'.[12]

Of Petre's last four churches only three survive, the Church of the Blessed Sacrament (1914), Gore, having been demolished in the mid-1980s. Like St Patrick's (1909), Waimate, it was a basilica and the only one of Petre's later churches to be completed according to his specifications. These two and St Mary's (1905), Invercargill, and the Church of the Sacred Heart (1910), Timaru, also show Petre's use of the Byzantine style of Westminster Cathedral in their arched windows and red and white decoration. There was little change in construction methods from those already established by the architect, despite the fact that Petre sold the plans to the parish priest and severed all connection with the Timaru church, which was then built by voluntary labour under the priest's supervision.

Because it was to be built for an Anglican rather than a Roman Catholic congregation, Early English Gothic was a not unexpected choice in 1902 for the Anglican Church of St Matthew-in-the-City, Auckland, designed by English architect Frank Loughborough Pearson, son of J. L. Pearson, architect of Truro Cathedral. Built in Oamaru stone, St Matthew's is strongly vertical in emphasis despite never

expense by specifying the use of prefabricated embossed-zinc panels on doors and ceilings.

The Christchurch basilica is so big because, as a cathedral, it had to accommodate large congregations, function as an administrative centre and include within its walls the traditional subsidiary chapels and altars. Of crucial

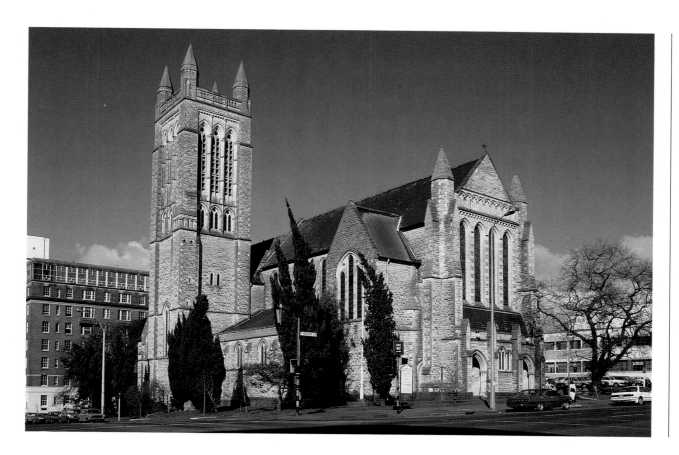

*Church of St Matthew-in-
the-City (1902), Auckland,
by Frank Loughborough
Pearson.*

achieving the spire designed for the tower. The
architect used the stone in an austere and
undecorated way so that the vertical lines of the
interior soar uninterrupted to the open timber
roof. The chancel arch is unusually narrow to
emphasise its height; the vaulting of choir and
aisles has a similar effect. Anything more
different from Invercargill's First Presbyterian
Church, designed by J. T. Mair in 1909, can
hardly be imagined.

J. T. Mair (1871–1959) had been a pupil of a
local engineer before joining the New Zealand
Railways Department, where he worked from
1901 to 1906 in the architectural branch. Then,
after two years in the U.S.A. at the University of
Pennsylvania, he returned to New Zealand and in
1910 commenced practice in Wellington. The
First Presbyterian Church was his first job and,
although his design was accepted, its
extraordinary exterior caused controversy from
the first. Such an eclectic mixture of Italian
Romanesque and Byzantine elements might have
been fashionable in Philadelphia or Boston,
where the eminent H. H. Richardson had
designed his elaborately patterned brick and
stone Trinity Church in a similar style as early as
1873. In Invercargill, however, it was considered
questionable by a congregation more familiar
with Gothic church architecture. Like
Richardson's Boston church, Mair's makes

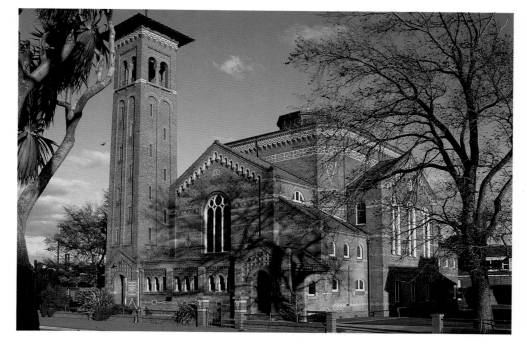

*First Presbyterian Church
(1909), Invercargill, by
J. T. Mair. The architect
was familiar with
Romanesque and Italo-
Byzantine buildings. Once
again, departure from the
usual Gothic made its
acceptance controversial.*

extensive use of differently coloured bands of
brick; Richardson's church used a traditional
plan but Mair's conforms to the more centralised
plan favoured by the Presbyterian Church. On
his way home, Mair had travelled extensively
through France and Italy looking at Romanesque
and Italo-Byzantine buildings; it is no surprise to
find that his campanile design is very similar to
that of the Church of San Michele, Lucca (1143),

St Faith's Church (1914), Ohinemutu, Rotorua, by E. La Trobe Hill. Although this was a Maori church, the architect had no qualms about using half timbering and decorative iron work. The inside of the church is adorned with traditional Maori weaving patterns.

where the tower, also positioned on the side of the church, has the same pointed roof and fenestration.

The significant numbers of 'Maori' churches built during the later part of the nineteenth century were mostly the work of Pakeha builders directed by Roman Catholic missionaries who, because of extremely limited budgets, preferred to build small-scale Gothic churches. These could then be decorated with Maori designs in an attempt to relate the natives' traditional skills to their more recently acquired Christianity. There was a revival of such activity by the church after 1880 when James McDonald, an Irishman, was appointed to the Catholic Church's northernmost diocese. His successor, the German J. B. Becker, and groups of clergy from St Joseph's Foreign Missionary Society identified closely with their Maori congregations and initiated a church building programme. Among those churches was St Gabriel's, Pawarenga (1899), which has one of the most spectacular sites of any church in New Zealand, on Mokora Pa overlooking the Whangape Harbour. Its design is of a sophistication which leads one to suspect the hand of an architect, yet there is no written evidence that its builder, Robert Shannon, received any such assistance.

St Gabriel's Church (1899), Pawarenga. This was probably designed by its builder, Robert Shannon. It is one of many isolated wooden Gothic churches in Northland.

At Waihi, on the south-western shores of Lake Taupo, the Church of St Werenfrid (sometimes called St Winifred's) was opened on Christmas Day 1895. St Werenfridus was the patron saint of the Dutch Roman Catholic priest Jan Smiers, who had arrived in New Zealand in 1888 and been appointed to Waihi–Tokaanu the following year. Like St Gabriel's, this church is entered from beneath a high square tower surmounted by a steeple and a cross. Inside, simple roof trusses and supporting rafters are decorated with Maori designs; one of a pair of stained-glass windows depicts the Madonna as a wahine.

The Gothic detailing on the Anglican St Faith's Church (1914) at Ohinemutu beside Lake Rotorua was certainly the work of an architect, E. La Trobe Hill. Since Rotorua already had one notable building in the Tudor style it was not surprising that Hill should use half-timbering capped with decorative Victorian iron work on its square tower. Inside, Maori carvings and traditional kowhaiwhai and tukutuku are a reminder that the combination of Maori and Pakeha architectural motifs had been used at Rangiatea sixty years earlier and often since. Under a carved canopy nearby stands a bust of Queen Victoria which the monarch had presented in 1870 to the Arawa tribes who had fought with British government troops during the Land Wars.

The later years of the nineteenth century saw many impressive public buildings erected throughout New Zealand. In both style and construction most reflected a desire on the part of their builders that this country should reflect established European, particularly English, architectural precedents. New Zealanders still saw themselves as colonials; they drew their values from a parent culture 20,000 kilometres away and their buildings replicated as closely as possible the architectural grandeur of London or Edinburgh. It was not long, however, before architects began to insist that some attempt be made to found a characteristically New Zealand architecture, particularly in the field of housing.

CHAPTER FIVE
Changing Influences in Domestic Architecture

Tauroa
(page 90)

During the first three decades of this century there was, not surprisingly, a considerable growth in the variety of architectural styles employed in domestic architecture. Many successful families wished to display their wealth and confidently engaged one of the growing number of competent architects who were only too eager to work for someone able to pay for their sometimes grandiose and frequently novel schemes. Some of the best of these were New Zealand-born, English-trained architects who returned home with firm ideas about matters of style. Their clients were to find that they had to pay dearly for the privilege of having a young, opinionated architect design them a house which turned out to be rather more expensive to build on the slopes of Remuera than it might have been in the shires of England. Usually, though, architects such as J. W. Chapman-Taylor, Samuel Hurst Seager in Christchurch, Basil Hooper in Dunedin, and R. K. Binney and Gerald Jones in Auckland were remarkably successful in blending Arts and Crafts principles, or those they derived from experience in offices like that of Sir Edwin Lutyens, with New Zealand conditions.

The career of J. W. Chapman-Taylor (1878–1958) is one of the most intriguing in the history of New Zealand architecture. Born in Bloomsbury, London, he arrived in New Zealand aged two. As a child in Taranaki he received only minimal schooling, eventually running away from home when his parents made him work for a blacksmith. At the age of thirteen he apprenticed himself to a firm of joiners at Taihape and later he took an American correspondence course in architecture and building construction. By 1900 he had married and set himself up as an 'architect-craftsman' in Wellington.

Familiar with the ideas of William Morris and John Ruskin and the work of the English Arts and Crafts architects and designers who attempted to put them into practice, Chapman-Taylor became convinced that the moral, aesthetic and technical aspects of an architect's work were interdependent. He believed that those who lived in his houses would be morally and spiritually improved by the experience. Often he gave his clients a 'housebook' which included drawings and photographs taken by himself from site clearance to final completion. His philosophy of architecture was carefully explained so that no client could remain unaware of the precise reasons for each room's layout and furnishings. Readers of *Progress* received a characteristic sermon when he contributed a description of his 1913 Burgess House, called Plas Mawr, in Standish Street, New Plymouth.

> The art of building is so subtle because it has to do with human moods and should influence them for the better. Are we dull? white walls cheer us. Are we fearful? thick walls and high set windows guard us. Do our hearts feel cold? A generous fireplace and red curtains warm our spirits to a glow again. Sentiment attaches itself to permanent homes and around them patriotism and public spirit grow and thrive.[1]

By 1953, when the old architect presented his clients the Bradshaws of Chatsworth, Silverstream, with their housebook, he was waxing autobiographical.

> As a young man in 1909 I went to England to study at first hand the work of men whose names were famous in the field of domestic architecture. To study them from here is not enough, one must see the REAL THING. In the beautiful work of C. F. A. Voysey, Baillie-Scott, Parker and Unwin, and others, I discovered the basic principles on which good domestic architecture is developed. I returned to New Zealand determined to follow these principles (not to copy their work in detail). Thus I was able to do as they did and build better than I know. Beauty is really a by-product and comes almost of itself if our motives are right.[2]

It is highly likely that when he was in England, Chapman-Taylor met the great English Arts and Crafts architect, C. F. A. Voysey (1858–1941), with whose work he would already have been familiar from the *Studio* magazine. He went to the Daneway Workshops at Sapperton in the Cotswolds and was taught by Ernest Gimson the

Plas Mawr (1913), New Plymouth, by J. W. Chapman-Taylor. Exterior walls of brick were coated with roughcast, then whitewashed to form a sharp contrast with the adze-hewn jarrah trim of windows and doors. There was no wallpaper or plaster inside, whitewash being applied directly to the brick.

technique of hand adzing, which became a Chapman-Taylor trademark.

In Plas Mawr, the first of his 'sun trap' plans, all the woodwork is of jarrah, adze-hewn, oiled and waxed, reflecting his belief that planing and printing machines cannot express thought anything like as well as a man working with simple tools. Chapman-Taylor believed that the craftsman must be able to express himself through hand work, so that 'our ornament may become living, beautiful, full of ensouling ideas instead of dull meaningless repetitions as in machine-made decoration'.[3]

In Chapman-Taylor houses, the windows, even the hinges, were made from hand-forged iron, and natural wood finishes were darkened with bichromate of potash to contrast more effectively with the whitewash applied either directly to brick or to a plaster covering. Exteriors of roughcast or concrete (to which he was devoted) were frequently moulded by his son Rex, who became a master of the trowel-stroke technique that gave such a distinctive texture to a Chapman-Taylor house. Inside, cleanliness was essential: the architect forbad 'useless ornaments making us slave to the duster',[4] his windowsills were often tiled to allow easy wiping, and his shelving was kept at least an inch away from the wall so as not to act as a dust trap.

In 1913 Chapman-Taylor moved to Havelock North, where he was involved with a hermetic order, known as Temple of the Golden Dawn, and designed houses for members. One of the largest was built for the order's founder, Dr

Felkin. Whare Ra (1913) sits low on a sloping site above the concrete temple where the order's adherents met to perform their ceremonies. In 1923 Chapman-Taylor worked in Auckland, but by 1928 he was back in Wellington, where he built prolifically until late in his career.

Whare Ra. The heavily buttressed concrete rear of the house gives no indication of the size of the windowless temple within.

Whare Ra (1913), Havelock North, by J. W. Chapman-Taylor. A long verandah extends between two gables, the nearest of which contains a formal entry into a large drawing room, where adherents of the Temple of the Golden Dawn met before descending via a circuitous stairway to the temple.

Wilkinson House (1928), Pukearuhe, Taranaki, by J. W. Chapman-Taylor. Built around a central courtyard, the house was constructed of concrete and clad in sandstone taken from an outcrop on a beach some distance away. The roof is laid with irregularly sized concrete tiles.

Wilkinson House. The long, narrow entrance to the inner courtyard is more monastic than domestic.

Interior of Wilkinson House. Chapman-Taylor's ability to manipulate large interior spaces to allow the inhabitants intimate privacy is clear. The open doors to the left lead directly to the inner courtyard.

In 1928 he moved with his family to Pukearuhe in Taranaki, where they lived in a barn on site for a year while he worked on a large house for his friend C. A. Wilkinson, M.P. Dramatically sited on the cliff above Wai-iti Beach and close to the ancient pa, Whakarewa, the atrium-type house was built of reinforced concrete, faced with hand-laminated sandstone quarried from an outcrop on the beach. Rata and puriri timber was obtained from the bush nearby; the huge rata beam which dominates the entrance was chopped out of a whole tree. The roof was made of irregularly sized concrete tiles laid like slate and coloured with sulphate of iron to varying depths

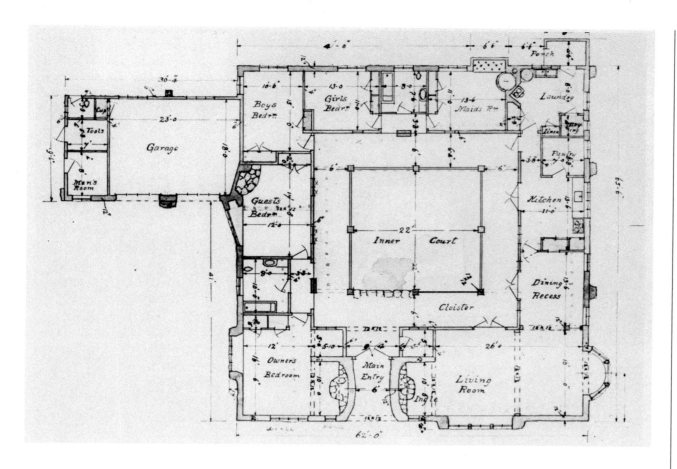

Plan of Wilkinson House.
AUCKLAND UNIVERSITY
SCHOOL OF ARCHITECTURE
LIBRARY.

*Spicer Beach Cottage
(1923), Rothesay Bay,
Auckland, by J. W.
Chapman-Taylor. Its walls
were made of 30-centimetre-
thick clay blocks, dug on
site and fixed together with
a mortar of clay and lime.
The surface was finished
with trowel-stroke cement
and whitewashed. The
architect's fondness for
sloping buttresses is evident.*

of colour, from pale biscuit to a warm burnt sienna. The architect intended to create something 'having the quality of old stone roofs of Europe'.[5]

Around the inner courtyard, cloisters give onto rooms proportioned according to their function. The bedrooms on the northern side are intimate and cosy. The enormous fireplaces have a raised hearth to break draughts and both the owner's bedroom and the living room feature inglenooks with cushioned settles at right angles to the fireplace. The windows are the usual small-paned casements, Chapman-Taylor believing that 'however beautiful a prospect may be, it is better to take it a little at time than to sit in a kind of shop window and gaze upon a scene from which there is no escape'. Each elevation illustrates in its plainness his dictum that there should be 'no senseless towers, no useless gables or imitation dormers'.[6]

Chapman-Taylor houses are easily recognised. Their trowel-stroke finish, hand-adzed front doors and windowsills, squared chimneys with side vents, cottage-like proportions and generally rustic appearance make them look as though they have grown naturally out of the ground. Chapman-Taylor, never a man given to false modesty, wanted them to look as though they would endure forever. This, he believed, was the supreme test of architecture.

In Christchurch, Samuel Hurst Seager (1855–1933) was keen to adapt predominantly Old World styles to suit the materials and climate of New Zealand, although he realised that only the most gifted architects would be equal to the task of creating a truly national architecture. In 1900 he published his ideas in an influential article for the *Journal of the Royal Institute of British Architects*.[7] At the same time he was involved in the design and building of a very large house called Daresbury Rookery (1897–1901) for the wines and spirits merchant George Humphries.

Daresbury (1897–1901), Fendalton, Christchurch, by Samuel Hurst Seager. This huge Arts and Crafts house was designed at the time its architect considered it necessary to adapt the best English styles to the materials and climate of New Zealand, to create a distinctive architecture.

Ground-floor plan of Daresbury.
AUCKLAND UNIVERSITY SCHOOL OF ARCHITECTURE LIBRARY.

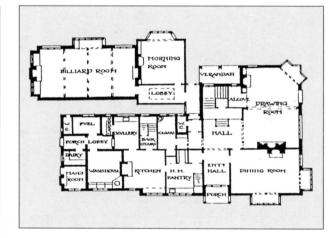

Daresbury Rookery was built in the Tudor style favoured during the English Domestic Revival and brought to its highest pitch in New Zealand by C. T. Natusch (1859–1951) in his Hawke's Bay and Wairarapa houses. Seager's forty-roomed, three-storeyed house is set among mature trees and stands on a lawn which gently slopes down to the Waimari Stream. With its wide, half-timbered gables and jettied upper floor, its dormers, porches and balconies, and its leaded casement and bay windows and terracotta ridge-tiled roof, Daresbury, as it is known today, is a perfect example of the transplanted English style which Seager was later so thoroughly to overturn.

Daresbury was illustrated in F. de J. Clere's article 'Domestic Architecture in New Zealand', contributed to *The Studio Yearbook of Decorative Art* (1916), but Clere commented that New Zealanders

are opposing in a vague and unconscious way those changes which a new environment and new conditions of living are of necessity forcing upon them . . . they have no particular desire to encourage anything native, preferring to import books, pictures, designs, fashions, etc., from the lands of their birth than to encourage a National style in the land of their adoption.[8]

He noted that architects were not having a great deal of success in introducing the general living room in place of the separate drawing room and dining room. Although Daresbury, with its additional morning room and magnificent timber-ceilinged billiard room, was backward-looking in its Englishness, it was also a highly fashionable example of the Old English manor style which became popular, particularly in Christchurch, during the following decade.

Adjacent to Daresbury in Fendalton Road is the much better known Mona Vale (1905), instantly recognisable because of its picturesque gate lodge. Originally built in about 1900 for Frederick Waymouth and known as Karewa, the house was designed by J. C. Maddison, who also favoured the Old English style. The property was subsequently bought by Annie Townend, daughter of G. H. Moore, the builder of Glenmark at Waipara, a vast Gothic mansion designed by Samuel Farr in 1880 but destroyed by fire ten years later. The architect of Mona Vale was probably R. W. England (1863–1908), creator of Holly Lea (see page 53), who also favoured the Old English style. He took advantage of the recently introduced Marseilles tile, creating a roof bristling with terracotta finials and cresting. Mona Vale has a brick ground floor and half-timbered upper floor, but its garden is more open to its grand surroundings than Daresbury's, the architect having designed a verandah for the ground floor and a balcony for the first. Two-storeyed wooden homesteads of forty years earlier had favoured such an arrangment, but it had been forgotten in the passion for the Old English style. From 1910 until the Second World War, leading Christchurch architects continued to build simplified versions of two-storeyed Old English or Tudor houses; with their slate or tiled roofs, half-timbered gables, and bay and leaded windows they are still recognisable in the city's western suburbs.

At the very turn of the century Seager had already in his own home begun to explore the possibilities of the truly New Zealand house. In 1899 he had bought and extended an unusual Colonial brick cottage in Cranmer Square, dating from 1864. Seager's wooden extension presents a

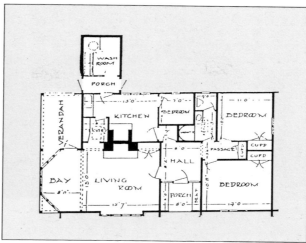

windowless facade to the street. Its appearance is so understated that the passer-by can easily miss it, although its pattern of arcaded battens and deep-set porch are worthy of attention.

Here, as Ian Lochhead has pointed out, we have the first example of a New Zealand architect alluding to another New Zealand building. Seager's porch is a direct quotation from his teacher Mountfort's 1859 arcade for the Christchurch Club in Latimer Square. According to Ian Lochhead, 'Seager was emphasising the importance of establishing an architectural tradition in a country which conspicuously lacked one.'[9] Seager also abandoned any historical reference in the Macmillan Brown Cottage (1898), built at the same time. It is New Zealand's first bungalow, constructed entirely of thick horizontal boards in log-cabin fashion and preceding the arrival of Californian bungalows in New Zealand by more than a decade.

In 1902 Seager began an enterprise which was to result in the most adventurous and distinctive of his houses. He purchased a perilously steep property on Clifton Hill, Sumner, known as The Spur and by 1914 had built eight timber bungalows with extensive sea views over Pegasus Bay. It was a singularly antipodean version of the English garden city movement with which Seager had become familiar during his two-year period of study in England.

No. 1 The Spur was built in 1902 by Seager for himself and he lived in it for the following eight years. The plans and photographs of the house reproduced in the handsome auction catalogue show that, although intimate in scale, it included a recessed entrance porch with seats, three bedrooms, an all-purpose panelled living room and an ample kitchen, in contrast with the tiny galleys in some of the other cottages. A bay window and verandah off the living room give a view to the beach. The long, low-pitched roof gives the house a snug appearance.

Interior of one of the houses at The Spur.
STEFFANO WEBB COLLECTION, ALEXANDER TURNBULL LIBRARY.

House at No. 5 The Spur (1902), Clifton Hill, Sumner, Christchurch, by Samuel Hurst Seager. A wooden bungalow designed for informal living and sited to take advantage of sea views. The rear gable is part of a later addition by Heathcote Helmore.

NEW ZEALAND ARCHITECTURE

House on the corner of Warrender and George Streets (c. 1906), Dunedin, by Basil Hooper. Newly returned from England, the architect demonstrated that there was an alternative to the omnipresent villa.

Moorcrag (1898), by Lake Windermere, is regarded as the most successful and typical house by C. F. A. Voysey.
BRITISH ARCHITECTURAL LIBRARY, R.I.B.A., LONDON.

'We notice,' observed a writer in *Progress* in May 1906, 'that an attempt has been made by Mr Hooper in designing these villas to strike off from the stereotyped style of former days.'[10] The comment pertained to a brick house which Basil Hooper had designed in 1906 for the corner of George and Warrender Streets, Dunedin. Taking full advantage of the site, Hooper's elaborate house bears very little resemblance to the Victorian villas which dominated the Dunedin cityscape at the time.

Its roof lines are complex. A double gable looks onto George Street, around the corner another gable announces the glazed porch which serves as the main entry, while still another indicates the existence of a hall. A large faceted bay is capped with a four-sided gable which, like the others, is topped with a terracotta finial. Ornamental tiles line the roof ridges. Casement windows with fanlights in amber and green glass show the influence of the English bungalow. Only the rear of the house bears any relationship to the older villa. Hooper announced his English training and admiration of Voysey by designing windows which have either gently curved tops outlined in contrasting brick or a delicately protruding curved cornice. Voyseyan, too, is the interesting play of contrasts between brick and roughcast. Here was something new.

Basil Hooper (1876–1960) was born at Lahore, India, his family emigrating to New Zealand from England in 1878. At first they settled in Cambridge, where Hooper was apprenticed to a builder before being articled to the Dunedin architect J. L. Salmond in 1896. Although domestic architecture was always his forte, Hooper worked on churches and public buildings with Salmond and he acted later as supervising architect for the building of Sedding & Wheatley's St Paul's Anglican Cathedral.

In 1901 he spent eighteen months in the London office of the eminent Edwardian architect A. Beresford Pite, a foundation member of the Art Workers' Guild, which also numbered among its members the Arts and Crafts architects W. R. Lethaby, E. S. Prior and C. F. A. Voysey. These architects rejected historicist styles based on non-English traditions; instead their work had a close relationship with the vernacular buildings of medieval and Tudor England.

In 1902 Hooper moved to the Housing Section of the London County Council Architects' Department, which was at the time producing innovative designs for workers' housing. In late 1904 he returned to Dunedin, where his reappearance as the first young architect with the letters A.R.I.B.A. after his name and with a folio of up-to-date ideas was welcomed. In an unpublished memoir he describes how he was regarded as an eligible bachelor, played the flute in the Dunedin Orchestral Society and was out most evenings. He got plenty of work.

By 1909 he had married and done well enough to be able to afford to build himself a substantial house in Wallace Street. Here he again showed his admiration of Voysey's work, using sloping corner buttresses and flat-roofed dormers which slice into the generous eaves line, itself supported with curved gutter brackets. Voysey had favoured brackets with a concave curve; Hooper follows the example of Josef-Maria Olbrich at Darmstadt, where the Austrian architect used large convex gutter brackets to great effect on his much-illustrated 1901 Habich House.

The same device is apparent on the 1911 Scoular House at 319 York Place, Dunedin, undoubtedly Hooper's finest. The facade is dominated by a subtly tapering central stair tower which includes two fanlight windows decorated with pairs of stained-glass tall-stemmed tulips. Again Voysey was the moving spirit behind many of the architectural features, although Hooper reduced the scale of the Voyseyan house, which would have been singularly inappropriate in urban Dunedin.

Hooper's later architecture was disappointing. In 1923 he moved to Auckland, attracted by the work opportunities he had discovered when he acted as competition assessor for Auckland University's Arts Building (see page 110) the previous year. He formed a partnership with J. W. Rough, but the firm collapsed when Hooper had to pay a large debt after Rough was declared bankrupt. Although he continued to practise until 1948, Hooper never recaptured the Voyseyan stylistic unity of the many Arts and Crafts-inspired houses he had designed in Dunedin as a young man.

The houses of Gerald Jones (1880–1963) in Auckland show that he and Basil Hooper had similar architectural influences. Born in Wellington, Jones received some of his education in Sydney, but was articled to Edward Bartley of Auckland and set up a practice there on his own in 1908. He returned from war service overseas with an back injury caused when a case of oranges fell on him on board a hospital ship. This, and a dislike of writing architectural specifications (though he was an excellent draughtsman), lead him to form a partnership with A. J. Palmer. Together they did a great deal of domestic work, as well as producing the Georgian City Mission House in Greys Avenue and the Dutch-fronted Mt Roskill Fire Station.

The partnership lasted until 1940, when Jones joined the architectural staff of the Ministry of Works.

Gerald Jones's finest house was the elegant and meticulously detailed Hanna House (1915) in Arney Road, which won him an N.Z.I.A. Bronze Medal. Set on a 23-centimetre brick base, its outer frame is of Oregon pine, lathed and covered with roughcast. Its dominant feature is a central two-storeyed tower bay used in a very similar way to Hooper's in the Scoular and Ritchie houses (see opposite). Here too we find gently outward-sloping, wide eaves, although Jones's windows are symmetrically placed along the facade. Inside, there is an Oregon-panelled hall and a dining room connected by folding doors to a large living room.

The interior spaces of the Hanna House prove that Jones practised what he had preached in a scathing article contributed to *Progress*. Headlined 'Our Dreadful Architecture', the article announced his agreement with the late Governor-General, Lord Plunket, who, 'after seeing most of New Zealand declared that our architecture is contemptible'. Among the solutions which Gerald Jones advocated were the abolition of the drawing room ('a showplace rarely entered'), the lowering of ceilings to improve the flow of air, the reduction in size of skirting boards and the avoidance of elaborate friezes. He fulminated against 'speculative jerry builders', calling such people 'the curse of the age . . . with their pretty-pretty villas'. An enemy of 'showy deceptions', he pointed out that constructive details should not be hidden, there being 'nothing to be ashamed of in a good nail'. More unexpected, perhaps, is a diatribe against trade unionism in the building trade.[11]

Scoular House (1911), Dunedin, by Basil Hooper. Though the house is smaller in scale, the sweeping roof lines, curved gutter brackets, shed dormer windows and sloping corner buttresses all indicate the architect's debt to C. F. A. Voysey.

Ritchie House (1911–13), 26 Heriot Row, Dunedin, by Basil Hooper. Corner buttresses in brick form an effective contrast with white-painted roughcast walls. The oriel window, bracketed eaves and half timbering are characteristic of the architect's insistence upon high standards of craftsmanship and attention to detail.

Hanna House (1915), Arney Road, Auckland, by Gerald Jones. This house demonstrates the influence of the great English Arts and Crafts architects on New Zealand practitioners, particularly if their clients happened to be wealthy.

Neligan House (1907–09), St Stephens Avenue, Parnell, by Noel Bamford. The house, originally called Bishopscourt, has very high chimneys, a central double gable and a variety of different windows, making clear the architect's debt to Lutyens.

Coolangatta (1911), Remuera Road, Auckland, by Noel Bamford.

Neligan, next to Thatcher's Selwyn Court (see page 27) on St Stephens Avenue, although work did not proceed until 1909. Built in warm yellow-orange brick, its eaveless double gables, dormered downward-sweeping roof line and variety of windows asymmetrically placed at once call to mind Lutyens's earliest houses. At the rear of the house Bamford has tried to come to grips with the problems of the sea-facing garden front, but his curving verandah with its exposed beams fanning around bays created a confusing effect.

Although the same problem occurs in his refined and compact 1911 Foster House, called Coolangatta, in Remuera Road, the pristine symmetry of its street facade seen behind an immaculately kept garden is one of Auckland's most elegant architectural sights. The entrance porch is an almost exact copy of Lutyens's at Fulbrook, Elstead, Surrey, built in 1897. The clean-lined effect is accentuated by the orange tiles that outline the ridges of the grey slate-tiled roof. Inside the small panelled hall one enters a corridor which occupies most of the length of the house and is so spacious as to be almost a gallery. Many Remuera Road houses of this period have a similar plan, with doors off a corridor into the main social rooms. Parallel to the street and to the sea front, this arrangement allows full advantage to be taken of the sea view.

Another Auckland-born architect who worked in Lutyens's office was Roy K. Binney (1886–1957). Educated in New Zealand, he returned to the city of his birth in 1912, saw overseas service during the First World War but resumed a flourishing practice on his return, designing some of Remuera's grandest homes. A flamboyant and prickly character, he left New Zealand abruptly in 1926 following official investigation into his work on the Hellaby House, Remuera, where the cost of the extras was said to have equalled the contract sum of £4000. Despite his undoubted talent, it is impossible to discover any record of architectural work done after his return to London, rumour having it that he became an elegant clubland sponger supported by his family.

Binney believed that New Zealanders should endeavour to hold on to the English traditions left by the pioneers 'and not be led away by the dazzling prettiness of some American modern architectural craze'.[12] In May 1927 the *Architectural Review* published an article by him called 'The English Tradition in New Zealand', which he illustrated with his own work, in particular the enormous house he had designed for himself on his return to Auckland after the

Noel Bamford was another Aucklander who was articled to Edward Bartley, but his horizons widened after a period of study in the office of the eminent Edwardian architect Sir Edwin Lutyens in London. A partnership with Hector Pierce ended in 1916 when Pierce was killed in France; by 1920 Bamford was working for W. H. Gummer but despite great ability as a draughtsman he was found to be unreliable, sleeping in his office and continually missing appointments. Two of Auckland's most magnificent houses are examples of his early work and both show his indebtedness to Lutyens.

In 1907, on returning from London, he designed Bishopscourt for the Anglican Bishop

war. On the plans the house is called Yennib Yor (Roy Binney spelt backwards), but it was later known as Guisnes Court and still later as Dynes Court. 'Mr Binney,' reads his own caption for a photograph of its rhododendron bedecked garden front, 'has founded his manner on the work of the greatest living English architect, Sir Edwin Lutyens.'

As in Lutyens's Daneshill (1903) and New Place (1905), Binney used brick, creating colour contrasts between dull red and purple, with lighter red bricks for the quoins. Stone work detailing is in the lighter-coloured Oamaru stone, while all joinery is in kauri. Exterior doors were originally painted apple-green and the roof covered with dull brown Marseilles tiles. A pair of multi-paned French windows with an arched fanlight lead onto a garden terrace from the central Big Room, which rises to the height of two storeys. Open balconies upstairs look over the Waitemata Harbour towards Devonport.

Binney's later houses are smaller and less grandiose, yet more adventurously planned and generally more pleasing. In 1922 he designed the unfortunately much-altered Fairley, now known as Awatea, for J. McCosh Clark, a former mayor of Auckland. Like the equally fine Mills House (1926) in Upland Road, it recalls Lutyens in its use of dark-stained wooden shingles on eaveless interlocking gables which come right down to door level and are further enlivened with eccentrically placed windows. Lutyens's house Homewood (1901) was obviously a favourite of Binney's and one to which he frequently alluded in the years immediately before he left New Zealand forever.

Mills House (1926), Upland Road, Auckland, by R. K. Binney. The large side gable shows Binney's extensive use of shingle cladding as well as his fondness for unusually shaped, eccentrically placed windows.

Cranston House (1916), Remuera Road, by R. K. Binney. This is one of a number of houses which reflects the architect's interest in Lutyens's Homewood (1901). The roof line sweeps right down to window-head level on each side but in the centre is interrupted by a projecting balcony.

Homewood (1901) by Sir Edwin Lutyens.
REPRODUCED IN *ARCHITECTURAL REVIEW*, FEBRUARY 1911.

Awatea (1922), Auckland, by R. K. Binney. The architect chose this photograph of the garden view to illustrate his article in the Architectural Review. *In those days the kauri joinery was apple green and the roof tiled. English readers were informed, 'The loggia is used as an outdoor sitting-room during the warm season.'*

Winstone House (1915),
Epsom, Auckland, by
W. H. Gummer. The
architect quickly adapted
his experience in Lutyens's
London office to New
Zealand conditions.

During the 1920s William H. Gummer (1884–1966) was Auckland's most prominent architect, known especially for his public buildings. His domestic work has been underrated, yet during his long career he designed some distinguished houses. Not surprisingly, the influence of Lutyens is again apparent, Gummer having worked in his office during 1911. His letters home give a vivid account of the long hours he worked on such notable buildings as Lutyens's Castle Drogo and The Salutation. In 1913 Gummer returned to Auckland to go into partnership with Hoggard & Prouse. He designed a group of houses which show a restraint which derived from his love of the proportions of Classical architecture. Three of his early houses were illustrated in the 1917 publication *Modern Homes of New Zealanders by Architects of Standing*, and all display this quality.

The Winstone House (1915) in Claude Road, Epsom, shows Gummer's readiness to adapt what he had learned from the Lutyens experience to Auckland's humid climate. An arched brick entry leads straight into a central hall, which gives on to a formal panelled living room which in turn leads into low-gabled, shady verandahs on two sides, one of which has now been glazed and turned into a sun room. There is a kitchen of generous proportions and a breakfast room distinct from the formal dining room, with a

magnificent classically detailed oak and marble fireplace.

The exterior is marked by a low, sweeping gable over the entry porch, but its proportions are disturbed by shingle-clad, flat-roofed dormers which look like unsympathetic additions but which are, in fact, original. The west face of the house has another large, low gable which is cut in half by a chimney rising from ground level, in the manner employed by Lutyens at Little Thakenham (1902) in Sussex. Gummer was probably attracted by the blend of English vernacular and Classical detailing in this Lutyens house.

If Gummer's Auckland houses looked primarily to his English training, those he built around the town of Havelock North in Hawke's Bay certainly did not. In 1916 he replaced Tauroa, a large two-storeyed wooden house belonging to the wealthy landowner T. Mason Chambers, which had been destroyed by fire. The result was extraordinary. Its walls are of double brick with a cavity between the two, covered with roughcast. Reinforced-concrete pillars and beams enabled the structure to survive the 1931 Napier earthquake without damage. Its plan radiates from the base of the stair of the ground-floor hall entry, which rises to form a circular gallery above. The disposition of rooms reflects Gummer's skills as a planner and, as is evident in

*Tauroa (1916), Havelock
North, by W. H. Gummer.
This extraordinary house
reflects an interest in
Lutyens's neo-Georgian
houses and in Californian
Spanish domestic
architecture, both
fashionable in England and
America at the time
Gummer visited those
countries.*

*Ground-floor plan of
Tauroa.*
REPRODUCED IN MORRISON,
IMAGES OF A HOUSE.

the exchange of letters between architect and client, his ability to listen to his client's ideas and to provide innovative solutions. Although such a plan was exceptional in New Zealand architecture at the time, Gummer would have been well aware of its fascination for not only Lutyens but also Shaw, Prior and Baillie-Scott. At Papillon Hall (1902), Lutyens had already solved the problem of the relationship between diagonal wings by putting a circular entrance court between them.

The carefully outlined, parapeted, flat roof lines, the square-columned balconies with Craftsman pergola verandahs, the plain stucco facades all show Gummer's familiarity with Californian domestic architecture, seen in 1909 on his way to Europe and again in the library of Daniel Burnham's Chicago office, where he worked briefly in 1912. This influence is also pronounced in the later Havelock North house, Arden (1926), which has a garden facade lined with arched French windows and, on its upper storey, a central open balcony flanked by two covered ones. In Gummer's own house, Stoneways (1927), at Mountain Road, Auckland, the subtle Spanish inflexion is again used, the architect obviously realising its appropriateness to the New Zealand indoor-outdoor life.

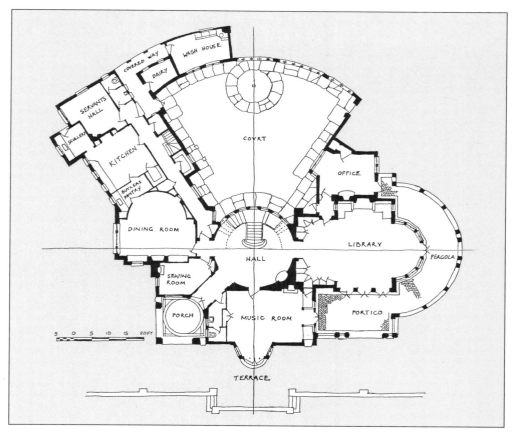

*House of Sir James Elliot
(1914), Cambridge Terrace,
Wellington, by William
Gray Young. The dormer
windows are a
comparatively recent
addition to a house which
shows the architect's
detailed understanding of
Georgian symmetry.*

The neo-Georgian interlude in New Zealand's domestic architecture was both long-lasting and widespread. It probably began in Wellington with William Gray Young (1895–1962), who built a charming little house for Sir James Elliot in Cambridge Terrace as early as 1914, although this owes rather more to Wren than to a strictly Georgian model. Gray Young had never studied overseas but would have been familiar with Lutyens's early Georgian essays at Great Maytham (1909), The Salutation (1911), Sandwich, and Ednaston Manor (1912) from architectural journals. These are, as Daniel O'Neill pointed out, still 'visually in the camp of revivalism', Lutyens unashamedly borrowing many details from Sir Christopher Wren.'[13]

Although Gray Young's intentions were much less grand than Lutyens's, Sir James Elliot's brick house, with its central, segmentally pedimented portico and symmetrical balance of all parts, makes clear reference to his admiration for the English architect's backward glance at Wren. Gray Young, an architect competent in many styles, also used the neo-Georgian manner for his timber-clad Adamson residence at Salamanca Road, Kelburn, in 1923 and again, as late as 1930, in his Young House in Pitt Street, Wadestown.

In Christchurch, Cecil Wood (1878–1947) also moved away from the English vernacular style

into neo-Georgianism. He had spent his formative years articled to Frederick Strouts and was next employed as a draughtsman by Clarkson & Ballantyne. It was inevitable that he should travel to England in 1901, where one might expect him to have taken advantage of the fact that his uncle was the great Queen Anne architect Richard Norman Shaw. Although he visited him at his home in Hampstead, Cecil Wood was determined to succeed on his own terms rather than rely on a family connection. His first employment was with the London County Council's Housing Section, at that time heavily involved in rehousing schemes. He then went to Arts and Crafts architect Robert Weir Schultz, and finally to Leonard Stokes, who, like Lutyens, specialised in designing large houses in either Tudor or neo-Georgian styles. Wood was extremely well qualified by New Zealand standards upon his return. This was a point not lost on Samuel Hurst Seager, who offered him a partnership in 1907, observing to Wood that he should consider himself the most fortunate young man in New Zealand to have such an association. The partnership, like several others Wood entered into, lasted only a short time.

Wood's first major job was a large country house for the extravagant H. A. Knight at Racecourse Hill, fifty kilometres west of Christchurch. The architect used roughcast, brick, wood, slate and leadlight glass in a much more restrained way than had previously been seen in Christchurch's Tudor Revival houses. There is no half timbering, chimneys are short, and the roof is not cluttered with crested ridges or finials. Inside there is an open-plan approach, with wide doorways which can be left open in summer and closed off by sliding doors in winter.

The influence of Lutyens is apparent in Wood's 1926 Fleming House, adjacent to Seager's Beech House on the corner of Park Terrace and Bealey Avenue in Christchurch. Here Wood achieves a notable harmony of materials in wood and brick; his gables are neatly asymmetrical but certainly less daring than Binney's in Auckland.

It was logical that Cecil Wood, an architect not wholly committed to the more eccentric characteristics of domestic revivalism, should be attracted by the balance and order of Georgian architecture. The garden front of his 1923 Weston House, on the corner of Park Terrace and Peterborough Street, utilises the full Georgian vocabulary, including a brick facade with a hipped roof, enlivened with two flat-headed dormers with sash windows. Below there is a deep cornice with modillions and dentils. The upper line of symmetrically placed sash windows is broken by a circular motif in brick which also serves to strengthen the central vertical accent created by the columned white-painted concrete

porch and the dormers. The corners are delineated by projecting brick quoins. Balance and proportion are beautifully achieved in this classic Georgian facade. Inside, the planning is characteristically straightforward and decoration restrained.

Although Cecil Wood was not to see American Colonial Georgian buildings for himself until 1927, he would have been aware that younger Christchurch architects had already created a

demand for such houses in the city. In 1926 he designed Bishopscourt, a 22-roomed mansion in Park Terrace, for the Anglican bishop. The once spacious garden has been converted into a retirement village, but it still allows an excellent view of the facade. Unlike the English Georgian Weston House, Wood faced the brick surface of Bishopscourt with cement which was left unpainted, creating a colour harmony of soft blues and greys with the painted window shutters and roof tiles. American, too, is the profusion of curved-headed shutters on ground-floor French windows. There are balcony porches at either end of the facade, each with garden access through more French windows. As befits a client as important as the bishop of a city which had its origins as a Church of England settlement, there are a number of elaborate features. A porte cochère opens off the entrance hall, and the drawing room is suitable for entertaining large numbers of people. The dining room, the morning room panelled in oak, and the study panelled in maple all open onto the garden. The plastered ceiling decoration also tends to be more ornate than in most houses by Wood.

His other large Georgian-styled house was Anderson Park, Invercargill, built in 1925 for Sir Robert Anderson. The vertical emphasis of the facade is achieved by the use of paired interior chimneys, a group of dormers, the central one of which is accented by an arched hood, and a matched pair of urns at either end of the upper balcony's solid balustrade. The house was built of reinforced concrete finished with white cement.

Changing Influences in Domestic Architecture

LEFT: *Weston House (1923), Park Terrace, Christchurch, by Cecil Wood. The architectural ancestry of this Georgian brick house is undoubtedly English.*

RIGHT: *Bishopscourt (1926), Park Terrace, Christchurch, by Cecil Wood. Although plainly neo-Georgian, this house looks towards colonial Virginia, U.S.A., rather than London.*

93

LEFT: *Anderson Park (1925),
Invercargill, by Cecil
Wood. An American bow
front replaces the central
open portico, no doubt out
of consideration for
Southland's cooler climate.*

TOP RIGHT: *Pinckney House
(1924), Holly Road,
Christchurch, by Helmore
& Cotterill. The architects
pioneered the adaptation of
American Colonial
Georgian models to local
conditions. Their small,
elegant houses were readily
accepted by Christchurch
citizens accustomed to
wooden housing, which had
the added advantage of
being cheaper than brick or
masonry.*

BOTTOM RIGHT: *Joseph
Bernard's 1768 Mulberry
House, Old Deerfield,
Massachusetts.*
REPRODUCED IN PIERSON,
AMERICAN BUILDINGS.

The sand for the cement was brought from Stewart Island in a ketch belonging to the builder, Alf Ball. The roof slates came from Bangor in Wales, and most of the interior fittings were imported from England. Wood is said to have visited the site only twice during construction. Interestingly, his knowledge of Georgian architecture was so thorough that he created two blind windows on the south side, in imitation of the practice of blocking up windows in order to avoid the window tax which was imposed in 1695.

At the same time, two men who were to become Christchurch's best-known domestic architects, Heathcote Helmore (1894–1965) and Guy Cotterill (1897–1981), were attracting clients in large numbers. Their partnership began in 1924 and lasted until Helmore's death. Both had attended Christ's College, served articles with Cecil Wood and attended classes at the Canterbury School of Art. They travelled to England where they first worked on garden city schemes as assistants to Lanchester, Rickards & Lucas, and devoted much of their time to cultivating friendships with members of well-known families.

In 1915, Helmore had been appointed aide-de-camp to the Governor-General, the fifth Earl of Liverpool, a position he held for four years. When he and Cotterill left New Zealand in 1920 they travelled on the *Ionic* with Lord and Lady Liverpool, sailing via New York. A chance delay in their schedule enabled them to make a car journey with their hosts to Yorktown, Virginia, where they saw at first hand examples of American Colonial architecture, a subject which was to occupy their minds greatly in the future. Equally important for their future practice was the time Helmore spent in the office of Sir Edwin Lutyens. The great architect had largely abandoned his interest in English vernacular revivalism and in the early 1920s was working on the neo-Georgian Queen's Doll's House for

Queen Mary, and the Government Buildings in New Delhi. Robert Esau has written that, despite the small size of the Doll's House, its influence on Helmore was enormous, especially the manipulation of ornate effects in interior decoration and furnishing.

By 1924 both men had returned to Christchurch and clarified their particular roles in what Esau called 'a patrician partnership'. For the next decade their designs were to be predominantly Georgian in spirit; indeed, they were to remain so for the rest of the partnership. Two houses in Wellington, the MacEwen House (1926) and the Crawford House (1927) owe much to Cecil Wood's Weston House. Earlier, in 1924, they embarked upon the Pinckney House in Holly Road, Christchurch, 'the first timber house to be erected in New Zealand which consciously emulated American Colonial antecedents'.[14] Esau points out that Helmore & Cotterill obviously had in mind William Byrd's 1730 tidewater plantation house, Westover, in Charles City County, Virginia. Like Westover, the Pinckney House is rectangular in shape, and has a single-pitch hipped roof and a symmetrical facade. Joseph Bernard's 1768 Mulberry House at Old Deerfield, Massachusetts, clad in weatherboard with sash windows, louvred shutters and a shingle-covered roof, was an even more important influence. The Pinckney House is provided with an entrance portico which consists of a projecting pediment, supported by wooden pillars flanked on either side by a wooden lattice.

Other much larger American-influenced houses followed: notably the enormous 1924 Georgian Revival mansion Fernside, near Featherston in the Wairarapa, and the Four Peaks (1925) homestead in South Canterbury. Both owe something to the neo-Georgian wooden houses of McKim, Mead & White who, among other contemporary American architects, were encouraging the fashion for domestic work in this manner, particularly in the eastern states of the U.S.A., where the restoration of Williamsburg, begun by J. D. Rockefeller in 1927, was a symptom of the re-evaluation of the country's architectural heritage. The American Colonial Georgian style was appropriate for New Zealand, as it was less expensive to build than the English brick Georgian. It is perhaps surprising that Helmore & Cotterill apparently made no reference to already existing wooden Georgian houses in New Zealand such as the Waitangi Treaty House or the Waimate Mission House, but their interest lay more in details of style than in fostering a national tradition.

In New Zealand's provincial cities interesting developments in domestic architecture were taking place. One of the more unusual figures was J. A. Louis Hay of Napier, an architect whose work has always been appreciated locally but who is largely unrecognised outside Hawke's Bay. The New Zealand-born architect Basil Ward (1902–76), who, with his partner Amyas Connell, was one of the leaders of the British avant-garde in the 1930s, had served his articles with Hay between 1918 and 1920 and always gave him credit. On his own curriculum vitae, Ward appended a footnote about Hay, describing him as 'a far from conventional member of a small town community whose architectural philosophy reflected the turn of the century avant garde. He was greatly influenced by the Art Nouveau movement, the Austrian Secessionists, Frank Lloyd Wright, Louis Sullivan and Charles Rennie Mackintosh.'[15]

J. A. Louis Hay (1881–1948) was born at Akaroa, Banks Peninsula, but moved with his family to Napier, where he joined C. T. Natusch as an articled pupil in 1896. In 1904 he spent a period of time working in the Lands and Survey Department, Invercargill, but by 1905 he was back in Napier, remaining there for the rest of his life. He made a brief trip to Sydney in 1908. Most of Hay's work before the 1931 earthquake was domestic and all of it proves that, even if he did happen to live in a small provincial town on the Pacific coast of New Zealand, it was perfectly possible for an intelligent, enthusiastic architect to keep himself abreast of developments in Darmstadt, Vienna, Glasgow and Chicago, by taking the right architectural periodicals.

Chateau Tongariro (1929) by Herbert Hall. Sited at the foot of Mt Ruapehu, this is surely New Zealand's largest and best-known neo-Georgian building. The architect, whose client was the Mount Cook Tourist Company, is said to have modelled it on Canadian Pacific Railways hotels.

Hay's first houses were for wealthy Hawke's Bay landowners who wanted something modern and spacious, often as a replacement for an original mid-nineteenth-century wooden house. The architect sometimes gave a nod in the direction of half-timbered English Revivalism, as in the single-storeyed, villa-style 1912 Rathbone House, called Glenalvon, at Tikokino. The house displays a confusing and indecisive blend of influences, including some obviously drawn from Hay's years with C. T. Natusch, but also shows that he was familiar with the work of the Arts and Crafts architects, particularly in the inglenooked living room. Here too one finds the profusion of floral motifs in stained glass which indicate considerable familiarity with Mackintosh's work.

Vigor-Brown House (1915), George Street, Napier, by J. A. Louis Hay. This unusual house draws on a variety of architectural influences, including Californian bungalow exterior treatment, Arts and Crafts interior fixtures, and Scottish Art Nouveau and Viennese Sezession decoration.

By 1915, when he came to design the Vigor-Brown House in George Street on Napier's Bluff Hill, Hay was prepared to allude to some of the features he had absorbed from his copy of the 1910/11 Wasmuth folios of Frank Lloyd Wright's work, which remained a lifelong inspiration.

While not the first architect to see the potential of the Californian bungalow in New Zealand, Hay incorporated many characteristics from the Craftsman bungalows which had been illustrated in books and periodicals since the turn of the century and which were the source of R. K. Binney's dismissive remarks about 'some modern American craze'.[16] Both Craftsman homes (the name given to Arts and Crafts derived houses in the United States by their chief architect, Gustav Stickley), and Wright's prairie houses were perceived as being distinctly un-English. Such geographical niceties were of little concern to Hay, whose Vigor-Brown House incorporates details from both. Although its exterior is the familiar white-painted roughcast rather than timber, one's attention is immediately drawn to the extraordinarily wide eaves line, which gives the whole house a typically Californian low-slung

look. Inside, a spacious sitting room which merges into a dining room occupies the centre of the house and is extended at the front to become a wide sun porch. The inglenook is a reminder of Arts and Crafts, while complex arrangements of intertwining rose stems in stained glass again speak of Mackintosh. Beneath the street facade's wide-eaved, flattened gable are four green tiles arranged in a diamond pattern. This decorative motif, or close variants of it, is a recurrent feature in Hay's work, being found on stair posts, verandahs and fences; it is unmistakably drawn from the square decorations which were an all-pervasive feature of design by artists and architects of the Sezession, the avant-garde movement in Vienna at the turn of the century.

In 1919 at Hatuma, south of Waipukurau, Hay designed the 700-m² Hinerangi for the Estate of P. F. Wall. The specifications indicate that the job entailed entirely changing the character of the original six-roomed timber house. It was provided with a stone entrance verandah interrupted by semi-circular, slatted, wooden clere voirs, a favourite Hay device, and high supporting pylons. On either side there are balancing overhanging ventilated gables with exposed beams and tiled window hoods with carefully detailed brackets for support. The whole effect is undeniably imposing, as are the wide hall, beautifully glazed living room and brick-lined billiard room. Most elevations are provided with differently-posted verandahs, which frame extensive rural views.

Many of these features have a Californian origin but none of them gives any indication of the architectural direction Hay would take for his next house. In designing Waiohika (1920), outside Gisborne, Hay had an unrestricted budget and was working for the rich widow of the landowner, Charles Gray. Practical concerns were not uppermost in the mind of Emily Gray, who apparently expressed no surprise when the young architect presented her with plans for an enormous house, to be lived in by three people at the most. Louis Hay's unrestrained borrowings from Frank Lloyd Wright led to the creation of a house striking in its modernity.

The house has a distinctly horizontal emphasis because of its low-pitched, hipped roof with the edges flattened to form widely overhanging eaves, and its horizontally laid weatherboards. There is a severe, brick, central front entry with a solid balustrade above; at each side elevation, single-storeyed porches are subordinated to the principal two-storeyed mass. Windows are arranged in tall vertically accented bands but, in contrast to the prairie house, they are sash windows, not casements, and none has any coloured leadlight glass, a surprising fact considering that Hay had already used geometric patterns very similar to Wright's in the entry hall of his Dolbell House (1918) at Napier. A long verandah at the back has simple unornamented posts arranged in groups of three. Beside the front entrance projects a magnificent stairwell, its exterior and interior detailing offering ample evidence that Hay had looked hard at drawings of Wright's Little House (1900), at Peoria, Illinois. Never again was he given such an opportunity to display his enthusiasm for the work of his American idol, although many of the houses he built in Napier during the succeeding years make subtle reference to it.

The Californian bungalow had, ironically, made its first New Zealand appearance in Christchurch, a city which has traditionally been regarded as the country's most English. On the corner of Fendalton and Straven Roads, Fendalton, is Los Angeles, a house which in summer is almost invisible, so completely does its dark-stained weatherboard exterior blend with the leafy surroundings. It was built in 1910 by Captain McDonald, a trader between New Zealand and California, who obtained the plans in Los Angeles and imported North American cedar and Australian jarrah for his house. Construction of the house was presumably supervised by Christchurch architect J. S. Guthrie, who illustrated it on a page of his designs in *Progress* in 1913.[17] Despite the many different types of window and the two split gables beneath the main roof line, every detail has been aligned, creating a distinctly horizontal emphasis. A secondary roof extends above the main roof, but because it slopes downwards it does not disturb the emphasis. All the Californian features are in place: the river boulder verandah post, the wide eaves, the exposed rafters on gables and window hoods. All of these were features of the classic Californian bungalows being designed at the same time by the Greene brothers at Pasadena. Like the Pasadena bungalows, Los Angeles has a panelled, and consequently very dark, interior and a typically open plan.

Waiohika (1920), Gisborne, by J. A. Louis Hay.

Little House, Peoria, by Frank Lloyd Wright. Notes in Hay's copy of Wright's Studies and Executed Buildings *show that the book was a life-long influence.*

Los Angeles (1910), Fendalton, Christchurch, by J. S. Guthrie. From 1910 the New Zealand magazine Progress *reproduced plans and elevations of Californian bungalows. This house, one of the first of its type built here, has all the classic features.*

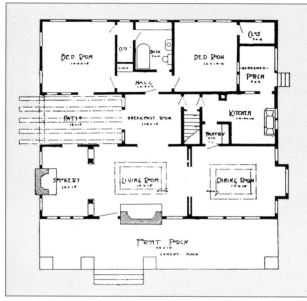

In Auckland in 1913, the architect R. Atkinson Abbott (1883–1954) was commissioned to extend a gardener's cottage at Wharua Road, Remuera, and he provided the new structure with a low roof with exposed rafter tails and overhanging eaves, as well as a bay window and verandah with shingled skirts. Familiarity with the Californian bungalow style had increased from 1910 onwards, when a column in *Progress* ('from Our Californian correspondent') illustrated large numbers of plans and elevations of bungalows, to the chagrin of most of the country's English-trained architects. Builders all over New Zealand took to them with such enthusiasm that excellent examples of the style can still be found in most

Plan of a Californian bungalow from the 'Just a Little Different' catalogue. The relatively open relationship of rooms differs considerably from the more closed villa plan (see page 45).

towns. In Wanganui, for instance, the builders Bassett & Co. made a speciality of the bungalow, building hundreds of 'Kosy Konka Homes' from over a thousand house patterns designed to encourage buyers to use the company's new concrete-sheet construction process.

Many architects realised that the bungalow was becoming increasingly popular with clients glad to be liberated from the omnipresent villa, and incorporated its features into their repertoire of styles. Some, like F. C. Daniell in Hamilton, produced two-storeyed houses. The house Daniell designed for the Murray family in Radnor Street in 1919 shares many features with the even larger Clunes, at Onewhero in Raglan County, which

An all-wood bungalow at Queen Street, Thames.

*Murray House (1919),
Radnor Street, Hamilton,
by F. C. Daniell. This large
family home shows how
readily architects adopted
the details of the
Californian style, sometimes
overusing certain of its
features, as the profusion of
projecting ornamental
brackets here illustrates.*

F. W. Mountjoy designed in 1914 for Duncan Campbell. Both have fairly traditional plans and merely allude to bungalow style in their exterior detailing. At Clunes window hoods are fixed to walls with the spindle brackets more characteristic of villa stickwork than the bungalow's much plainer decorative style. The transitional period during which Californian bungalow elements were tacked on to villas also produced many an interesting 'bungled villa', as Jeremy Salmond named them.

In New Plymouth, the Australian-born T. H. Bates (1873–1954), a classically trained architect, operated a practice which produced work in a variety of different styles. He took many architectural magazines, cutting out articles and filing them according to style and function for later use. Although Bates declared himself irritated by the bungalow craze, he realised that it was wise to give his clients what they wanted, and even incorporated some bungalow features into the fine house he built for himself in Pendarves Street in 1924. Gradually, as the bungalow became more popular, the style which in the hands of architects like Bates had been manipulated with flair and finesse, became a cliché. Streets in Auckland and Wellington were filled with dull bungalows against which, in terms of quality, the early examples built in Wanganui stand out.

Clunes (1914), Onewhero, Raglan County, by F. W. Mountjoy. Recently restored after years in a derelict state, this house is an interesting example of the blending of the villa style with that of the bungalow. The turret is a particularly fanciful touch.

Bates House (1924), Pendarves Street, New Plymouth, by T. H. Bates. Even an architect who expressed reservations about the spread of the bungalow craze was not averse to appropriating some of its features on his own house.

However eager architects like Seager and Clere might have been to see the establishment of a truly New Zealand architecture, it is quite plain that most of the large and expensive houses described in this chapter were scaled-down versions of the work of eminent English architects. New Zealand architects, deprived of formal academic training in what many still regarded as a colonial outpost, could only become acquainted with modern trends by travelling to England. It was there that even those born in New Zealand felt intellectually and spiritually at home, surrounded by great architectural monuments of the past, something their own country so conspicuously lacked. Like New

Zealand writers and musicians, the architects of this period felt displaced. It is perhaps surprising that more did not follow the example of Binney, who came back to New Zealand briefly, then left forever. Those who returned were, however, determined to graft English notions onto antipodean ones, and their clients were more than happy with such a solution. It was not until many years later that New Zealand's domestic architects, by then imbued with the spirit of a modernism which their professional forebears had regarded only with suspicion, were able to realise the long-held hopes for an indigenous architecture.

CHAPTER SIX
The Conservative Solution

Old Arts Building
(page 110)

In the years following the outbreak of the First World War and during the whole inter-war period the architecture of New Zealand's public buildings was characterised by a conservativeness which had its origins in the prevailing climate of economic uncertainty. Although, particularly in the 1920s, information was reaching this country about new European directions in architecture, the profession seemed unwilling to investigate their relevance to New Zealand. Instead, the Classical doctrines enshrined in the teaching methods of the Ecole des Beaux Arts in Paris, the most famous architectural school of the nineteenth century, continued to dominate the education of most architects, including those in New Zealand. Indeed, it was not until the mid-1930s that the functionalism of the German Bauhaus was to displace the Ecole's time-honoured curriculum. Between 1914 and 1930 competent New Zealand architects were to dress their buildings in a variety of stylistic garbs which, from a purely Modernist standpoint, appear to be a symptom of confusion, but which in fact produced some interesting public buildings.

Until the establishment of the Auckland University School of Architecture in 1918, no formal university training in architecture had been available in New Zealand. Aspiring architects served articles of apprenticeship with established architects; the best way to become educated was to go overseas and obtain work, sometimes unpaid, in the offices of some eminent architect. Examples of this procedure can be seen in the early careers of the two New Zealand-born avant-garde Modernists, Basil Ward and Amyas Connell.

Ward and Connell both made their names in England, but they had begun their architectural education articled to J. A. Louis Hay in Napier and Stanley Fearn in Wellington respectively. Between 1924 and 1926 they had both studied at London University's Bartlett School, eventually winning scholarships to the British Architectural School in Rome. Although already on the road to Modernism, they had reverted to their traditional Beaux Arts training in order to win the competition. An editorial in the *New Zealand Institute of Architects' Journal* attributed their success to the sound foundation of this typically New Zealand training, pointing out that they had, in fact, been in London only a relatively short time. 'Go and do likewise,' exhorted the magazine's editor, 'either at the School of Architecture in Auckland or by study in England.'[1]

In Wellington, the Architectural Students' Association was established in 1918; like the Ecole des Beaux Arts in Paris it created an *atelier* in which students carried out graded exercises in design. Few of those who attended the classes could afford full-time study in Auckland although some, like Paul Pascoe in Christchurch, submitted student drawings to the Auckland school for the N.Z.I.A. professional qualification. Many Wellington and Christchurch candidates felt that the standards applied to their work by the Auckland authorities were unfair, a common complaint being that no explanations were ever offered for the failure of many of their drawings. To counteract this, Christchurch students formed their own *atelier* in a High Street attic, where they worked late into the night refining their submissions, helped by older architects Cecil Wood, Heathcote Helmore, R. S. D. Harman and J. G. Collins.

Perhaps today's distinct architectural rivalry between Auckland and Christchurch had its origin in these difficult times. Certainly many of the Christchurch students avoided the final professional year at Auckland's architecture school, preferring to travel to the Royal Institute of British Architects in London, safe in the knowledge that the letters A.R.I.B.A. after their names would confer added status upon their return.

Although many of these students were aware of modern developments in architecture overseas from their reading of the *Architectural Review* and *Pencil Points*, their reliance upon the advice and teaching practices of older architects meant that a conservative attitude dominated architectural thinking. It was not until the late 1930s, as Ian Lochhead has pointed out, that New Zealand architects chose to adopt styles that reflected the radical changes in direction that had taken place earlier in Europe. Instead, most relied on stripped-back Gothic or Classical forms, although some more exotic styles were to be seen too.

One of the most unusual and immediately arresting buildings of the time is the enormous Spanish Mission edifice that R. Atkinson Abbott (1883–1954) had designed for Auckland Grammar School in 1911. Before setting up practice in Auckland with C. Le N. Arnold in 1910, Abbott had travelled widely in Europe and even studied for a period at the Ecole des Beaux Arts in Paris. Given the preference for Gothic educational buildings, it was surprising that a Spanish-styled building should be chosen at this time as the winner of the competition to design a New Zealand school; that Abbott should so readily

*Auckland Grammar School
(1913), by R. Atkinson
Abbott. The Spanish
Mission style was quite
exceptional in New
Zealand, where educational
buildings had usually been
in the Gothic style.*

cast aside his particular academic background is
even more surprising. In fact, the Californian
Spanish Mission style had been widely publicised
internationally since the 1890s. We have already
seen that Abbott was familiar with Californian
bungalow architecture in his 1909 Wharua Road,
Remuera, house. At Auckland Grammar School
he again incorporated certain Craftsman features,
such as the wide overhanging eaves and exposed
rafters. The rest of the building is a harmoniously
proportioned assemblage of the classic Mission
features: the long, arcaded entry porch; curved,
pedimented gables on the massive symmetrical
corner towers; terraced bell towers with lantern
and arched windows; and low-pitched, tiled roof
lines. Only the projected central tower
incorporating a flagpole remained unbuilt.
Perhaps Abbott had seen photographs of George
Costerisan's Long Beach High School of 1898, a
building Weitze has described as 'replete with all
the stylistic keynotes of the Mission revival'.[2] The
Auckland building's cream-painted brick rubble
surface has a natural vigour which responds to
any light conditions.

Inside, the Californian Mission church
courtyard has become an assembly hall in which
large square brick columns and more exposed
rafters support a magnificent arcaded ceiling lit by
a clerestory. Abbott's fondness for the Spanish
idiom was later demonstrated when he designed

the Dilworth Agricultural Farm School at East
Tamaki, where a single *campanario* very similar to
the four he designed at the Grammar School
crowns the roof line.

Other architects looked fondly back to the
elaborations of the Victorian Gothic. J. J. Collins
(1855–1933) and R. S. D. Harman (1859–1927)
were probably the first Christchurch architects to
be born, educated and trained in New Zealand.
They had both been articled to William Armson
and continued his practice after his death in
1883. In 1903 they were joined by Collins's son
J. G. Collins (1886–1965), and it was during this
period of their partnership that they designed the
Dominion Farmers' Institute (1917), now called
Seabridge House, on the corners of Ballance,
Featherston and Maginnity Streets, Wellington.
The design applies a mixture of Tudor and
Victorian Gothic imagery to a building which
was intended to be a centre where farmers could
co-ordinate their city activities. The top floor was
to be laid out as a kind of hotel, where delegates
to conferences and 'the ordinary man of the land
could stay and exchange views with kindred souls
from other districts'.[3] Built in ferro-concrete, the
Farmers' Institute has a highly ornamented
exterior, although some of this was removed
during alterations in 1948 and in 1964. Its
verticality is emphasised by soaring banks of bay
windows, capped with triangular pediments.

Seabridge House (1917), Wellington, by Collins & Harman. Although considerably altered and modernised the building, originally the Dominion Farmers' Institute, retains its highly decorated character.

Sarjeant Gallery (1916), Wanganui, by Donald Hosie. It was the studied simplicity, relative absence of decorative effects and fine proportions which impressed Samuel Hurst Seager, who judged the architectural competition to design a gallery for the city.

Beneath each pediment a flattened Gothic arch brings the upward movement to a gentle conclusion. The corner tower is particularly imposing: its Gothic-arched portal, quatrefoil-decorated balcony and oriel window announce a building of some significance.

This was also the great era of architectural competitions. Large numbers of anonymous competition entries were invariably received and the results were eagerly awaited by the profession. In November 1916 an extraordinary chain of events followed the announcement by Samuel Hurst Seager, chairman of judges of a

competition to design a new art gallery for the city of Wanganui, that submission number sixteen had won. On 16 November the Mayor of Wanganui, Mr C. Mackay, revealed in a letter to the *Dominion* that the reason for the delay in announcing the winner's name was that Seager had decided that the winning design was not in fact the work of its signatory, well-known Dunedin architect Edmund Anscombe, but of his pupil, Donald Hosie. Seager went on to recommend that Hosie should be appointed architect for the erection of the building, but his plan was thwarted because by January 1917 Lance-Corporal Hosie was a member of F Company of the 23rd Reinforcements, stationed at Featherston Military Camp. Despite the Mayor's long correspondence with military personnel, including Major-General Sir Alfred Robin, Hosie was conscripted for overseas service. Just before he left New Zealand, Hosie posted his working drawings to Wanganui in order that building could proceed. On 5 December 1917 the *Otago Witness* announced that Donald Peter Brown Hosie had been killed in action in France on 12 October, aged twenty-two years.

These facts about the design of the Sarjeant Gallery have remained buried for many years. Anscombe's name appears on the foundation stone; a photograph and a drawing of the gallery were proudly displayed in his private publication of 1934, *Modern Architectural Service*; Anscombe's obituary in *Home and Building* specifically mentions the Sarjeant as one of his buildings. However, there is probably nothing sinister in the fact that Hosie's drawings were submitted to the competition under Anscombe's name. At that time the work of articled pupils was rarely signed personally, usually bearing instead the imprint of the office in which it was produced. Seager's insistence that Hosie's work be recognised was more surprising, and was testimony to the quality of the design.

Hosie's Sarjeant Gallery was commended by Seager for the simplicity of approach which distinguished it from the thirty-three designs submitted. Freely interpreted Classical decoration on both exterior and interior is characterised by a restraint typical of the times; the central sculpture gallery, although small, has a pleasant airiness contributed by its domed ceiling; the architect's clever use of bays on either side of the sculpture court gallery has ensured that even today the Sarjeant remains one of the country's most adaptable galleries. On the small hill above the city, the building's palm-surrounded low profile presents an unusual sight from all viewpoints.

Little is known today about the English-born Auckland architect A. Sinclair O'Connor, who in 1919 designed fifteen self-contained residential apartments, known as Courtville, for the corner of Waterloo Quadrant and Parliament Street. O'Connor was certainly active in the city by 1911 when, with A. M. Bartley, he submitted a design for Parliament Buildings, but his practice had ceased by 1943. The subject of vigorous anti-demolition protest during the 1980s, Courtville is part of the complex of Edwardian residential buildings which is fast disappearing as commercial developers realise the potential of the inner-city sites. Both Corner Courtville and its neighbour, Middle Courtville (1914), are part of the work which O'Connor did for Ernest Stanton and William Potter, as are Tanfield, Potter & Co. business premises in Queen Street (1928), which remain one of the city's last surviving examples of Edwardian shop design.

Built of reinforced concrete, Corner Courtville's most noteworthy feature is its splayed, domed, corner elevation; no less skilful is the contrast between projecting bay windows and receding balconies. The large cornice and plaster ornamentation on the high pilasters indicate that the architect was familiar with the work of the

great Viennese architect Otto Wagner (1841–1918), whose use of carefully placed decorative pendants and swags as well as the pronounced Italianate cornice encouraged a host of imitators in Europe and the U.S.A.

Wagner's use of decorative ironwork is also reflected in the former George Court's Building (1924) on Auckland's Karangahape Road, which was once thought to be the work of Sinclair O'Connor but is now known to be that of Clinton Savage (d. 1957). Here the projecting cornice, the banks of multi-paned metal windows and the third-storey iron verandah painted in the shade of green still seen in Otto Wagner's buildings all over Vienna today, indicate that both O'Connor and Savage were probably familiar with some of the bulky volumes of sketches which Wagner produced between 1890 and 1922.

The 1920s saw the zenith of the career of the remarkable theatre architect, Henry Eli White (1877–1952). Born in Dunedin, White first worked with his father, a small contractor, as bricklayer, joiner, plumber, carpenter and painter. By the age of nineteen he had educated himself at night school and, always an adept self-promoter, talked his way into the contract for a huge tunnel scheme from the Waipori River, near Dunedin, to the city. Contracts in Christchurch followed and it was here that he developed a fascination for theatre design. His first theatre was built there in 1900 for John Fuller & Sons, who also commissioned him in 1911, following a host of other successful ventures, to build His

LEFT: *Courtville (1919), Auckland, by A. Sinclair O'Connor. These inner-city apartments were given decorative treatment which calls to mind similar structures built in Vienna at the turn of the century by Otto Wagner.*

RIGHT: *George Court's Building (1924), Karangahape Road, Auckland, by Clinton Savage. In its day one of the most modern of department stores, it is still an impressive part of a street in which many fine older commercial buildings survive.*

Interior of St James Theatre (1911), Wellington, by Henry Eli White. Pilasters supporting theatre boxes were ornamented with terms (figure statues whose lower half forms part of the structure of the pillar).

Interior of St James Theatre. Boxes were covered in floral motifs of all kinds made of plaster and painted.

Majesty's, now known as the St James Theatre, in Wellington. With seating for 2355 people, this was to be the country's biggest and best theatre, and was built in an opulent Edwardian Baroque style in a mere nine months. It was at the time the largest theatre in Australasia and the first steel-framed, reinforced-concrete theatre in this part of the world. By using the cantilever principle to transfer the weight of the dress circle and gallery through joists to the main steel framework, White ensured that no pillars obscure any patron's view of the stage. The deeply modelled, symmetrical pattern of decorative elements which extends across the wide street frontage gives the building a very grand appearance, while inside, a profusion of elaborate, mainly classically inspired, plaster motifs extend from the central dome to the stalls. It is little wonder that White was immediately snapped up by Australian theatre tycoon Hugh D. McIntosh, who gave him a contract for £110,000 to build theatres on the other side of the Tasman.

Besides being fascinated by acoustics, structural engineering and new constructional techniques, White was a master of many styles. His 1914 Municipal Theatre, Hastings, has a Spanish

Municipal Theatre (1914), Hastings, by Henry Eli White. Anticipating by two decades the city's fervour for the idiom, the architect designed a theatre in monumental Spanish Mission style.

facade, while inside the auditorium tiers of boxes on either side of the stage are decorated with the sinuous long-stemmed plant forms which Olbrich had used to such effect on the 1897 Sezession Building in Vienna. In 1916, White applied similar motifs to his Strand Theatre in Christchurch, but the building's 1944 conversion into the Plaza Cinema by Cecil Wood saw much of this detailing wiped away. White's masterpiece, the magnificent Midland Hotel (1917) in Lambton Quay, Wellington, was another entirely successful blending of Spanish and Viennese influences, but was demolished in 1980 to make way for a park. White himself fell on hard times during the Depression, when some of his major contracts were cancelled; he retired to a dolomite mine near Bathhurst, New South Wales, taking all his drawings with him. He is reputed to have spent his later years throwing parties and sailing his schooner, the *Matangi II*, on Sydney Harbour, dressed as an admiral.

New Zealand's most spectacular theatre building is the Civic (1929) in Auckland's Queen Street. Built for the daring business entrepreneur Thomas A. O'Brien by Bohringer, Taylor & Johnson of Melbourne, the Civic was designed in the period when the talkies were revolutionising cinema-going. O'Brien had toured England and the U.S.A. looking at cinema design and decided that what this part of the world needed was an 'atmospheric' theatre with an oriental decorative scheme. All the details were available in Sir Bannister Fletcher's *History of Architecture*, although the Civic's decorative plaster work includes such western motifs as the fleur-de-lis and the scallop, as well as Hindu and Moorish features.

The Conservative
Solution

*Civic Theatre (1929),
Auckland, by Bohringer,
Taylor & Johnson of
Melbourne. The exterior's
fashionable stripped
'skyscraper' styling added to
its public appeal. By the
mid-1980s the need for a
thorough restoration of the
building had become clear.
New Zealanders watch the
fate of this unique
atmospheric theatre with
great interest.*

The vestibule's interior decoration is constructed from fibrous plaster painted to resemble ivory. Two identical staircases lead to the circle foyer, which has the appearance of a Moorish courtyard, while the main auditorium is a Persian walled garden with domes and minarets silhouetted against a ceiling of seemingly limitless blue sky with twinkling stars. The exterior of the Civic has similarities to the stripped-back skyscrapers that were appearing in so many architectural periodicals of the late 1920s. Large fretwork screens add to the vertical thrust provided by the corner tower; the surface is decorated with panels of sun bursts, dancing maidens, floral spirals, volutes and swags, designed by Arnold Zimmerman, a Swiss scenic artist who had studied at the Ecole des Beaux Arts in Geneva before moving to Sydney.

Many of the large commercial buildings designed in this period showed that New Zealand architects were aware of the high rise structures which were by now such a feature of the American and English urban environments. Some Wellington examples, like Hoggard, Prouse & Gummer's State Fire Insurance Building (1919), White's Midland Hotel (1917) in Lambton Quay, and Hennessey & Hennessey's Colonial Mutual Life Building (1933) are severe losses; that other fine buildings of the 1920s should still be under threat is difficult to understand. 'None of

*Interior of Civic Theatre.
The circle foyer is a riot of
luridly lit Moorish and
Hindu plaster decoration
painted to look like ivory.*

these Wellington buildings is recognisably historic,' conservation architect Chris Cochran pointed out as long ago as 1980.

> They lie in the transition period between the Victorian and the Modern; they are not loved by the layman for the richness of their decoration, nor are they thought valuable by architects because they don't quite mark the beginning of the modern movement . . . but they do stand as landmarks of our social and architectural history.[4]

LEFT: Landmark House (1929), Auckland, by Wade & Bartley. The highly decorated surface was made of moulded cement panels. The strong vertical accent and set-back top give the building (formerly Auckland Electric Power Board) the appearance of a miniature New York skyscraper.

RIGHT: General Buildings (1927), Shortland Street, Auckland, by Bloomfield & Hunt. This modern office block (formerly Yorkshire House) with Neo-classical detailing is much in the manner of Sullivan & Adler's Wainwright Building (1890–94), St Louis.

Hamilton Nimmo Building (1929), Wellington, by F. D. Stewart. Like most office buildings of the 1920s, this one has a structural steel frame which supports concrete columns and beams. On its angled corner, diagonally arranged bricks in two contrasting colours rise above the parapet line, giving a sense of verticality. Originally, like Landmark House, Nimmo's had a corner tower, but it collapsed in the 1942 earthquake.

Of those that remain, some, like the Auckland Electric Power Board Building (now called Landmark House), which Alva Bartley and Norman Wade designed in 1929, have been adapted for modern use. Very much in the vertical skyscraper tradition, this ornate seven-storeyed structure was constructed from pressed and moulded cement panels. By contrast, the Hamilton Nimmo Building which F. D. Stewart designed in the same year for Willis Street, Wellington, uses a much starker treatment of brick and plaster ornament to achieve a similar effect. The commercial building of Louis Sullivan in Chicago also provided inspiration in 1927 for Grierson, Aimer & Draffin's South British Insurance Building and Bloomfield & Hunt's 1928 Yorkshire House, now called General Buildings, both of them in Auckland's Shortland Street. These reinforced-concrete structures exhibit Sullivan's three divisions of base, shaft and capital for tall office buildings; both have Neo-classical detailed facades and elaborate cornices.

It has been suggested that the Auckland architects T. C. Mullions and Sholto Smith alluded to château style in their Chancery Chambers (1923). French-born Sholto Smith

(1882–1936) had come to Auckland via Saskatchewan in 1920. He practised with T. Coulthart Mullions (1914–57) for a decade, until war disabilities forced him to give up work. The original drawings for Chancery Chambers show a much more elaborately decorated version of the scheme eventually adopted; a dispute over estimates which saw the building reduced in cost from £70,000 to £37,000 is probably the explanation. The street elevations clearly express the building's ferro-concrete frame; the heraldic shields at first-floor level and the corner tower, originally provided with elaborate flying buttresses, suggest some interest in the Gothic, as do the finials on the same architect's elegantly proportioned facade for Shortland Flats (1924).

Beaux Arts Classicism was in this period the dominant force in the design of New Zealand's public buildings, but not surprisingly, the Gothic remained predominant in church architecture. Unmistakably Gothic is St Mary of the Angels Catholic Church (1918) in Boulcott Street, Wellington, the work of Frederick de Jersey Clere (1856–1952). Clere was born in Lancashire but in 1872 was articled to the ecclesiastical architect Edmund Scott of Brighton. In 1877 he arrived in New Zealand, practising in Wellington and Wanganui before settling permanently in the capital, where he was to dominate the various partnerships he entered into during his long career. In 1883 Clere was appointed Wellington Diocesan Architect and built traditional modest, wooden-steepled churches clad in vertical timbers, before moving to brick and reinforced concrete. His little St Oswald's (1914) at Westmere and St Mary's (1911), Karori, were both steel-reinforced concrete churches. The distinctly Californian appearance of St Mary's seemed strange to contemporary commentators, who preferred to describe it as an Italian hillside church.

TOP AND BOTTOM RIGHT: *Chancery Chambers (1923), Auckland, and Shortland Flats (1924), Auckland, both by T. C. Mullions and Sholto Smith, show how modern architects were prepared to adapt traditional styles, such as the Gothic, to concrete construction.*

LEFT: *St Mary's Church (1911), Karori, Wellington, by Frederick de Jersey Clere. One of the first concrete churches to be built in New Zealand, St Mary's has Californian features including a wide eaves overhang and prominent brackets.*

109

LEFT: *St Mary of the Angels (1918), Boulcott Street, Wellington, by Frederick de Jersey Clere. The use of steel-reinforced concrete permitted the particularly delicate proportions of its Perpendicular Gothic detailing.*

RIGHT: *Old Arts Building (1920), University of Auckland, by R. A. Lippincott and Edward Billson. The controversy occasioned by this prizewinning design from an American and an Australian architect has seldom been equalled in New Zealand's architectural history.*

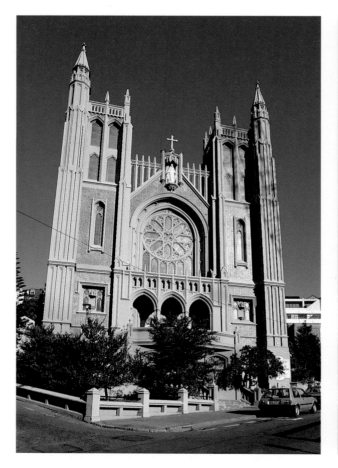

For St Mary of the Angels, Clere chose the Perpendicular Gothic style as being particularly suited to concrete construction; a document in the church archives states that the building was actually modelled on the cathedral church of St Michael and St Gudule in Brussels. Traditionally such a church would have been built in stone, but by 1918 Arts and Crafts objections to concrete were abating. Certainly Clere was sensible in advocating its use in earthquake-prone Wellington. The facade is a high gabled wall containing a rose window and flanked by two pinnacled towers. The two upper storeys of the towers have open tracery; at the front and outer angles square turrets contain a circular staircase which gives access to the roof. Wayne Nelson described the richly ornamented Gothic structure as 'a tour de force in the art and craft of the machine . . . particularly as Clere's design was executed not by trained stone masons but by day labourers with no more skill than the ability to handle a concrete mixer and a mould'.[5]

The inspiration behind the controversial competition design submitted in 1920 by R. A. Lippincott and Edward Billson for the Auckland University College Arts Building was also Gothic. Roy Alstan Lippincott (1885–1969) was born in Pennsylvania and studied architecture at Cornell

University between 1903 and 1909. In 1909 he became associated with Walter Burley Griffin, the architect of Canberra and former pupil of Frank Lloyd Wright. Wright had gone to Europe, closing his Oak Park Studio and leaving his incomplete work to Griffin, H. W. Von Holst and Marion Mahoney, the last of whom had worked in Wright's office for eleven years. The newly graduated Lippincott joined the Von Holst office and was given the job of supervising work on Wright's Robie House. In 1911, Griffin and Mahoney were married, and in 1914 Lippincott married Griffin's sister. The two couples moved to Australia, where Lippincott worked with Billson, arriving in Auckland in 1921 to supervise the erection of his university building. He was to remain in New Zealand until 1939.

The acrimony which greeted the decision to award the prize to Lippincott & Billson has seldom been equalled in New Zealand's architectural history. In *Building* magazine, the caption for a reproduction of the Princes Street elevation spoke of 'freak architecture' in which

the laws of architectural balance and proportion are entirely ignored; though as a piece of bluff the designers claim that they have been influenced by English gothic architecture. The low monotony of the wings, the humps called gable ends, the hideous tower springing out of a medley of ridiculous buttresses, brand the design as the work of a child rather than of matured architects and certainly the acceptance of it is not creditable to any body concerned.[6]

The magazine also illustrated a number of extremely dull entries for the competition. Reference was made to 'new art Yankee notions', which suggests that some were annoyed that an American architect should have won the competition at all. Lippincott pointed out that he merely wished to suggest English collegiate Gothic architecture and that he had referred to Oxford's Tom Tower in designing his tower. One letter to the *Herald* branded the building 'Indo-saracenic', another referred to its 'nuptial style'. An editorial in the paper on 18 March 1926 expressed the hope that 'the building will grow upon the community as its erection proceeds'.

The Wrightian angular geometry of the tower finials and tracery, the cloisters, the string course at ground floor sill height, the flared window reveals and the gable end elevations are all strongly influenced by Walter Burley Griffin's highly expressionistic design for Newman College (1915), Melbourne, a similar amalgam of medieval and modern design precepts. Lippincott had taken charge of its plans and specifications after Griffin had completed the basic plan. Like Newman College, the Arts Building was constructed from poured concrete, but the Arts Building is faced with gleaming Mt Somers stone. Interior stonework is Oamaru stone, while the tower is reinforced concrete. The steel windows and the tiles for the impressive entry vestibule mosaic were imported from England. Lippincott regionalised many of the building's decorative elements, as he was to in the buildings he designed in 1927 for Massey University in Palmerston North. Stone kea cling to ledges and

under bays, capitals sprout flax flowers rather than acanthus leaves, and the pinnacles have unfurling ponga fronds instead of oak leaves. Over the windows there are carved crests, designed to bear the coats of arms of universities throughout the world.

When Lippincott designed the Smith & Caughey Department Store (1927) on the corner of Elliott and Wellesley Streets, he looked more to Louis Sullivan than to Wright or Griffin. Like the General Buildings of Bloomfield & Hunt, he designed the store as a monolithic mass; the vertical emphasis is given by pilasters which soar upwards to protrude above the parapet line. They are decorated with pre-cast tinted concrete units incised with organic motifs like the ones Sullivan used on exterior surfaces, but less sinuous in conception than his. On the lower floors ornamental cast-iron relief surrounds the windows. The building was designed without the projecting cornice, which is an unfortunate later addition. Lippincott later gave Smith & Caughey's Queen Street facade an Art Deco profile but in its currently neglected condition it is very much a poor cousin to its predecessor.

New Zealand's most prominent architectural practice during the 1920s was that of Gummer & Ford in Auckland, which started operations in 1923. William Henry Gummer (1884–1966) served articles with W. A. Holman in Auckland, then travelled overseas between 1908 and 1911. He qualified as an associate of the Royal Institute of British Architects, and worked in Lutyens's office, then briefly in Daniel Burnham's in

The Conservative Solution

LEFT: *Interior of Old Arts Building. The integration of the building's English collegiate Gothic detailing is one of its most admirable features.*

Smith & Caughey Department Store (1927), Auckland, by R. A. Lippincott. The pre-cast concrete panels of this Chicago School commercial building are covered in incised organic motifs.

New Zealand Guardian Trust

Chicago. In 1913 he returned to New Zealand, joining the Auckland and Wellington firm of Hoggard & Prouse, where he remained until he set up practice with Ford.

Charles Reginald Ford (1880–1972) was born in England. As a youth he served in the Royal Navy and was the youngest member of Scott's 1901–04 Antarctic expedition. At its conclusion he went with Scott on a lecture tour of England, then travelled to Canada and Australia, where he embarked on architectural studies. In 1909 he was living in Christchurch and practising as a real-estate agent, but by 1919 he was a partner in the firm of Ford & Talboys at Wanganui. This partnership lasted until 1922, when Ford left to travel the west coast of the U.S.A., before settling in Auckland the following year. A cultivated and sociable gentleman, he was for many years honorary curator of the Auckland Institute and Museum's English china collection, obtaining many important items for the museum and often giving fascinating lectures on English ceramics and Scott's Antarctic Expedition, once being billed as a 'Hero of Polar Exploration'.

Ford has left a vivid description of life in the practice of Gummer & Ford during the 1920s, when competitions were much in vogue.

They were in general a nuisance, interrupting the normal working of the office — to have any chance of winning meant a great deal of work, mainly out of usual office hours. All worked every night in the week up to midnight and frequently until one or two in the morning . . . I can see now our office one night forty years ago — Gummer in his office laying washes of colour on one of his beautiful renderings or designing some further detail, draughtsmen at their desks, working away occasionally stopping to ask a question of Gummer, leading the whole team . . . A draughtsman would sometimes be driven almost demented by Gummer saying that a line in a perspective was, perhaps, a sixteenth of an inch out. But it was all taken as part of the game.[7]

In 1911, from London, Gummer had sent an entry for the competition to design Parliament Buildings; in 1913 he had produced a submission for the Auckland Grammar School competition which came second to Abbott's. Gummer later incorporated details of this design into the one he produced for the Auckland Railway Station in 1926. In 1918 Gummer's first important building, for New Zealand Insurance in Queen Street, now known as the New Zealand Guardian Trust, was opened. It is an enormous L-shaped structure with a main frontage of unusual severity compared with other office buildings of the period. Its riveted steel frame, encased in concrete, was faced with Kairuru marble quarried in Nelson. A strong verticality is created by the piers which rise from the second floor uninterrupted because of the dark recessed spandrels and wide, steel-framed windows between. Here too are the impressive bronze based and capped columns which were to be an essential feature of New Zealand Insurance premises built by Gummer throughout New Zealand. Inside, a polished marble corridor leads to the company's main offices, which were appointed in a manner befitting its image.

In 1925 Gummer & Ford designed the magnificent Dilworth Building for the corner of Queen and Customs Streets, Auckland. A watercolour by Gummer entitled *Urbis Porta* indicates that he envisaged the building as having a mirror image on the other side of Queen Street, forming a gateway to the city from the harbour. In designing the Dilworth, Gummer used the stripped Classical style favoured by American architects during this period, particularly Paul Cret (1874–1945). John Stacpoole has described the building as 'pure Lutyens, and splendid',[8] but it is also clear that the architect has followed Louis Sullivan's three-part ordering of high rise buildings. The building's most attractive feature is

*Dilworth Building (1925),
Auckland, by Gummer &
Ford. Gummer's
watercolour, entitled* Urbis
Porta, *shows that he
envisaged the building as
having a mirror image on
the other side of Queen
Street. At this time it was
common practice for
architects to indicate their
intentions to their clients by
means of such watercolour
perspective sketches.*
AUCKLAND UNIVERSITY
SCHOOL OF ARCHITECTURE
LIBRARY.

*Dilworth Building. The splayed corner and tower with
pagoda roof are still a focal point in Queen Street.*

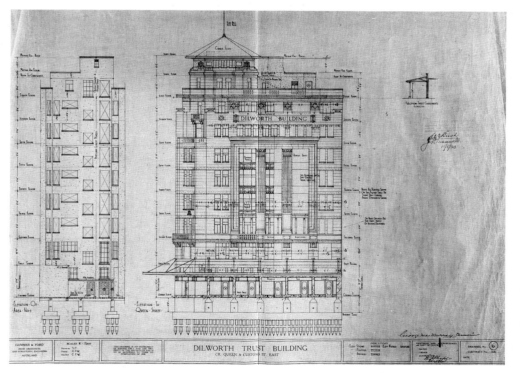

its recessed corner, which at the second-floor level
culminates in a balustrade. At the set-back sixth-
floor level it continues upward to form a tower.
The central bays of both facades are surrounded
by vertical mouldings and capped by a horizontal
entablature between the fifth and sixth floors.
These bays are defined by giant order pilasters,
four storeys high, which feature a stylised lotus
and fret motif capital. The lowest level of

*Dilworth Building. Ink on
linen. This working
drawing shows the
disposition of Portland
stone, marble, plaster and
bronze over the building's
facade.*
AUCKLAND UNIVERSITY
SCHOOL OF ARCHITECTURE
LIBRARY.

113

*Dilworth Building. This
photograph appeared in the
New Zealand
Architectural and
Building Review of
January 1927. Much was
made of the fact that
electric rather than
hydraulic lifts had enabled
the building to be
constructed more rapidly
than was usual. The
reinforced-concrete frame is
clearly visible.*

windows are framed by aedicules; the upper
spandrels are composed of bronze panels. The
area which surrounds this central block is entirely
unornamented and comprises pairs of windows
within ashlar stone work.

The Dilworth Building is faced with Portland
stone, although some of the detailing is of cast
plaster made with Portland stone dust to match
the actual stone work. In the mid-1980s, in an act
of conspicuous vandalism justified as
modernisation, the magnificent black and grey
marble vestibule and staircase were ripped out.

In 1926, Gummer & Ford won an N.Z.I.A.
Gold Medal for their Remuera Library and began
work on the Auckland Railway Station. The
railway station owes much to Charles Follen
McKim's Pennsylvania Railway Station (1910).
This immense New York structure, demolished in
1963, had a classically decorated entrance lobby
with a coffered ceiling. Like Pennsylvania Station,
Gummer's main concourse included a number of
dining rooms and waiting rooms, a barber's shop,
dressing rooms, lavatories, an ambulance facility,
and book and fruit stalls. Nothing like it had
been seen in New Zealand before, and it is ironic
that the building has never been tested to its full
design capacity, owing to the Auckland City
Council's decision not to proceed with the
underground system designed for the city.

*Auckland Railway Station (1926), by Gummer & Ford.
The scale and expense of this building was quite new for
the time but the building was never to realise its
intended purpose.*

Construction began in late 1927 and continued
until November 1930. It was the largest contract
ever undertaken in New Zealand, costing
£320,000. The building's foundations are piles
over 2 metres long, because the station is on
reclaimed land. The piles were tied together at
ground level with reinforced concrete beams, and
great care was taken in their construction to
allow for seismic movement and vibration from
trains.

individual, reached a conclusion in the work of Nazi architects like Paul Ludwig Troost. No doubt Gummer would have preferred an analogy with Edwin Cooper's St Marylebone Town Hall of 1911, which exhibits similar features.

Ian Lochhead has drawn attention to the fact that, although Gray Young, Morton & Young's Wellington Railway Station did not open until 1937, its architects favoured the American brand of Neo-classicism which Gummer & Ford had utilised in 1927. Its massive portico may be more traditional in approach but inside the entrance lobby, the effect is even more monumental than at Auckland.

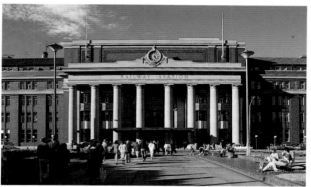

Auckland Railway Station. Detail of central clock showing terracotta crests and classically derived ornament in terracotta tiles, including the Roman fasces which appears on many of Gummer & Ford's buildings.

The station won Gummer & Ford another N.Z.I.A. Gold Medal in 1931, by which time they were working on Wellington's National Art Gallery and Museum, another competition victory. Here again they employed the vocabulary of restrained Classicism, this time producing a building which in its monumental austerity is a reminder that the stripped Classical style, with its symbols of the power of the state over the

In addition to his major commercial designs produced during the 1920s, Gummer, working both with Hoggard & Prouse and later with Ford, was called upon to design most of the country's largest war memorials, following the First World War. His understanding of Classical principles was to stand him in good stead when he came to work on the Bridge of Remembrance (1919), Christchurch, the Dunedin War Memorial (1921) and the Wellington Dominion Museum and Art Gallery (1930), in front of which he placed the country's National War Memorial.

The competition to design New Zealand's largest war memorial, the Auckland War Memorial Museum was, however, won by Grierson, Aimer & Draffin in 1922. It was to be built on the spectacular hill site overlooking the harbour which Potatau Te Wherowhero, later the first Maori king, had named Pukekawa, the hill of bitter memories, to commemorate the place where the northern Ngapuhi tribe under Hongi Hika had made their final peace with Waikato, led by Te Wherowhero himself, in 1828.

The Auckland War Memorial Museum is the most monumental Greek Revival building in New Zealand. Its double function as museum and war memorial made it almost inevitable that such a

The Conservative Solution

Interior of Auckland Railway Station. The lobby was conceived on the grandest scale using marble and mosaic tiles. The press of the day made much of the fact that Auckland's station now exceeded Dunedin's in its splendour.

Wellington Railway Station (1933), by Gray Young, Morton & Young. Although not opened until 1937, by which time its stripped Classicism looked a little old-fashioned, the Doric colonnaded entry portico is undeniably impressive.

115

Auckland War Memorial Museum (1922–29) by Grierson, Aimer & Draffin. New Zealand's largest Greek Revival building.

style should be chosen; it also determined the plan of the building, which carefully distinguishes between the two functions. The massive facade, with its portico of fluted, Doric pillars, closely resembles that of the Parthenon in Athens. Above the portico the rather heavy proportions of the attic storey indicate that, although the architects had ransacked the textbooks in their determination to be accurate in matters of detail, they were equally intent upon reflecting a distinctly modern approach to Greek architecture. The ornate bronze cresting has corner acroteria, while on the entablature there are carved bas reliefs depicting military scenes. The Portland stone exterior is inscribed with the names of battles fought during the long struggle. The lettering was the work of Vernon Brown who was, however, not responsible for a spelling mistake which necessitated the removal of a whole block of the expensive imported stone.

Inside the building, massive groupings of Ionic columns form a peristyle which further increases the building's solemnity. M. K. Draffin actually designed a wrought-iron screen to ensure that the bargeboard diagonals of the meeting-house Hotunui should not disturb the Classical verticals of this enormous space, which rises to the height of three storeys. Yet, despite its almost pedantic

Classicism, the museum is a fervently nationalistic building; it is even said that a decision was made not to have its crest approved by the Royal College of Heralds in London. The leaves on the bronze wreath of the upper floor's marble altar are kawakawa not laurel; on the solid balustrade a taiaha spear-head is made to shoot out of a Greek key pattern; traditional Maori decorative motifs in varying degrees of elaboration are found on capitals, friezes and door mouldings.

The ceremonies of consecration on 28 November 1929 of both the museum and the cenotaph, a replica of the one Lutyens designed for Whitehall, were impressive. Morning rain cleared as the Governor-General, Sir Charles Fergusson, delivered an oration on the heroes of ancient Hellas and of Anzac, Palestine and France. After knocking with a carved mere on the front doors, the Governor-General led ten thousand people into the building. The following day their Excellencies and the elderly tohunga Tutanekai Taua reopened the meeting-house, Hotunui, re-located from Parawai, Thames, to the museum's Maori Court. Today, the Auckland War Memorial Museum remains a powerful architectural symbol in which classical and modern meanings are fused into a convincing whole.

During the period of 1914–30 the public buildings of New Zealand reflected an international tendency for all but the most innovative architects to dress large structures in styles dignified by the practice of the past. The Beaux Arts training which was standard for most architects was backward looking in its respect for Classical styles in particular; few New Zealand-born architects experimented with anything daringly new, although some of them, like Gummer and Ford, were to strip the Classical forms back to their bare essentials in a manner which seemed to give them new life. It was left to the American, Lippincott, or the eccentric Henry Eli White to break out of the mould. In the following decades the Beaux Arts Classical forms which had dominated the design of public buildings in this period were to gradually fade from the scene as New Zealand architects began to respond to other influences.

CHAPTER SEVEN
Modern, Moderne and Deco

Masonic Hotel
(page 128)

In the decade of the 1930s, architects were faced with a number of unusual challenges, all of them crucial in determining the direction New Zealand architecture would take in future years. Despite the use of a diversity of styles during this period, most architects met the challenges unimaginatively, retreating behind a range of conservative solutions which may have pleased wary clients but which produced few major buildings. The most significant architectural achievement of the decade was that initiated by the Government in 1936, when the Department of Housing Construction began its extensive building programme.

Throughout these years the whole country was in the grip of the Great Depression. It was a time of 'acute financial difficulties', as F. E. Greenish observed in his gloom-laden editorial, 'The Outlook for 1932' in the *New Zealand Institute of Architects Journal*. Contrasting the current economic climate with the boom years of the 1920s, he pointed out that it wasn't at all surprising that architects should be suffering, because 'from the data given in the New Zealand Year Book for 1932, the number of persons employed in building is stated to be 11,312, the greatest number in any occupation except farming'.[1] Many of these were now unemployed and this fact, combined with the reduction in capital available for building, meant that work for architects was scarce; few of those talented young architects who had graduated from the schools of architecture could afford to set up offices of their own; what large-scale work there was remained in the hands of established architects, whose response to such difficult circumstances was generally to fall back on familiar solutions.

The challenge from the European Modern Movement was met with incomprehension from New Zealand architects. Although the work of the great Modernists, the Swiss-born Le Corbusier and Walter Gropius of the Bauhaus, was known here it was treated with nothing more enthusiastic than a guarded respect. Basil Ward, Amyas Connell and Brian O'Rorke made their careers as Modernists in England, although they scarcely had an easy time of it there either. It was difficult for architects brought up in the Beaux Arts tradition to look sympathetically on a radical departure from the academic exercises in applied ornament they had been taught to admire. According to the Modernists, the form of a building should be determined by its function and be closely related to the lives of the people it served. Instead of covering a building's structure with various stylistic disguises, the Modernists advocated the use of simple forms which revealed both the structure and the materials. They were at pains to point out that aesthetic considerations were not absent from their theories or their buildings, and that it was wrong to imagine that the more decorative aspects of a post-Art Deco style, which the public tended to label 'modern' had any resemblance to real Modernism. Such an architecture was bogus Modernism and gradually attracted to itself the label 'Moderne'.

Articles on Modernism were printed in the *N.Z.I.A. Journal* throughout the decade, most of them conveying a barely disguised contempt for the subject. The worst were the two papers by a Warsaw-domiciled French architect, known only as M. Francastel, who accused Le Corbusier of elitism, of 'having conceived art as a superfluous luxury' and of 'setting utilitarianism in all his works as a high road to contentment'.[2] Others, like Christchurch architect V. J. R. Hean's reprinted paper, 'Modern Architecture', employed a tone of cautious tolerance in attempting to persuade readers that the Modern style was more than just 'a style of queer crazy cubes, or of futuristic foolishness and distorted idea'.[3]

Ian Lochhead has pointed out that 'we no longer feel compelled to regard those architects who worked in different modes as failed modernists'.[4] Some of the major figures of the previous decade — Lippincott, Cecil Wood, Helmore & Cotterill, and Gray Young — while maintaining an allegiance to an established architectural vocabulary, showed that they were not impervious to change. Although the New Zealand Institute of Architects exhibited its values by giving Gummer & Ford two Gold Medals, for the modest but accomplished Remuera Library in 1928 and the Auckland Railway Station in 1931, few could have foreseen how the style of the country's premier architectural practice was to change by 1939. A group of younger architects, among them Horace Massey (1895–1979), came to prominence during the decade and, like Anscombe, sometimes embraced an Art Deco stylishness which passed for Modernism.

The tension between the two came to be characterised as a battle between the 'Modern' and the 'Moderne', which was often fought in the periodicals of the day. The debate was academic as there were very few examples of the Modern style in New Zealand; Humphrey Hall's Corbusian villa (1938) in Lysaght Street, Timaru, was almost the only example. Although it is now compromised through alteration, the house

Park Lane (1938), Lysaght
Street, Timaru, by
Humphrey Hall. Now much
altered, this house was
designed as a Corbusian
villa. Behind the still visible
metal railings there was an
open sun deck, but
otherwise there was
minimal decoration to
disturb the simplicity of its
white painted cubes.

originally had a roof garden in clear imitation of
Le Corbusier's Villa Savoie (1929–30) at Poissy.
Hall's use of simple cubic construction, his play of
solids and voids, and his use of pilotis to support
the bedroom wing on the street facade all
indicate a familiarity with Corbusian Modernism.

In 1937, under the heading 'Versatility', the
magazine Home and Building illustrated two
Remuera homes designed by Horace Massey, one
labelled 'Tradition' and the other 'Modernism'.
The first, called Craigmore, is a large-scale, two-
storeyed, brick and shingle house, very much in
the English manner but clumsy compared with
Binney's houses, which it resembles. The Abel
House may look modern by contrast, but its
brick garden facade, made up of a huge metal
bay-window sweeping curve and a rectangular
block, is unpleasantly monolithic in appearance.
It certainly appeared modern to observers in
1937, even attracting the nickname 'Massey's
Folly'. To many architects, Modernism often
meant merely simplifying masses and giving
traditionally planned buildings some subtle
exterior Art Deco detailing.

Other architects side-stepped the issue by
employing a Georgian architectural vocabulary
which could pass as Modern because of its
simplicity. The Georgian Group in London had
been formed in London in 1937 in response to
the rebuilding of Nash's Regent Street; the
adoption of the Georgian style allowed English
architects to design with a fashionable restraint,
one dignified by history but not un-modern in
appearance. In Wellington, William Gray Young
was awarded the N.Z.I.A. Gold Medal in 1932 for
his Wellesley Club, which was designed in 1925
'in the tradition of the London clubs of Pall Mall

Villa Savoie (1929), Poissy,
France, by Le Corbusier. It
took many years for New
Zealand architects to see the
relevance of the
interpenetration of outer
and inner space evident in
this house, now regarded as
a locus classicus of
Modernism.
REPRODUCED IN GIEDION,
SPACE, TIME AND
ARCHITECTURE.

NEW ZEALAND ARCHITECTURE

in a well-mannered neo-Georgian style'. The architect's own explanation for his choice of the Georgian style was that 'the name of the club commemorated the family name of the Duke of Wellington, who had had his famous career mainly in Georgian times'.[5]

It was predictable that those enthusiastic neo-Georgians, Heathcote Helmore and Guy Cotterill, should also have chosen the style for their Cook & Ross Building (1926–27) in Christchurch's Victoria Square. This academically correct building sits on a concrete rather than stone rusticated base; above are two storeys in brick punctuated with symmetrically placed sash windows, while at the top there is a line of dormer windows. Robert Esau pointed out that this structure was more in keeping with the work of Sir Reginald Blomfield, an implacable foe of Modernism in England, than the work of Lutyens, who was much more inclined to an experimental, if not Modernist, approach. New Zealand architects who agreed with Blomfield would have felt their own conservatism legitimised when they read his notorious book *Modernismus*, which was published in 1934, the same year Blomfield joined battle with Amyas Connell in a wireless debate which was reported in the *Listener*.

But, like many architects of this period, Helmore & Cotterill were quite prepared to employ a variety of styles in their work, although their concern for order and symmetry remained an abiding one. They used a Spanish Mission idiom for their concrete Hanmer Springs Lodge in 1930, yet Helmore & Cotterill turned, unexpectedly, to a Colonial New Zealand model when they designed the Doctor's Consulting Rooms in 1932 at Palmerston North. The Langlois-Etévenaux Cottage (see page 19) at

Akaroa has had a considerable influence on the proportion of the consulting rooms; both have weatherboarded walls, louvred shutters, sash windows, flared eaves and wooden pilasters around the entrance and windows. In 1932 they designed Vogel House at Woburn, Lower Hutt, for James Vogel, a house much illustrated in recent times since it became the official residence of the Prime Minister of New Zealand. The architects returned to their familiar Colonial Georgian style using steeply pitched roofs, weatherboard cladding, overhanging eaves and dormer windows.

Coldstream Lodge, designed for the wealthy Christchurch retailer Kenneth Ballantyne in 1933, stands alone in the work of Helmore & Cotterill in its allusion to the Modern Movement. The huge house, like Humphrey Hall's in Timaru, has a white-painted, cubically massed, concrete exterior, with a flat roof, wrought-iron railings and cantilevered balconies. Inside, however, there is no merging of rooms; instead the architects followed their standard practice of linking rooms by a straight corridor connected to the front entrance. Robert Esau has drawn attention to the striking similarity between the window panels above the main entrance and those used by Peter Behrens in the design of New Ways (1926), Northampton. While some features of Coldstream Lodge suggest that its architects had a superficial understanding of the principles of Modernism, the chevron detailing on doors, windows and ledges indicates the tension between the Modern and the Moderne.

In 1937 Helmore & Cotterill were engaged by Ashburton landowner J. H. Grigg to design a replacement for his homestead, Longbeach, which had been destroyed by fire. Three design solutions were produced: one involved a Colonial Georgian rectangular block with the familiar sash windows, shutters and pilasters. Another, more

*Longbeach (1937),
Ashburton, by Helmore &
Cotterill. Indebted to
Lutyens's early Surrey
cottage style, this house was
built in brick to allow it to
blend with surrounding
gardens established fifty
years earlier.*

richly decorated, provided an adjoining wing, extra gables, columns and an entrance adorned with elliptical windows and a fanlight above the doorway. In the final design these Georgian features were discarded in favour of a pared-back building with steeply pitched gables and asymmetrical massing. As in the earlier plans, the house was built in brick. At Longbeach, Helmore was obviously inspired by the magnificent established gardens around the site to look at Lutyens's early houses such as the famous Munstead Wood, which he had designed in 1893 for landscape gardener Gertrude Jekyll. But Longbeach is plainer than any of these early Lutyens houses, reflecting its architects' acquaintance with the sparseness of Modern architecture.

Cecil Wood's response to the challenge of Modernism was to continue with the progressive abstraction of the stripped Classical manner of his Dunedin Public Trust in 1926. His State Insurance building (1934) and particularly the Hereford Street Post Office (1937), both in Christchurch, show that Classical proportion still dominated Wood's thinking, although he removed all hints of Classical ornament. During 1937–38, Wood had his former pupil Paul Pascoe as his assistant. Not yet thirty, Pascoe was an undoubted Modernist who had just returned from an extensive period in London, where he

had worked with the Architectural Press and the Tecton Group.

Robyn Ussher believes that, because of this experience, he 'must have been the most up-to-date architect in New Zealand at the time'.[6] Pascoe's hand is certainly visible in the entrance to the Post Office, with its circular concrete canopy, and it is even more evident in the unbuilt side wings which, unlike the stripped Classical central block, had a distinctly horizontal emphasis. When Cecil Wood embarked upon an extensive overseas journey in late 1937, he went armed with a list of Modern buildings which Pascoe though he should see. Among them were Tecton's High Point Flats and Maxwell Fry's Kensal House at Ladbroke Grove, although Wood was apparently more impressed by what he saw in Sweden, including Ragnar Ostberg's Stockholm Town Hall (1911–23), than by the English Modernist buildings he visited.

The purpose of Wood's journey was principally to look at church architecture before he began work on the design for Wellington Cathedral in 1938. Because of the earthquakes in the capital, reinforced concrete was essential. At first Wood was tempted to build in the Gothic manner, as Edward Maufe had in his Guildford Cathedral (1932), and was said to have been considerably taken aback by Maufe's negative reaction when Wood showed him a preliminary sketch. In the final event, Wood designed a vast Spanish Colonial structure which was destined to be finished by others and to excite a good deal of criticism, most notably from the members of the Auckland Architectural Group, which in the August 1946 edition of *Planning* devoted some terse pages to a building which it regarded as highly anachronistic.

In Wanganui, R. G. Talboys's Ridgeway Street Post Office (1938) adopted strongly vertical, stripped Classical proportions, with fluted bronze spandrels to delineate two upper storeys. The restrained detailing is not Classical but Maori; koruru heads, vestigial moulded pilasters and canoe prow spiral motifs mark the stepped parapet.

Departmental Building (1938), Wellington, by J. T. Mair. The Government Architect's monolithic office block resembles contemporary inner city buildings in London. Its windows, curving around corners, dramatically illustrate how a steel-framed structure can take the load formerly carried by walls.

Wanganui Post Office (1938) by R. G. Talboys. Classical proportions are here so stripped back as to give the impression of Art Deco styling. A number of traditional Maori motifs can be seen where Classical ones would usually have been placed.

Wood's Modernism was no more tentative than that of the Government Architect, J. T. Mair, who in 1938 designed the Departmental Building in Stout Street, Wellington, and the Jean Batten Building (now New Zealand Post) on the corner of Shortland Street and Jean Batten Place in Auckland. The Wellington building was, at the time it was built, the largest office building in New Zealand, having frontages on Ballance and Maginnity Streets and a floor area of more than 2 hectares. Its steel framework was put up using electric welding instead of riveting; its base is granite up to first-floor level, the remainder of the street frontages being faced with a substance called Vitric Tuff stone. The sculptural qualities of the Departmental Building owe something to the work of a number of London architects. The colossal Shell Mex House (1931) by Joseph Brothers has a stepped-back central tower topped with a clock which, like Mair's, looks as though it would be more suited to a mantelpiece than an office building. Francis Lorne's Mount Royal Hotel (1932) in Oxford Street sweeps around a whole block with the same smart streamlined styling as Mair was to employ.

Horace Massey was widely regarded as a progressive architect in his day yet his achievement seems less significant now. The Wellington Provincial Centennial Memorial (1940) at Petone, with the prow of the settler ship *Aurora* sticking out of a central glazed arch, is an unfortunate conception in every way; James Turkington's recently restored murals inside are more interesting. Yet this was the building which won the N.Z.I.A. Gold Medal in 1940. So too in 1933 had the Roman Catholic Church of St Michael, which Massey designed for Beatrice

*Church of St Michael
(1930), Remuera,
Auckland, by Tole &
Massey. This brick church
is very correctly dressed in
the Romanesque style
fashionable, particularly in
the U.S.A., in the late
1920s and early 1930s.*

Road, Remuera, Auckland. Built in brick, its
construction supervised by his partner George
Tole, the church is in an Italian Romanesque
style and bears an unmistakable resemblance to
Donaldson & Meier's St Benedict's Church at
Detroit, Michigan, a building Massey was familiar
with from his copy of Cram's *American Church
Buildings of Today* (1923). The west front of
Massey's church has an arcade of lancet windows,
a rose window and a double-doored arched entry
flanked by twisted Spanish columns. The
campanile and church have gabled, tiled roofs
which are given prominence by the corbel table
just below the eaves. Inside there is a barrel-
vaulted ceiling, although only the sanctuary is
coffered. The arch above the main door is
decorated with an impressive sculpture by R. O.
Gross, of St Michael slaying the dragon.

The building which brought Massey greatest
acclaim as a Modernist was Cintra Flats (1936) in
Whitaker Place, Auckland. Although *Building
Today* was careful to reassure its readers that the
flats were 'modern without being revolutionary',
it pointed out that 'its modernism lies in its being
planned to fulfil a useful purpose in the most
direct manner; its distinction and beauty lies in
its simplicity of design and lack of superficial
pretentiousness'.[6] Built of reinforced concrete
faced with textured brick, Cintra's cubic blocks
step elegantly down Grafton Gully, offering a

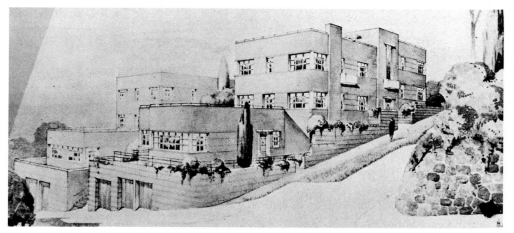

visually satisfying play of carefully organised
sharp angles and curves, softened by the creepers
which were to hang from window boxes. Massey
made use of such Modernist devices as horizontal
bands of metal windows, metal balustrades, flat
roof lines and absolutely plain facades. Inside,
compactness and simplicity were the determining
factors: floors were covered not with carpet but
cork tiles; metal work throughout was chromium
plated; walls were plaster, 'with modern sand and
hair effects' in light pastel shades; bathrooms and
kitchens had ornamental panels of Vitrolite and
floors of pastel-coloured terrazzo.

Further down Symonds Street, the young
Richard Toy, working in the office of E. Rupert

*Cintra Flats (1936),
Auckland, by Horace
Massey. The Modernism of
this building was
appreciated for its 'sanity'
which, it was thought,
would ensure that it 'would
not go in and out of style
with every veer of the
fashion weathercock'. In
sadly deteriorated condition
for many years, it is
currently undergoing
restoration.*
REPRODUCED IN *BUILDING
TODAY*, OCTOBER–DECEMBER
1936.

123

TOP RIGHT: *Smeeton House (1927), Remuera, by R. A. Lippincott. The very wide eaves with raked fascia are a feature deriving from the prairie houses of Frank Lloyd Wright.*

BOTTOM RIGHT: *Scott House (1935), Auckland, by R. A. Lippincott. The most Wrightian of Lippincott's Auckland houses, this one has a cruciform plan.*

Morton, designed Berrisville (1937) in a style *Home and Building* was pleased to call 'continental'.[7] In conscious emulation of Massey's Cintra Flats, Toy stepped his flats down to suit the slope of Symonds Street and faced the building with brick so that it harmonised with the Supreme Court across the road, even providing a promenade roof, from which the historic neighbour could be viewed. Designed as flats for professional city dwellers, Berrisville had simple but nonetheless luxuriously appointed interiors, while its plain exterior wall surfaces indicate the architect's familiarity with Dutch Modernism.

Berrisville Apartments (1937), Auckland, by Richard Toy, in the office of E. Rupert Morton. The architect has emphasised horizontality, contrasting it by rounding one corner of the stairwell.

Throughout the 1930s R. A. Lippincott, despite the straitened times, managed to attract work from wealthy clients. He continued to design within the context of his American training with Wright and Griffin, as his Smeeton House (1927) showed, despite its Binneyish shingle cladding. The Scott House (1935) at Paritai Drive, Orakei, is distinctly Wrightian in plan and its use of emphatic brick piers, low-gabled roof and overall horizontality, emphasised by wide eaves with a broad lined soffit, and bricks laid in such a way that the vertical dimension is apparently reduced. Lippincott has also used the Wrightian trick of concealing a gutter behind an angled fascia, a device of great elegance which is found on all his Auckland houses. Inside, the studs are of moderate height and the windowsills low; the sitting room has a shallow coffered wooden ceiling and picture rail at head height, both

features adding to the prairie house-like feel of the whole house. Despite the fact that the Scott House's American derivation entirely removed it from the Modern versus Moderne debate, a revealing sentence in *Home and Building*'s coverage of it shows how threatening the whole issue had become: 'Modern, up to the minute in every line and detail, it yet carries an atmosphere of comfort, warmth and gracious living that is conspicuously absent from most of the so-called "Modern" work. Unlike these latter, it will never date.'[8]

In 1934 Lippincott was approached by the English textile millionaire Arthur Broadhurst to design the buildings for St Peter's School, Cambridge. Broadhurst, wanting his school to have the appearance of an English country estate, insisted that the many existing trees must remain. He also needed it to be built quickly. Lippincott used both wood and concrete in designing the school buildings on earthquake-resisting principles, wherever possible keeping structures as low as possible to conform with the site's rural environment. He had some of his early designs returned to him by his client with the request that they be made more English; it is difficult, for example, to imagine Broadhurst's being pleased with the proposal for a concrete chapel with its window heads raised to a sharp point, its parapet interrupted with aggressively faceted pilasters, and its sills steeply inclined. Such a building, however subtle its Gothic allusions, was clearly unsuitable, although its replacement is still, ironically, more Californian than English.

There was no such difficulty with the school's other buildings. Lippincott provided the main two-storeyed administration and dormitory block with a steeply pitched, English-style, eaveless, tiled roof, complete with rows of gabled dormers. The classroom and refectory blocks were clad, like the chapel, in bevel-backed cedar weatherboards stained to give a warm, brown

finish. The classrooms have generously proportioned windows, to enable pupils to see outside while they are working. The dining hall is distinctly manorial in design; it is lined with broad redwood panels and, like the chapel, provided with a magnificent trussed roof. Today these school buildings stand as testimony to a talented architect's ability to respond to the client's demands without compromising his individual style.

Nearby, at Ngaruawahia, under the farsighted and energetic leadership of Te Puea Herangi, the Waikato people were shaping the marae called Turangawaewae. The traditional Maori pa culture had long since been dispersed and fragmented except in the most remote areas; Maori now lived much as Pakeha did, although usually in less favourable circumstances. As Michael King described in his biography of this remarkable woman, Te Puea led her people from Mangatawhiri to Ngaruawahia in 1920 in order to set up a marae which would eventually grow to be a central rallying point for the King Movement, and, she hoped, for the Maori people. Her inspiration for the creation of a settlement for the kingitanga was a whakatauki (prophetic saying) of King Tawhiao, who, dispossessed of tribal lands during the land confiscations of the 1860s, 'wandered disconsolately among homes at Whatiwhatihoe, Pukekawa and Parawera'.[9]

Ko Arekahanara toku haona kaha
Ko Kemureti toku oko horoi
Ko Ngaruawahia toku turangawaewae.

Alexandra will be a symbol of my strength of character
Cambridge a washbowl of my sorrow
Ngaruawahia my place to stand.

St Peter's School (1934), Cambridge, by R. A. Lippincott. The dormitory block shows how the architect blended his own preference for simple, angular shapes with his client's desire for a distinctively English building. Originally the building's concrete surface was covered with a textured red plaster tinted to a soft beige.

BOTTOM LEFT: *Interior of St Peter's School chapel. New Zealand's traditional wooden Gothic architecture is integrated with the distinctive forms Lippincott inherited from Wright and Walter Burley Griffin.*

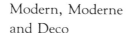

LEFT: *Mahinarangi (1927), Turangawaewae Marae, Ngaruawahia. This large whare whakairo, built along traditional lines, was originally intended to be a hospital. The tekoteko at the top of the gable is Potatau Te Wherowhero, the first Maori king, depicted in welcoming attitude.*

RIGHT: *Turongo (1934–38), Turangawaewae Marae, Ngaruawahia. Built as a residence for King Koroki, this extensively carved house is partially clad in ponga logs. It is said that Te Puea admired an angled-corner tower room on a house in Hamilton East and asked that something similar be built here.*

The first building to be erected at Turangawaewae was Ahurewa, a miniature house to protect tapu relics, including the bone chisels with which Tawhiao had been tattooed. The shrine was framed in front by carvings from the canoe Taheretikitiki. Early dwellings were small whare made from frames of lashed manuka or ponga poles with walls and ceilings of tied raupo and roofs of thatched nikau. Their pressed-earth floors were swept daily and sprinkled with water and pumice sand from the river.

Te Puea then organised that a hall at Mangatawhiri be dismantled and floated down the river to become Kimikimi, a dining room and assembly hall. Her Maori Concert Party, called Te Pou O Mangatawhiri, raised enough money to build a second and larger Kimikimi, which was opened on Christmas Day 1923. Next Te Puea decided to build a large meeting-house which could act as a hospital; its first post was driven into the ground by Sir Apirana Ngata in October 1927. It was he who named this house Mahinarangi, after the woman who linked the Waikato and East Coast genealogies by marrying Turongo, a Waikato chief of Kawhia.

own and its building process was tapu. The weatherboard exterior was built by a Pakeha builder and a team of Turangawaewae men; outside carving was done by Waikato men, while the interior was the work of Arawa carvers. Tukutuku and kowhaiwhai rafter panels were made under the direction of Sir Apirana and Lady Ngata.

The Waikato exterior carvings appropriately feature taniwha on the maihi and the pou tahu. The tekoteko standing at the apex of the maihi is Potatau Te Wherowhero, the first Maori king, depicted in the act of welcoming visitors. The head of the maihi apex is Mahinarangi herself. The full-length figure at the top of the pou tahu is Hoturoa, captain of the Tainui canoe. Below him is the curling body of Taniwha-rau, symbolising all taniwha of the Waikato River. Over the window, the carved lintel depicts Tainui, the paddle of Te Hoe O Tainui, and a kete said to have been given to one of the migrants by a tohunga of Hawaiki. At the bow and stern there are two birds also given by the tohunga: the front one is Pirakaraka, who had the ability to see in the dark and to utter cries of warning when the canoe went off course, while the other bird gave warning of the approach of dawn. Mahinarangi never functioned as a hospital for a variety of reasons, becoming instead a reception hall furnished in European fashion where such relics of the Tainui peoples as Te Puea thought fit were displayed.

It was essential to Te Puea that her hospital have the familiar and therefore comforting shape of a conventional meeting-house. Some modifications were necessary in view of the building's function: windows were placed between the wall panels to allow for proper lighting and ventilation and no poles blocked the central aisle. As with other meeting-houses, Mahinarangi was regarded as having a mauri, or life force, of its

In 1933, Koroki succeeded his father, Te Rata. Te Puea decided that the new king needed a residence suited to his position at Turangawaewae and immediately set about the long process of raising funds. Built by voluntary labour to Te Puea's own design, the new house was named Turongo and features a large sitting room, private bedrooms and kitchens. A covered walkway joins Mahinarangi to Turongo, thus making them 'linked in architecture as in life'.[10] Turongo's most notable exterior features are the partial cladding of ponga logs; the carved hexagonal tower supported by seven posts, each symbolising a major migration canoe; and the carved pataka set into its roof, which function as dormers and house relics formerly held in Ahurewa. On 18 March 1938 a crowd of five thousand people attended the simultaneous opening of Turongo, investment of Te Puea as a C.B.E., and the launching of the rebuilt canoe, Te Winika.

Another influential Maori leader of this period was Tahupotiki Wiremu Ratana (1870–1939), who, following a divine revelation in 1918, founded the religion which bears his name. Like Te Puea, his mission was to unite a dispersed people and, also like her, he chose a location in country long familiar to him. At the Ratana Pa near Wanganui in 1926 he laid the foundation stone of the Temepara or temple, based on plans drawn up by a Wanganui architect, Clifford Hood. Te Mangai (Mouthpiece of God), as Ratana was addressed by his people, was also said to have been influenced by a building he had seen in Japan but, whatever its precise origin, the building is one in which the traditional shapes of Maori architecture did not find a place. The probable reason for this is that, in the wake of the severe 1918 influenza epidemic Te Mangai, himself bereaved, wished to weaken the reliance of Maori people upon the tohunga and traditional medical remedies, which were perceived to be powerless in the face of such a virulent illness. The front of the Temepara, with its twin bell towers and central porch, bears a distinct resemblance to many large Gothic churches in New Zealand. Its windows have pointed arches, buttressing is clearly visible, and there are no carved surfaces. It was from the central balcony that Ratana addressed the crowds

of followers who assembled for his birthday, which coincided with the opening of the building. The design of the Temepara formed the pattern for many other smaller Ratana churches that were built in the following years.

The Napier earthquake and subsequent fire of February 1931 destroyed a Victorian Colonial seaside town in a few minutes and in doing so sent more than a tremor through New Zealand architectural circles. The need for radical reappraisal of building practices and codes was now apparent; despite the increase in steel-reinforced concrete buildings during the previous decade, the Government took the lead in introducing a national code for the first time.

The rebuilding of Napier offered architects and tradespeople a golden opportunity to sidestep the effects of the economic depression. The city had to be rebuilt quickly and local architects formed themselves into an association mainly, it is said, to prevent architects and builders from outside the city coming in and grabbing all the work. Students from the Auckland School of Architecture suddenly found that their draughting skills were in demand and hastened to the devastated city. Much of the characteristically Art Deco detailing of Napier's buildings is due to the extreme pressure of work on senior partners in architectural practices, who were only too keen to give young, competent employees a chance to show what they could do.

The appearance of the new city was much discussed. Some, including R. A. Lippincott, favoured a Spanish Mission townscape for which

LEFT: *Turongo. The north-facing pataka, named Hinana ki Tai (Look up to the Land), is one of two which function as dormer windows.*

RIGHT: *Temepara (1926), Ratana. A Wanganui architect, Clifford Hood, drew the plans according to the instructions of T. W. Ratana, who wished for a building which had no allusions to the traditional shapes of Maori architecture. The twin towers are decorated with the whetu (star) and marama (crescent moon) symbols, which represent the Light of the World, or Christ.*

*Hotel St George (1930),
Wellington, by W. J.
Prouse. Art Deco patterns
decorate the corner-sited
concrete expanse of one of
New Zealand's classic
hotels.*

*Masonic Hotel (1932),
Napier, by W. J. Prouse.
Many victims of the Napier
earthquake had been killed
by falling masonry parapets
and ornamental overhangs.
The severely stripped-back
style of this hotel is typical
of the new Napier.*

the Californian city of Santa Barbara, itself victim of a severe earthquake in 1928, was the model. While some of the new Napier's most attractive buildings were to be in the Spanish style, the majority of them were erected in the style which had its origins in the 1925 Paris Exposition Internationale des Arts Decoratifs et Industriels Modernes, abbreviated to Art Deco.

The clean, geometric lines of the style were eminently suited to the predominantly concrete-constructed buildings of the new Napier. Many of those who had died in the earthquake had been hit by falling masonry; stripped-back Art Deco buildings had no such dangerous ornamental cornices or overhanging parapets. Ornamentation was instead reduced to sharply defined zigzags, chevrons, sun bursts, and abstract motifs derived from plant forms, placed in panels on the plane surfaces of buildings. In the U.S.A., Art Deco skyscrapers were the symbol of the modern; in struggling Napier, Art Deco buildings reached no higher than two storeys, yet were in many cases elaborately decorated with fashionable motifs familiar from architectural magazines such as *Pencil Points* and the *Architectural Record*. Despite the fact that the earthquake had presented the citizens of Napier with the clean slate so desired by the European Modernist avant-garde, the architects of the new city preferred to build according to familiar notions, keeping abreast of the times by using a decorative vocabulary which their contemporaries regarded as having the hallmark of modernity. Today Napier has an international reputation as an Art Deco city whose uniformity of appearance, dictated by economic, seismic, geographical and stylistic features, makes it unique.

Among Napier's first new buildings were two hotels, the Masonic and the Criterion, both built in 1932 in styles which were shortly to be seen all over the city. Although the Wellington architect W. J. Prouse (1878–1956) had no formal architectural training and had been suspended from N.Z.I.A. membership for the year 1931–32, his reputation as a designer of hotels was secure since the completion of his magnificent Hotel St George, Wellington, in 1930. The corner-sited Hotel St George was constructed of steel-frame reinforced concrete and its floors were of Wingflor reinforced-concrete block. Its method of construction was as advanced as its styling, which, with its step-like massing and rhythmical arrangement of rectangular projections, seemed the very epitome of the modern hotel.

The Masonic Hotel in Napier has an even more

severely stripped back exterior, although Prouse softened the effect by providing the upper storey with a wooden pergola to enable guests to promenade, much as they had done behind the old Masonic's three-storeyed iron balconies. The new hotel's Tennyson Street entrance was given a starkly geometric parapet beneath which a suspended metal and glass canopy proclaimed the hotel's name in Art Deco-styled red leadlights.

Across the street is the Criterion, designed by E. A. Williams (1875–1962) in Californian Spanish idiom. Upon arriving in the city from London in 1908 Williams had worked with the veteran Napier architect Walter P. Finch as a draughtsman. After a period with the Napier Borough Council, Williams set up his own practice in 1912; by 1931 it had greatly expanded, ensuring that its principal partner got a good deal of the reconstruction work that followed the earthquake.

The Criterion is constructed in brick and plaster with terracotta roofing. The authentic Spanish touch is contributed by tilted Cordova half-tile roofs which project above the parapet, and window hoods which flank a group of three centrally placed arched windows. Spanish, too, is the corbel table beneath the roof line, and the use of 'barley twist' columns. In 1930, E. A. Williams had used Spanish detailing on Harstons Building, a small building which survived the earthquake; his 1931 Central Hotel and 1932 Daily Telegraph Building are among Napier's classic Art Deco buildings. Another is the Borough Architect J. T. Watson's Municipal Theatre of 1937, which was built after Louis Hay's Sullivanesque prizewinning theatre design was rejected as too costly. Watson's theatre is today a positive museum of Art Deco fittings, all of which are carefully maintained in their original condition.

The Wellington partnership of Crichton, McKay & Haughton combined Maori and Art

Deco motifs, while using the Classical facade composition of column, frieze and entablature, when they designed Napier's Bank of New Zealand premises in 1932. Lintels above the main entrance exploit the similarity between the zigzag and a kowhaiwhai pattern; inside, around a coffered glass ceiling, another kowhaiwhai border is used and a taiaha head motif defines the corners.

The Crichton, McKay & Haughton partnership was to spearhead the Bank of New Zealand's renovation programme, which resulted from findings by the Government's Buildings Regulation Committee, set up following the Napier earthquake. The Standards Institute, founded in 1932, advocated a single construction standard for all local authorities.

Ministry of Works (1936), Napier, by J. T. Mair. Stripped Classical proportions dominate the building behind a horizontally banded Art Deco light which stands on a fluted column.

The Government Architect J. T. Mair cast a wider allusive net when he decorated the otherwise conventional, stripped Classical Napier Ministry of Works building in 1936. Outside, on the circular pavement which leads to the impressive entrance, Mair placed a columnar light-stand which bears a distinct resemblance to the aluminium air-conditioning units designed by Otto Wagner in 1903 for the main banking chamber of his Postsparkassenamt, Vienna.

As a member of the Napier Reconstruction Committee, J. A. Louis Hay was in the forefront of the rebuilding of the new city and it was a position he clearly relished, on the evidence of

Modern, Moderne and Deco

TOP LEFT: *Criterion Hotel (1932), Napier, by E. A. Williams. The Spanish appearance of the hotel is probably due to the interest of the rebuilders of Napier in the Californian city, Santa Barbara, which had been largely rebuilt in Spanish style following an earthquake in 1928.*

BOTTOM LEFT: *Municipal Theatre (1937), Napier, by J. T. Watson. An earlier, more elaborate theatre designed by J. A. Louis Hay did not proceed for reasons of economy. Although Watson's was simpler in its exterior massing and decoration, it eventually cost as much as Hay's prizewinning building would have.*

*Watercolour perspective by
Leonard J. Wolfe of
proposed Albion Hotel,
Napier, designed in 1933
by J. A. Louis Hay. The
architect was unable to
persuade Australasian
brewing companies to
finance the building of an
extravagant scheme which
owes much to Frank Lloyd
Wright.*
PETER SHAW.

*Webb House (1938),
Auckland, by Horace
Massey. Its form echoing
the shape of the peninsula
on which its sits above the
Waitemata Harbour, this
house, called Valpré,
originally had a more
Spanish aspect, which was
compromised in 1940 when
the architect closed in the
open balcony on the right
with another bank of
curving windows.*

the outlandishly extravagant schemes he put
forward for an entertainment centre to straddle
the city's Marine Parade, the huge Albion Hotel
and the Municipal Theatre — all of them unbuilt.
He was lucky, however, in his wealthy client
Gerhard Husheer, founder of the National
Tobacco Company, whose 1933 mid-Depression
profit was a staggering £35,000. Husheer's sense of
display accorded well with Hay's interest in the
elaborately decorated work of Louis Sullivan, as
the National Tobacco Company Building (now
the Rothmans Building) of 1934 shows. Hay took
his basic shape of an arch within a square from
Sullivan's 1890 Carrie Eliza Getty Tomb.
Decorative panels on either side of the richly
carved doorway feature an arrangement of raupo
and roses in sculpted concrete; the arch sits on
two engaged piers, reminding the viewer that
Hay's other great enthusiasm was for the much
more pared-back horizontality of Frank Lloyd
Wright. Hay's eccentric combination of influences
can also be seen on the A.M.P. Building, which
he designed in 1933 for the company which
played a crucial role in financing the loans that
enabled the reconstruction of Napier to proceed
so swiftly. The A.M.P. also has Sullivanesque
floral decorative panels on the capitals of giant
order pilasters and the abutments of two arched
entrances, while a third entrance utilises the
stepped vertical construction of Mayan
architecture, another motif frequently borrowed
by Art Déco designers. Hay took his design for
the interior light-fittings from Wright's in the
Larkin Building (1903), Buffalo.

Napier's rebuilders usually looked to their
immediate American contemporaries for ideas;
Louis Hay's many post-earthquake buildings are
unusual because he adapted to his immediate
purpose an earlier enthusiasm for German
Jugendstil and Austrian Sezession architects, for
Sullivan and the prairie houses of Wright. His
essays in the Spanish and Art Deco styles were
few and less successful.

Architects outside Napier were also willing to
turn their hands to the designing of houses in
both these fashionable styles. Horace Massey in
Auckland was responsible in 1938 for the large
Webb House, called Valpré, at Paritai Drive,
which he handled with much greater finesse than
he did its close contemporary, the brick Abel
House. Both houses make much of the double-
storeyed curved bay window. At Valpré, an
angled plan and entry porch with balcony above
seem to indicate acquaintance with Gummer's
Spanish-styled houses. More obviously Art Deco
is the stucco-finished Curtis House (1936) at
Forbury, Dunedin, the work of local architects

Wood & McCormack. Its corners, instead of being curved, are chamfered and give the house a geometric rigour further emphasised by clear and textured glass arranged in sharply angled decorative patterns. In the spacious stairwell a stained and painted window depicts a ruined Scottish castle. By contrast, the Blackie House (1947) at Victoria Street, Hamilton, is so curvaceous that it has become known as a 'waterfall' house. The enduring popularity of such large Art Deco-styled residences is evident from the fact that the house was built as late as 1947.

Modern, Moderne and Deco

Avon Cinema (1934), Christchurch, by L. E. Williams. The hallmarks of the 'streamlined' Deco style are apparent.

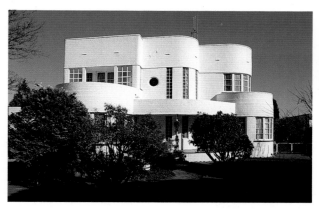

All over New Zealand smaller, single-storeyed Deco houses sprang up, relatively few of them the work of architects. Most were constructed by local builders quick to grasp the essentials of a style closely resembling that of 'modern' state houses. Many such smaller houses exhibited the proportions of the Deco box but were given a Spanish dress with the addition of angled Cordova tiles on parapets, obscuring their flat roofs.

Elsewhere in New Zealand, businesses which did not feel the economic pinch employed architects to design cinemas, transport centres, swimming pools and insurance companies in the modern Art Deco style. The so-called 'streamlined' Deco with its futuristic obsession

with movement made little impact here, although two cinemas, the State (1935) in Nelson by H. Francis Willis and the Avon (1937) in Christchurch by L. E. Williams exhibit the swooping linearity which characterised the style. Dunedin's Road Services Passenger Station (1936) by Miller & White owes its impressive appearance in part to an unusual site, which is a triangle nearly 125 metres on its longest side. Despite this, the architects designed a long, low building which actually curves smoothly around the site and is given definition by symmetrically placed, cobalt-blue metal sash windows, incised panels of vertical decoration and a superb entrance that was originally given even stronger vertical emphasis by a contrasting colour scheme of cream, brown and orange. Inside, three types of marble in black, pink and green, relieved by polished metal bands, created a stylish effect; on the second floor above it a social hall was provided with stage, dressing rooms and a jarrah floor for dancing. This was indeed a building

RIGHT: *Road Services Passenger Station (1936), Dunedin, by Miller & White. This is one of a number of fine Art Deco buildings in a city which is surprisingly rich in examples of the style.*

TOP LEFT: *Curtis House (1936), Forbury, Dunedin, by Wood & McCormack.*

BOTTOM LEFT: *Blackie House (1947), Hamilton. The exploitation of the smoothly curving stucco surface of houses such as this has led to the adoption of the descriptive term 'waterfall'.*

*First State House (1937),
Miramar, Wellington,
designed in the Department
of Housing Construction. It
was opened by the Prime
Minister, Michael Joseph
Savage, who helped to carry
the first inhabitants'
furniture into the house.*

which reflected the preoccupations of the Jazz Age rather than those of the Depression.

When the first Labour Government was elected to power in 1935, the exigencies of the time immediately commanded its attention. A housing survey revealed some shocking statistics about overcrowding in substandard buildings; there was an estimated shortage of 20,000 houses and still more were needed to cope with population growth. The Government's response was to establish the Department of Housing Construction in September 1936, under the dynamic leadership of John A. Lee, as Under-Secretary in charge of Housing.

John A. Lee abhorred English barrack-type terraced workers' housing; he insisted that the majority of houses should be individual units, each on its own plot of ground, and that no two houses in a particular area should be of the same design. The choice of areas to be developed for state rental housing was governed by their proximity to an existing urban area and the availability of cheap land. Lee insisted on a high standard of construction in New Zealand materials and, convinced that people's lives are influenced by the quality of their environment, was concerned that houses should be built in attractive locations rather than unobtrusively tucked away out of the view of wealthier property owners. The spectacular views available from the two early Auckland state housing subdivisions of Orakei and Mt Roskill are testimony to this enlightened socialist thinking.

Architects were invited by the D.H.C. through a competition to prepare designs and working drawings to the Department's standard requirements. It specified the need for four-roomed houses, three types of five-roomed houses, and six-roomed houses. Every group of ten houses was to have a different plan; every one was to be varied in elevational treatment and in materials used. Each architect was encouraged to impress his individuality on the basic design. Specifications, tendering, grouping, site placement and supervision were all to be handled by the Department's own architects.

Not surprisingly, given the depressed state of the profession, over 400 designs were received from architects in private practice. Among the designs accepted by the Department were those by S. S. Alleman and Horace Massey in Auckland; K. Cook, Bernard Johns and Swan & Lavalle in Wellington; P. H. Graham in Gisborne; England Brothers in Christchurch; and Stone & Sturmer in Dunedin.

They are mostly in the English Cottage style,

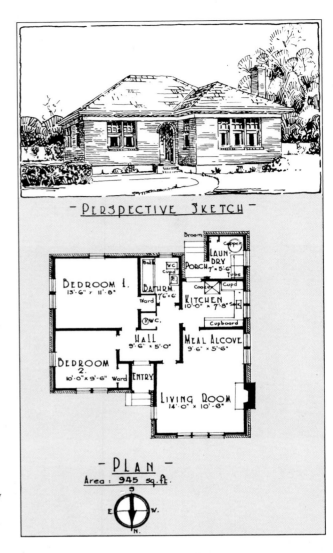

- PERSPECTIVE SKETCH -

- PLAN -
Area : 945 sq. ft.

although some, like the First State House in Fife Lane, Miramar, Wellington, had a Georgian aspect while others made oblique reference to Modernism. The Californian bungalow did not feature at all, having run its course in the previous two decades and been supplanted by buildings reflecting English rather than American origins. The Department's guidelines favoured an English rural cottage model because it was compact and economical to build, which goes

State houses built in brick
at the Dunedin suburb of
Pine Hill and others built in
wood at Mt Roskill,
Auckland, indicate that
despite early intentions,
state housing suburbs
quickly came to have an
appearance of uniformity.

State house (1939) at
Remuera, Auckland.
Modernist in every respect
except its planning, this
house draws attention to the
fact that the Viennese
Modernist Ernst Plischke
worked alongside New
Zealanders in the
draughting office of the
Department of Housing
Construction.

some way towards explaining the conventional appearance of the majority of the early state houses. It is perhaps significant that the first Minister of Housing was the English-born Walter Nash, although John A. Lee, as Under-Secretary, was its most ardent propagandist.

The Department's planning reflected a highly specialised, even inflexible view of family life: the small separate rooms had designated functions which were underlined by windows of varying sizes, ceilings of differing heights, bays and fireplaces. In the kitchens there was some confusion of public and private spaces; a dining table was frequently placed in a small recess off the kitchen; the entry hall all but disappeared, visitors entering the central passageway from a front porch hardly wide enough to accommodate

two people standing side by side. Both the separation of parents' bedroom from other bedrooms and the family-oriented front living room suggests a European origin.

Externally, the early state houses were characterised by steep-pitched roofs, either hipped or gabled, with a small eaves overhang. Windows varied according to the function of internal space, but were generally three-light, high-silled casements more appropriate to the climate of England than New Zealand. Clay or concrete tiles were the favoured roofing materials for 1930s state houses; most had timber soffit-linings with spouting and fascia board returns at gables to mask the ends of the boxed eaves. Although Lee favoured brick veneer construction, most of the houses were clad in

NEW ZEALAND ARCHITECTURE

A street of state houses under construction in Wellington. The target was to build 5000 houses a year, and carpenters were brought from England to help achieve this.
NATIONAL ARCHIVES.

Centennial Tower (1940), Centennial Exhibition, by Edmund Anscombe. This streamlined Deco structure, clad in asbestos for convenience, was dismantled at the exhibition's conclusion.
ALEXANDER TURNBULL LIBRARY.

depression . . . they represented security'. She also observed realistically that the Department of Housing Construction was a government department and was thus dependent on electoral success. 'It was politically expedient to respond to conservative taste . . . it was all right to experiment with flats and apartments as long as the standard house looked like a "house" and not a "cow shed".'[11]

The sitting room of this state house has the standard open fire because there is no central heating. The wooden floor is covered with linoleum.
NATIONAL ARCHIVES.

weatherboard, except in Dunedin where bricks were plentiful. Two state joinery factories were established, in Auckland and Wellington, to reduce delays in supply.

Wendy Fitzpatrick pointed out that these houses 'were born of a desire to build well but not extravagantly . . . to many a New Zealander they were a luxury in the aftermath of the

The celebration at the end of what turned out to be the Depression Decade had long been planned. Edmund Anscombe was commissioned as early as 1929 to design the New Zealand Centennial Exhibition of 1940. Exhibitions, 'timekeepers of progress' he called them, had always drawn him like a magnet, even before he designed the 1925–26 New Zealand and South Seas International Exhibition at Dunedin. He moved from Dunedin to Wellington, where he became one of the main driving forces behind the centennial project. In 1933 he visited the Chicago Exhibition, and in 1939 both the New York World's Fair and the Golden Gate Exposition at San Francisco. Small wonder then that Art Deco styling dominated his extravagant designs. Most of the exhibition buildings at Rongotai were clad in asbestos to enable convenient dismantling at the event's conclusion. The 52-metre-high Centennial Tower at the centre of the exhibition was a triumph of soaring, streamlined Deco, designed to uplift a nation by that time at war. The 1940 Centenary also resulted in a belated official interest in Maori buildings. As a result a number of historically important structures were restored and some new ones built.

The Kaik (1878), Onuku, Banks Peninsula. This Maori church was restored at the time of the Centenary of New Zealand.

Whare runanga (1934–49), Waitangi. A building of national rather than tribal significance, its foundation stone house was laid by Lord Bledisloe on 6 February 1934. The opening was delayed until 1949.

Centennial Memorial Church (1940), Otakou Marae, Otago Peninsula. Built in concrete to a design by Miller & White, the church follows a conventional layout but is decorated with carvings cast in concrete.

Interior of whare runanga, Waitangi. A great diversity of carving styles characterises the interior, because ancestors of many iwi are represented. The pou tokomanawa represents Rahiri, the Ngapuhi chief. The fourteen poupou are arranged in pairs, the first three displaying carving styles from Ngapuhi, Waikato and Ngati Maru.

Tama-te-Kapua, Ohinemutu, Rotorua. Built in 1878 to ratify the peace between Arawa and Waikato, the whare whakairo was demolished in 1939 then rebuilt, opening in 1943.

and loved so well in Prague. I was at home in Durham Street.'[12]

But when Porsolt designed a corner facade consisting of a severely Modernist glass-brick wall, interrupted only by entrance doors, with stairs and landings floating freely behind it, Bartley produced a radio station building elevation from California which had a curved corner similar to Porsolt's design but which was more conventionally dramatised by full building-height square pillars. The 'Prague solution' was dropped, as were other Modernist features, although the curved facade remained. The main innovation of the building was its two straightforward and uncompromising facades with identical window patterns, which radiated away on either side of the corner. Great care was lavished on the interior, which also incorporated many continental Modern features, as contemporary photographs clearly show.

On his 1935 Miller's Building (now Civic Offices) in Tuam Street, Christchurch, G. A. J Hart (1879–1961) created another distinctly Modernist facade by means of cantilevering, so that an uninterrupted line of windows could be used along the whole frontage without piers of any kind. On Gummer & Ford's 1936 Dingwall

Towards the end of the 1930s a number of buildings were constructed which clearly indicated that some architects now felt confident about employing Modernist notions in their work. One building became Modern in appearance by chance. In Auckland, when Alva Bartley designed Broadcasting House for Durham Street, he was fortunate that 'a chap with some new continental ideas', the young Hungarian-born Jewish architect Imi Porsolt, had just arrived in Auckland looking for work. When Porsolt began with him, the plan of the building was already designed; Bartley looked at the young man's sketches from his Prague student days and decided that a Modern elevational treatment was called for. Porsolt has written that 'the vertically accented intimacy of Durham Street was exactly the sort of streetscape I had known

CIVIC OFFICES

Modern, Moderne
and Deco

*Civic Offices (1935),
Christchurch, by G. A. J.
Hart. The building,
originally called Miller's
Building, is clean-lined in a
Bauhaus manner regarded
here as advanced for its
time. It was functional, in
that it allowed light to
penetrate into the first-floor
offices and second- and
third-floor clothing factory.*

Building in Queen Street, the front facade of the
eight storeys was also cantilevered out to present
an almost continuous line of square glass across
the front. But the Dingwall, despite its Modernist
appearance, was tame compared with the
extraordinary State Insurance Building which
they designed for the corner of Lambton Quay
and Stout Street, Wellington, in 1936–37 and
which was built during 1940. Gummer & Ford
dealt with an irregular site by splaying the
building's front across the corner, producing a
bold entry wall from which two unequal serrated
side facades stepped back. In clear emulation of
Emil Fahrenkamp's Shell Mex Building (1932),
Berlin, the building's undulating sides give the
whole structure a striking individuality, quite
distinct from the applied decorative Classicism
which Gummer & Ford had so recently
employed almost as a house style. The State
Insurance design, like the Dingwall Building,
allows a great deal of natural light to enter the
building. The architects could not resist
providing this Modernist structure with a
conventionally granite-sheathed base and an
entrance porch which exhibits slight touches of
Art Deco ornament. The free-standing pair of
columns framing the entrance are a reminder of
those which flank the entrance of the 1934 Royal
Institute of British Architects Building, London,
by G. Grey Wornum.

DINGWALL BUILDING

*Dingwall Building (1936),
Auckland, by Gummer &
Ford. The principle of
cantilevering was again
used to allow an
uninterrupted line of glass
across the building's facade.*

State Insurance Building (1938–41), Wellington, by Gummer & Ford. The significance of this building in New Zealand's architectural history made it the subject of a conservation controversy when in 1989 there were strong suggestions that it could be demolished.

The State Insurance Building is one of New Zealand's most important buildings because, as Wellington architect William Toomath pointed out in a submission made in response to the company's intention to demolish its historic building, 'it was designed at a period when the time honoured formulae of the past were being supplanted by the powerful modern simplification of functionalism and it exemplifies the best of the restrained transitional work of the period'.[13]

The decade of the 1930s was not one of great architectural innovation in New Zealand, despite the opportunities. The Depression brought about the enforced closure of many architectural offices, and those who remained to do the available work were frequently older practitioners whose training and experience led them towards familiar solutions. The architectural challenge occasioned by the Napier earthquake produced a great many stylish buildings but did not encourage an examination of the principles of Modernism. Similarly, the political decision to embark upon an extensive programme of state-sponsored housing resulted in buildings which mostly referred back to English Cottage models. It was largely left to architects who were refugees from Central Europe to introduce a Modernist outlook; their efforts during the following decade were to meet with considerable resistance.

CHAPTER EIGHT
The Search for the Vernacular

Dixon Street Flats
(page 142)

*Berhampore Flats
(1938–40), Wellington, by
Gordon Wilson in the
Department of Housing
Construction. European
Modernist in conception
and design, this was the
first example of multi-unit
housing in New Zealand.*

In the 1940s, despite the war, architecture changed direction. A significant number of younger, New Zealand-born architects had by now served their articles in the offices of senior practitioners both here and overseas and had returned with the intention of ensuring that Modernist thought and practice should no longer be ignored. New Zealand was to become the new home for a group of established European architects who sought refuge in a country free from anti-Semitism and Fascism. They were hopeful that the democratic socialist ideology which lay behind their Modernist forms would be well received by a Labour Government which had already initiated a progressive housing policy.

A young architect called Gordon Wilson (1900–59), decided in 1936 that he had had enough of the concessionary approach to Modern architecture in the practice of Gummer & Ford and applied for and was appointed to the position of Architect to the Department of Housing Construction. Wilson had been employed by Gummer & Ford for fourteen years. He had detailed their National War Memorial Carillon in 1929 and had been an associate partner with the firm during the period when it produced the designs for the Dingwall Building and the State Insurance Building (see page 137).

From the start, Wilson was keen that the D.H.C. design and build small blocks of unit housing. This contrasted sharply with both the politicians' determination that there should be no houses in rows anywhere in New Zealand and the desire of most applicants that they should be able to live in detached houses. There was also a degree of political expediency involved; the figures for construction of individual houses could be made to look much more impressive to the electorate than could those for multi-unit housing. Despite this, Wilson, always a forceful advocate for his new ideas, began to experiment with semi-detached units which could accommodate two to four families but which looked like single houses. John A. Lee, eventually persuaded of the usefulness of multi-unit housing in central city locations, even went so far as to damn 'cottage construction' in a pamphlet called *Worker Housing*, which was suppressed by the Cabinet because it did not conform with government policy. Of the early multi-units, most repeated the English Cottage stylistic formula to considerable ill effect; others which exhibited a more severe and pared-back appearance in line with Modernist notions were hardly more successful.

The same cannot be said for Wilson's Berhampore Flats, in Adelaide Road, Wellington, which were designed in 1938 and completed in time for the New Zealand Centennial in 1940. They consisted of fifty medium-density flats or 'multi-units' built in four blocks comprising bedsitters, one- and two-bedroom units, and three-bedroom flats. As Kenneth Davis has pointed out, the external appearance shows that Wilson had completely thrown off the elevational symmetry of his Gummer & Ford work. Nor was there any trace of the vestigial Art Deco ornamentation of earlier stripped Classical buildings. 'Both in form and content the Berhampore Flats were one of the first expressions of the ideals of European Modernism in New Zealand and their design recalled mass social housing in Berlin by Bruno Taut and Hans Scharoun between 1926 and 1931.'[1] Like J. J. P. Oud's 1926 worker housing scheme at the Hook of Holland, the main public space of Berhampore centred on a circular recreation hall which protruded into a landscaped, communal grassed area, which has unfortunately now become a car park. The recreation hall failed to live up to the communal ideal and was eradicated from future schemes.

Wilson also replicated Oud's long horizontal first-floor balconies in his two-storeyed blocks; he even used the same light metal grilles to separate individual terraces in the rear access balconies. The flats were built of reinforced concrete specially designed to resist earthquake shock and spread of fire. External forms were devoid of ornament but from every angle there is a fine play of abstract shapes created by gravity-defying, cantilevered balconies and port-hole windows on doors. The wooden-framed windows, mass produced in one of the Government-owned joinery factories, are less interesting; metal windows would have been more in keeping with the building's Modernist style.

The D.H.C.'s concern that living spaces be oriented towards sun and light ensured that living rooms and balconies faced north; the scale of the block on the northern boundary was reduced to single-storey height to allow sunlight to enter the central courtyard. Interior planning ensured privacy for each flat and followed traditional lines rather than the free-planned approach favoured by so many European architects of the time.

From 1939 onwards the ranks of those employed at the D.H.C. were swelled by the arrival of a number of refugee European architects. All thoroughly familiar with Modernist principles, as Kenneth Davis has pointed out, they were probably less interested in finding a way of blending these principles into a truly New Zealand indigenous style, 'given their recent exposure to nationalism in Europe'.[2]

Among this group were Friedrich Neumann (who quickly changed his name to Frederick Newman), Ernst Gerson, Frederick Farrar, Helmut Einhorn and, most notably, Ernst Plischke.

Ernst Plischke came to New Zealand with a firmly established international reputation. As a young man under the influence of Le Corbusier's *Towards a New Architecture* he rejected the conventional educational process in order to study with Peter Behrens at the Vienna Academy. Plischke's work was so brilliant that, upon graduation, he was first taken into Behrens's office and then later into Josef Frank's. In late 1929 Plischke left Vienna for New York, where he found work with the eminent architect Ely Jacques Kahn and met Frank Lloyd Wright. As economic circumstances worsened he decided to return to Vienna where, in 1930, he set up in private practice and was asked to contribute a design to the Vienna Werkbundsiedlung, the Vienna State Council's experimental housing research project, under the direction of his former employer Josef Frank. Plischke found himself working alongside such luminaries as Hugo Haring, Josef Hoffmann, Adolf Loos, Richard Neutra and Gerrit Rietveld. When the Werkbund became subject to political pressure from those who felt it was dominated by Jews and Left-wing sympathisers, Plischke, a gentile, did not resign. He was responsible for a two-unit building in reinforced concrete finished in white stucco, with a flat roof and with built-in interior furniture. Its austerity and restraint were akin to Oud's terraced houses at the Weissenhofsiedlung, Stuttgart, and were to be characteristic of Plischke's later work in New Zealand.

Next Plischke designed an Employment Office in the Viennese suburb of Liesing, and from this time his work became the subject of much attention in the international architectural press. When he was awarded a prestigious state prize by the Austrian Government his career seemed assured. Following the *Anschluss* with Germany in 1938 he realised that, as a man with a Jewish wife and two children, he must emigrate. In the Fascist climate of the day he was endangered because his Modernism and past allegiances allied him with socialism.

Plischke's decision to come to New Zealand was made because he knew people who could facilitate his family's immigration and because he imagined that this would be a 'country ideally suited for the successful transplanting of his brand of International Style architecture'.[3] His New Zealand sponsor, Otto Frankel, found him a position in the newly formed department of

Design for Mt Eden Flats (1942), Auckland, by Ernst Plischke in the Department of Housing Construction. The innovative architect located laundry facilities on the open roof, but was to see his plans drastically altered.
NATIONAL ARCHIVES.

Interior of Dixon Street Flats. The careful geometry of the entrance hall is Modern in its sparseness.
NATIONAL ARCHIVES.

Housing Construction — as a draughtsman! This did not, however, disappoint Plischke, who was sure that his international reputation would ensure his quick promotion.

At the time he was not to know how difficult life could be in New Zealand for a German-speaking architect. He did not imagine for a moment that he would have to reckon with jealousy from his associates, with a profession deeply suspicious of Modernism, with a boss who clearly felt intimidated by the arrival of such an eminent figure in his office, and with a country whose inhabitants despised the very idea of high-rise urban multi-unit housing. Plischke was to remain in New Zealand for twenty-four difficult years, from 1939 to 1963.

His first work at the D.H.C. was the detailing of back porches of state houses. The salary was so inadequate that he also worked in the evenings on interior designs for the Government Court at the New Zealand Centennial Exhibition. Then, as the result of intervention by the Director of Housing, Arthur Tindall, Plischke was given his own office and a special assignment to design semi-detached housing units for the Government's housing development at Orakei, Auckland.

It was a controversial scheme from the start. In 1929 the police, acting on a request from the Commissioner of Crown Lands, had forcibly removed the remaining Maori from their tribal land; next, a planned Garden Suburb scheme foundered and the land, which gave spectacular views over the Waitemata Harbour, was eventually put aside by the Labour Government for housing development after private section-buying tailed off during the early years of the Depression. In mid-1937 tenders were called for the building of 212 houses, of which all but three were eventually built by the Fletcher Construction Company. Plischke was apparently aware that Lee had a political motive in encouraging potential Labour voters into the suburb, but he accepted the brief because it was a chance for him to work in a familiar area and to exhibit his skills to colleagues.

Plischke's watercolour perspectives for the units at Kupe Street, Orakei, were exhibited in the Government Court at the Centennial Exhibition. Although they bore a significant resemblance to Mies Van der Rohe's 1927 steel-framed apartment building in Stuttgart and to his own work at the Vienna Werkbundsiedlung, their planning was entirely conventional and included separate living, dining and bedroom areas. When the units were built in 1940 the original flat roof was

replaced with a pitched one, the skylights were dispensed with, and the open sun balconies roofed over. A block wall was built to screen off each entrance.

In 1942 a similar fate was to befall his proposal for the design of thirty-five flats at Mt Eden, Auckland. Here he used the Orakei plan, but arranged the blocks in a U shape around a grassed quadrangle. The Corbusian roof garden made an appearance on the main block of sixteen flats; only five flats faced the street, the remainder facing inwards towards the courtyard. These plans, too, were considerably altered within the D.H.C. to enable more flats to be squeezed in, thus reducing the size of the courtyard.

The following year Plischke began work on the enormous Dixon Street Flats in Wellington. This time his brief was to design 50 one-bedroomed flats in a ten-storey building on a tight central-city site. Unlike the Berhampore Flats designed by Plischke's superior, Gordon Wilson, the Dixon Street Flats are a monolithic unit with a group of lifts at the centre. This was to be Plischke's only major Housing Department design which was not drastically altered from its original conception, the only change to the flat facade being the addition of flower boxes. The rear facade, with its

solid balcony lines, is even more severe. At each end the stairs are encased behind a curved wall punctuated by square windows, forming a sharp contrast with the rectilinear solidity of the main block.

It rankled with Plischke that the Dixon Street Flats won for Gordon Wilson, as head of the department responsible for their design, a New Zealand Institute of Architects Gold Medal in 1947. Plischke's signature was, according to standard practice at the time, erased from his designs once they had been submitted to the draughting room. These designs were further adapted for the Gordon Wilson Flats on the Terrace in 1952 and in other high-rise blocks of flats built during the next twenty years. From 1942 all work on civilian housing was halted for the duration of the war, and Plischke was transferred to the office of R. Hammond, the Town Planner and Assistant Director of Housing. His troubled relationship with Gordon Wilson came to an end.

A Viennese colleague of Plischke's at the D.H.C. was Frederick Newman (1900–64), who had arrived in Wellington in 1938. A graduate of the Ecole des Beaux Arts in Paris, Newman spent the years 1933 to 1937 designing hospitals, sanitoria and other buildings in Moscow at the invitation of the Soviet Government before returning to Vienna, where he too designed flats. After coming to New Zealand he worked at the D.H.C. until 1948, when he transferred to the Power Design Office and was responsible for the distinctive architecture of major hydro-electric stations at Maraetai, Whakamaru and Roxburgh.

Newman, like Plischke, identified fully with the life of his adopted country; both men were active polemicists on behalf of Modern architecture. Plischke, unlike Newman, did not sit the examinations for admission to the Royal Institute of British Architects and was only admitted to the New Zealand Institute in 1969 as an honorary member on a return visit to this country. Plischke was a member of the editorial board of the magazine *Design Review*, to which he often contributed articles, while Newman preferred to publish his carefully researched lectures in the *N.Z.I.A. Journal*. Both men frequently lectured to enthusiastic audiences, particularly in Wellington. In 1947 Plischke applied to be appointed to the Chair of Design at the University of Auckland's School of Architecture but was passed over. One can only speculate on the effect had he been appointed. Instead he left New Zealand at the age of sixty to become head of the Academie der Bildendekünste in Vienna.

In a sentence ringing with a Modernist's confidence in architecture's ability to transform society, Newman wrote that 'high blocks of flats will lead to a more dynamic interpretation of the new society and should greatly contribute towards bringing about our very own architectural expression'.[4] Before the war, while still with the D.H.C., he had designed the Symonds Street Flats in Auckland, although they were not built until 1947. Both the Symonds Street Flats and the Greys Avenue Flats, which were built in the same year, are usually ascribed to Plischke, but he probably had no influence on the design of the latter, while the former are certainly the work of Newman.

The Search for the Vernacular

Interior of Dixon Street Flats. This view up the stairwell shows how severely and simply the architect conceived every detail.
NATIONAL ARCHIVES.

Symonds Street Flats (designed 1939, built 1947), Auckland, by Frederick Newman in the Department of Housing Construction. Another modern monolith, this time with a slightly curved facade.

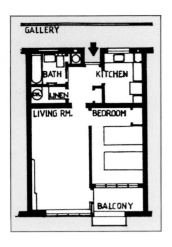

Plan of a one-bedroom flat in Symonds Street Flats.

Smaller than Dixon Street, the Symonds Street Flats consist of forty-five units built as a T-shaped block. One wing, with a distinctive concave facade, runs parallel to the street, the other juts out into the slope of Grafton Gully. Unlike the Greys Avenue Flats, which are made up of four separate blocks of flats, each with its own entrance, the Symonds Street Flats are entered below street level from the footpath by means of a bridge which leads to a central vestibule at the junction of the two wings. The building is constructed around a reinforced-concrete column with beam-and-slab framework; each flat is a virtually solid concrete shell, filled at each open end with brick work and glazing. As at Greys Avenue, there are 8-centimetre spaces between each block and these are covered with flush face panels, designed to slide should any seismic movement occur.

Greys Avenue Flats (1947), designed by the Department of Housing Construction. Four separate blocks step down the slope of the street.

In a burst of post-war enthusiasm both blocks of flats were opened on 13 September 1947 at a large public event, and the Minister of Housing Bob Semple took the opportunity to deliver to the assembled crowd a homily about 'the need for goodwill, co-operation and enthusiasm in facing today's problems', and exhort them to indulge in less 'snivelling'.[5]

Also working in Auckland at this time was an architect who, unlike Newman, believed that an indigenous architectural expression would spring not from high-rise flats but in the field of detached housing. London-born Vernon Brown (1905–65) was destined to have an enormous influence on a whole generation of architects who studied with him at the Auckland School of Architecture, where he taught from 1942 until his death. Educated at the Northern Polytechnic Institute School of Architecture, London, he arrived in New Zealand in 1927, spending the next ten years gaining experience in various offices, including Grierson, Aimer & Draffin, where he was one of a team of draughtsmen summarily sacked early in the Depression when the firm was forced to cut back. This unfortunate experience was repeated when he was employed by Bloomfield, Owen & Morgan, and he was forced to earn money digging useless ditches across the streets of Grey Lynn. There was little casual work for qualified draughtsmen in the early 1930s, but Vernon Brown was not too proud to work with a building contractor. Then, despite the straitened times, Aimer took him on again as a salaried employee because he was capable of producing a great deal of work in a short time. Recalling these days, Brown used to say that if the office boy told him, 'We've lost one of them,' he knew immediately that it was one of the office's four drawing-pins that was missing.[6]

In 1936, when Aimer was awarded the N.Z.I.A. Gold Medal for his Marina Garden Flats in Mt Eden Road, Auckland, he gave full credit to Vernon Brown as 'the man who should have got the medal'. By the early 1940s Vernon Brown had parted company with his final employers, Wade & Bartley, and gone out on his own. His work was principally domestic, but even that dried up as the war continued, and Brown was forced to undertake the supervision of military works for the Public Works Department. At the war's conclusion he was joined in practice by Robin Simpson, a talented architect who had worked for Gummer & Ford and reputedly had more than a little influence on the facade of their State Insurance Building on Lambton Quay. It was a happy partnership which resulted in a fine building for the Auckland Glass Company (1948), but ended just two years later with Simpson's death at the age of forty.

Vernon Brown, like his European Modern contemporaries in Wellington, had little interest in perpetuating the English Cottage tradition which had, after state encouragement, replaced the Californian bungalow as the commonest form of housing in New Zealand. A man whose command of the *bon mot* was second to none, Brown said that these cottages were to him like over-sweet cake: they damaged the organism they purported to nourish. Instead, he wanted to build houses that were like wholemeal bread. It is said that he looked for inspiration not to houses or 'homes' by other architects but to sheds.

In fact, he looked rather more closely at Scandinavian domestic architecture, of the type produced by Blakstad and Munthe-Kaas in Norway, and the work of William Wurster, who from 1927 to 1942 designed over 200 houses and became the recognised leader of a group of San Francisco Bay architects. Wurster, too, was fond of a culinary metaphor. 'I like an unlaboured thing that looks as inevitable as something that comes out of a frying pan just right, like an omelet in France, for instance.'[7] Frank Lloyd Wright called him a 'shanty builder', and to others he was known as 'Redwood Bill' because of his dislike of concrete. Like Vernon Brown he preferred to make use of the plentiful supplies of good timber, keeping building costs to a minimum. Neither architect was interested in the tags of the International style, making no fetish of the flat roof or of the avoidance of projections and overhangs as a matter of principle. In both their utterances and their buildings the organic replaced the mechanical analogy.

A country house in Norway by Blakstad and Munthe-Kaas, illustrated in the Studio Yearbook 1936, *exhibits striking similarities with Vernon Brown's houses.*

Brown's houses are instantly recognisable because of their informal, understated character. Many were built during the 1940s in Remuera, a suburb of Auckland not otherwise noted for the avoidance of ostentation. Vernon Brown's clients were invariably Left-leaning academics, professional people or artists only too eager to escape the uniformity into which state-sponsored housing schemes seemed to be plunging. Brown was a genius at planning; his style allowed these clients the satisfaction of owning a carefully designed house which was both cheap and

unobtrusive. He designed from the inside out, carefully tailoring interior spaces to client needs, precisely observing the fall of light in each room, and adopting a low-key approach to exterior detailing.

The Vernon Brown hallmarks are the low, single-pitched roof, the cut-out patio or porch painted white to contrast with the black, creosoted boards, and the carefully placed double-hung sash windows stretching from floor to ceiling. Inside, bookshelves were recessed; the mantelpiece, if there was one at all, was narrow so that the occupants could not clutter it up with photographs. Sometimes he put his foot down. When Honey Haigh wanted her piano in the sitting room Vernon Brown said 'You're not having that awful thing in *my* lovely room', and designed an alcove into which it could be unobtrusively fitted.

TOP RIGHT: *Wright House (1942), Takapuna, by Vernon Brown. The architect's houses invariably had a single-pitched roof, walls of creosoted weatherboards and white window trim.*

BOTTOM RIGHT: *Interior of Haigh House (1942), Remuera, by Vernon Brown. The sitting room exhibits Vernon Brown's ability to design with great simplicity and elegance. There are no pelmets or elaborate scotias, fireplace surrounds are of wood, and large windows carefully placed to catch afternoon sun.*

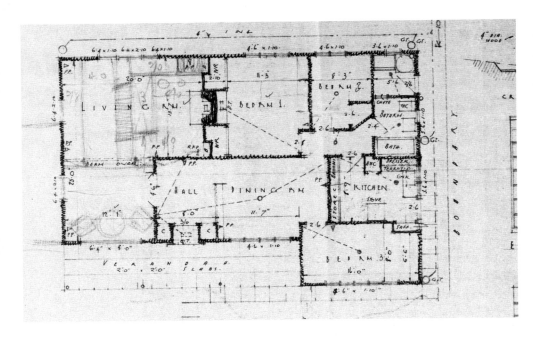

Plan of the architect's own house (1939), Arney Road, Remuera, by Vernon Brown.
AUCKLAND UNIVERSITY SCHOOL OF ARCHITECTURE LIBRARY.

Two cartoons painted by A. R. D. Fairburn in 1935 and given to his friend Vernon Brown. Their satire is directed at C. R. Ford (of Gummer & Ford) who, in Fairburn's and Brown's eyes, represented an architectural establishment which disapproved of Brown's 'chicken coops'. The second cartoon, entitled When Reginald met God, *shows Ford shaking hands with the deity.*
MRS LESLIE VERNON BROWN.

Although he seldom built outside Auckland, Vernon Brown's houses became widely known as the result of their illustration in the magazine *Home and Building* and in the *Yearbook of the Arts*. In the immediate post-war years these publications fostered an interest in New Zealand culture by illustrating the work of writers, artists and architects. The English *Studio* magazine, reviewing the first *Yearbook of the Arts* in 1945, wrote of its 'quiet assurance and national pride' being a good augury for future development, reminding its readers that because Britain was still 'home' for the New Zealander, libraries and museums there should stock it. In its first number, Charles Brasch's *Landfall*, another magazine devoted to the encouragement of New Zealand culture, included an article by the Christchurch architects Paul Pascoe and Humphrey Hall called 'The Modern House'.

Like Vernon Brown, Paul Pascoe, whose mentors in London were Lubetkin and the Tecton Group, wished to encourage a specifically New Zealand architectural 'vernacular'. The New Zealand house was to be a Modern house rather than the '"modernistic" house of the arty, streamlined exterior; a false cloak to a dull, stereotyped plan'. Pascoe & Hall described their 'contemporary home for intelligent contemporary living' as growing on the natural characteristics of the site. As retreat, hub of family life and centre of entertainment it was to be entirely free-planned; shadows cast by over-dominant interior walls were to be eliminated by the use of large windows; glass close to the floor line would bring the garden 'into' the house but overheating avoided by the use of wide, overhanging eaves. It was to be 'emancipated from the doctrines of historical styles' and built using materials truthfully. With almost missionary zeal Pascoe and Hall informed *Landfall*'s intellectual, literary readership that

> there is a group of architects in this country who apply modern principles to house design. The spirit is vigorously alive, and the ideas that brought success in the best designs abroad have been developed here already. The conditions in this young country are wholly suitable to modern design. Our indigenous materials are suitable. Our earthquake risk demands studied structural systems which confirm the cantilever principle, the simple forms and other features of modern design.

Humphrey Hall's 1938 Timaru townhouse (see page 119) and the Christchurch house Pascoe designed for Hall in 1946 illustrated the article, which ended with a list of recommended reading, including such source books of Modernism as Giedion's *Space, Time and Architecture*, Frank Lloyd Wright's *Autobiography*, F. R. S. Yorke's *The Modern House* and 'various works by Le Corbusier'.[8]

Houses by Pascoe, Hall (the Timaru house again) and Vernon Brown had already been illustrated in the section devoted to modern homes in the Centennial publication *Making New Zealand*, two issues of which Paul Pascoe had written in 1940. As Robyn Ussher has observed, 'Pascoe seeks in the buildings of the past the simplicity, functionalism and fitness to purpose of a modernist and the delight in craftsmanship and truth to materials of an Arts and Crafts architect.'[9] Plischke's *Design and Living*, published in 1947, and Pascoe's two *Making New Zealand* issues were the most influential architectural publications of the decade. The drawing and plan of his L-shaped 1940 Harris House in Dunedin would have seemed very modern to readers of *Making New Zealand*.

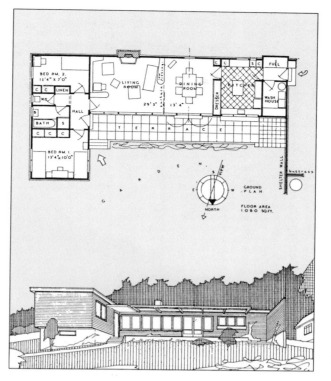

Harris House (1940), Dunedin, by Paul Pascoe. The house is inexpensive, L-shaped, passageless, never more than one room deep, and the flow of space indicates how successfully Pascoe could design for convenient family living. The house has many similarities to the work of Vernon Brown, for which Pascoe had great respect.
REPRODUCED IN *MAKING NEW ZEALAND*.

Pascoe House (1948), Sumner, Christchurch, by Paul Pascoe. The very long, narrow, two-storeyed house with its cantilevered wooden sunscreen and sloping mono-pitch roof is unconventional in all respects.

Pascoe refused to copy the International Modernist detailing that characterised his partner Hall's 1938 concrete Timaru house, ensuring instead that the timber-framed interior functions of the Harris House determined its weatherboard-clad external appearance. Influenced by a number of English architects experimenting with timber construction, and by Frank Lloyd Wright's 1936 board-and-batten Usonian house for the Jacobs family, Pascoe arrived at a very similar solution to the same problems Vernon Brown had set himself in forging a New Zealand style of domestic architecture.

The search for the vernacular was hardly a primary concern for Plischke or other European architects who began designing houses in New Zealand at this time. When he left the D.H.C. in 1948, Plischke went into partnership with Cedric Firth and began building houses again. Because of the building restrictions in force at the time these houses were mostly one-storeyed, built in local materials and simple in design. Large expanses of glass were common, as was a wide overhanging flat roof; again, Wright's 1937 Jacobs House, the first low-cost Usonian house, was a major influence. Plischke preferred not to designate internal spaces according to a specific purpose. There was rarely a formal dining area; kitchens and bathrooms were invariably very small and built-in furniture predominated. Not unexpectedly there are considerable similarities between Pascoe's Harris House and Plischke's Frankel House, built in Christchurch in 1939.

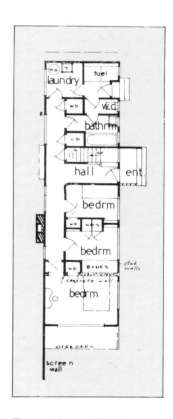

Pascoe House. The New Zealand Arts Yearbook 6 (1950) illustrated the plan of the downstairs bedrooms and bathrooms, placed to allow convenient access for visitors returning from a swim at Sumner Beach.

147

Sutch House (1953–56), Brooklyn Heights, by Ernst Plischke. The long, low profile of this house is as alarmingly Modern today as it was in 1958.

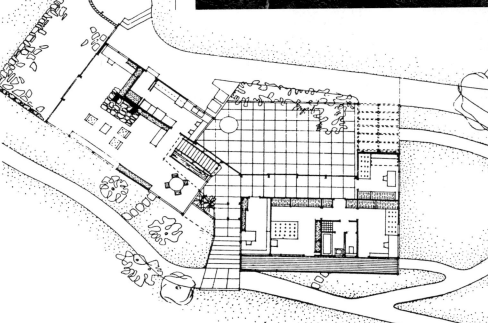

Plan of Sutch House. The house is angled to follow the path of the sun.
REPRODUCED IN PLISCHKE, EIN LEBEN.

RIGHT: *Sutch House. Only upon turning the corner does the visitor discover the entry, at the junction of the upper and lower levels.*

Plischke's largest and most innovative New Zealand house was built for Dr W. B. Sutch and his wife, lawyer Shirley Smith, on Brooklyn Heights, Wellington, in 1953. His clients encouraged him to take his time designing a house without compromises to occupy a very difficult site; eventually he produced plans for a house on three levels which moves down and around the contour of the hillside. The result, as Linda Tyler has remarked, 'eloquently encapsulates Plischke's whole intent to express lightness and transparency through structural daring'.[10] Of particular interest is a long rimu-panelled picture gallery, the outside wall of which is floor-to-ceiling glass, leading without interruption to an inner courtyard paved with smooth Sydney sandstone. The very large living room has three nearly fully glazed walls, one of which slides back to allow access to another stone-paved terrace. The absence of any steps leads to a feeling that the indoor and outdoor areas are scarcely differentiated. Most surprising of all is the way the visitor has first to approach the bedroom section of the house, with its balcony projected over its base, and only then, turning the corner, is confronted by the upper living room wing and glazed entrance hall, from which the minimalist stairway ascends.

*Krukziener House (1962),
Auckland, by Henry Kulka.
The studied asymmetries
and extreme simplicity of
the house are typical of
Kulka's work.*
MRS MARU BING.

Two Czech-born architects who lived in
Auckland were Heinrich Kulka (1900–71) and
Imric Porsolt (b. 1909). During the 1950s they
built a number of houses that illustrated the way
in which European-trained Modernist architects
were able to adapt their familiar world of
concrete and brick to New Zealand timber
construction. As Imi Porsolt wrote, Kulka had to
'learn' weatherboards. He had worked so closely
with the great Viennese architect Adolf Loos
from 1923 to 1933 that he was known to Vienna
as 'Der Loos-Kulka'. When Kulka arrived in New
Zealand as a refugee in 1940, he hoped for work
at the D.H.C. alongside other European
Modernist architects. He failed in this and was, in
Imi Porsolt's words, 'spared the disappointment
which was in store for the others when the initial
élan was spent, the most popular designs sorted
out, and there was little else to do than to shuffle
the well worked out plan-types about on the sites
available'.[11] Instead, Kulka obtained employment
in Auckland with the Fletcher Construction
Company, with whom he remained until 1964.

Kulka, like Loos, was an advocate for the
Raumplan, or 'spatial planning', which involved a
three-dimensional approach to design instead of
treating it as the creation of separate floor areas
on a plane. He was not in favour of radical open-
plan methods, but instead designated function
through height and floor modulation. The
Raumplan at first proved to be a luxury in New
Zealand, where the country's equable climate did
not dictate a simple, severe, cubic external form,
inside which rooms had to be economically

*Interior of Strauss House
(1959), Auckland, by
Henry Kulka. Great care
was taken with the
proportions and colour
relationships of this small
clerestory-lit sitting room.*

disposed. But post-war floor area restrictions gave
the concept an immediate application here.
Kulka's concern was, above all, for liveableness;
as a Loosian Modernist he disliked structural
exhibitionism.

A man of great culture, he numbered among
his friends composer Arnold Schoenberg, satirist
Karl Kraus, poet Peter Altenberg and painter
Oskar Kokoschka. His Viennese clients had
mostly been wealthy people; now Kulka was to
build more modest houses in New Zealand where
he could live in a free society. An anglophile and
a Jew, he resented his distinctly Germanic first
name, and was always known in New Zealand as
Henry Kulka. Many of his clients were European
immigrants who, like Wolf and Alice Strauss, for
whom he designed a house in 1959, recognised
the value of his concern for detail, his unique
blend of the aesthetic with the practical, and his
ability to use local materials sympathetically.

*Goodman House (1956),
Auckland, by Imi Porsolt.
A pentagonal plan
generated the striking
appearance of a house
designed to encompass
extensive views of the
Waitemata Harbour.
The living rooms are on the
upper floor and bedrooms
below.*

*Auckland Electric Power
Board Building (1951),
Auckland, by Lew Piper.
Around the curved corner
the eye is led down the
bands of windows, their
elongation accentuated by
thin concrete strips which
have a practical function as
sun shields. This massive
building exhibits a
Bauhaus-like attention to
detail.*

Imi Porsolt's 1956 two-storeyed house for the bookseller Robert Goodman and his wife also showed how imaginatively these European architects could use their new environment. Built on a tiny Parnell subdivision, the Goodman House has neither flat roof nor rectangular plan, but is characterised by a pentagonal plan. Because of its pronounced gable and vertically laid cedar weatherboards, it was comfortingly dubbed 'the chalet' by neighbours, to whom it must have looked outlandishly modern. There is a generous roof overhang shading the interior space, which fans out in three directions towards the view of the Waitemata Harbour. The colour effects in the main upstairs room come from various wood finishes which were to become popular during the decade. At Fletcher, Kulka was a pioneer of plywood finishes, and he made extensive use of them in many of his houses: in his now demolished 1941 Fletcher Plywood premises and in the greatly altered 1954 Dalgety

Building, Hamilton. A striated matai bonded onto ply, called Weldtex, had formed the exterior lining of the German-born architect Helmut Einhorn's 1951 Modernist house in Donald Street, Karori, Wellington.

The major New Zealand-born architectural figures of this period are, probably deservedly, better known for their public buildings than their houses. Although Gray Young's 1939 Christchurch Railway Station was not built until 1954, its elements of Dutch Modernism did not strike an anachronistic note, neither had Colin Lamb's Ovaltine Factory (now Helene Curtis), built in Christchurch a decade earlier. In 1951, Lew Piper designed four huge blocks for the Auckland Electric Power Board, and cast more than a glance at the Bauhaus with the curved entrance facade on Remuera Road. The building was described in *Home and Building* as 'entirely utilitarian, simple in exterior elevations and in keeping with the modern trend in architecture'.[12] The upper floor, designed by J. I. Van Pels, was added in 1965.

Helene Curtis Building (1944), Christchurch, by Colin Lamb and Christchurch Railway Station (designed 1939, completed 1954) by Gray Young, Morton & Young. Both have much in common with Dutch Modernist buildings.

In 1952 Gordon Wilson was appointed Government Architect, ushering in a period of unprecedented Government-sponsored building activity. Wilson had travelled to the U.S.A. in 1947, where he met Walter Gropius. On subsequent journeys to Europe and England in 1954 and 1957 he studied developments in office building design, sending back copies of plans and samples of materials so that his staff had access to the latest information. In his major buildings Wilson showed the clear influence of the rectilinear forms of Gropius, Le Corbusier and Mies Van der Rohe, but he later also introduced such structurally expressive devices as walls of glass, exposed columns and pilotis, blocks of colour to give planar form, and lightweight horizontal elements which give his buildings transparency. Such features contrast sharply with the bulky solidity of his earlier multi-housing schemes.

shading drapes failed to arrive in time for occupation, the building has faded into obscurity as more elaborately detailed buildings have risen around it.

Wilson made greater use of colour and pattern in the 1954 Dental School of Otago University, Dunedin, where he repeated the rectilinear form, glass curtain wall, recessed ground floor and free-standing columns. This time, however, he enlivened the structure by using greater amounts of coloured glass and by articulating the stairwell, which he had buried within the walls of his earlier buildings.

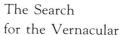

RIGHT: *Dental School (1954), Otago University, Dunedin, by Gordon Wilson. Constructed using the same principles as the Bledisloe Building, the Dental School's glass skin is more colourful and its stairwell articulated in an attempt to enliven the facade.*

The Bledisloe Building in Auckland designed by Wilson in 1950, was a Corbusian eleven-storey slab. Its column-and-beam shear wall structure allowed the use of extensive glazing, which adds to the building's sense of lightness. At the time, its one-and-a-half acres (6000 m²) of glass, its height, and its resemblance to Le Corbusier's United Nations Building (1947–53) in New York were made much of in the press. The Bledisloe was followed in 1955 by the Bowen State Building, Wellington. Its structure consisted of two cantilevered structural cores which carried building services and seismic loads, allowing for flexible planning and creating a model for office design which was to be much emulated in the future. The building's ground-floor walls are recessed, so that the structure appears to rest on rows of granite-clad columns. Again, like the Bledisloe, east and west walls are glazed within aluminium jambs. Labelled 'an inferno' by its office workers after regulation government sun-

Plischke's Massey House (1951–53), commissioned by the New Zealand Milk and Dairy Board, is an eight-storey office block. Its plan adopts the familiar technique of disposing office space around a central core containing lift and stairs. It too has a glass curtain wall and stands on four round, white columns, which are repeated on the top floor giving, according to the architect's intention, a sense of organic growth. The building is divided into halves; the well-known Lambton Quay front being two storeys higher than the shorter rear section on the Terrace. Fenestration is regularly patterned by the use of projecting aluminium frames which surround the whole glass wall at each level, while, within this larger frame, individual window frames have both structural and aesthetic importance.

The interior of the building is open and uncluttered too because of the extensive use of glass, natural wood veneers, built-in furniture,

LEFT: *Bowen State Building (1955), Wellington, by Gordon Wilson. The size of such government buildings was a focus of public criticism. It was also reported that office girls wore colourful sunhats and sunglasses inside to combat glare and heat.*

Massey House (designed 1951–53, completed 1957), Wellington, by Plischke & Firth. Hemmed in by later buildings of similar height, its design replicated on the neighbouring site, Massey House now looks less innovative than when it was one of the first curtain-walled buildings in New Zealand, and seen as a symbol of Modernity.

panelled surfaces devoid of frames or architraves, and concealed utilities such as air-conditioning units. Visiting New Zealand the year after Massey House was completed, the architectural historian Nikolaus Pevsner singled it out as the best major building in the country, particularly praising its 'very sensitive and excellently executed interior details'.[13]

Paul Pascoe had to wait until 1955 for the opportunity to design a major building. Christchurch International Airport occupied him for nearly twenty years, involved him in extensive international travel, and eventually won him the N.Z.I.A. Gold Medal for 1960. With the high central control tower, long curved facade, and folded and cantilevered roof canopy, Pascoe again looked back to the 1930s and his London years with Tecton.

Functional principles governed the layout of the interior, Pascoe having experienced at first hand the many frustrations of air travellers. Efficiency of movement and an impression of spaciousness were major determinants of his design. The pleasing harmony of his original colours and long internal vistas have in recent years been sadly compromised by lurid carpet and a proliferation of signs.

When he designed the N. M. Peryer Building in 1958, Pascoe used pilotis for structural support, freeing the ground floor for off-street parking. The building, like Tecton's Highpoint Two in London, is topped with a pent-house; below, projecting concrete floor slabs separate the three floors and function as shading balconies, each one divided by vertical columns. Robyn Ussher is surely correct in pointing out that Paul Pascoe was singularly unfortunate in having been prevented by economic circumstances from designing large-scale buildings until so late in his career, by which time he 'could no longer compete against the advanced buildings of the next generation'.[14]

A portent of things to come had already been designed for the city of Wanganui by three precocious architects still in their twenties. Geoffrey Newman, Gordon Smith and Anthony Greenhough, all graduates of the Auckland School of Architecture studying overseas, designed the Wanganui War Memorial Hall in 1956 on a dining-room table in Putney, London, and won the competition ahead of forty-two other entries. It is said that Gordon Wilson, one of the assessors, was particularly enthusiastic about their design, which David Mitchell has described as 'paying scrupulous respect to the principles of international modernism'.[15]

Christchurch International Airport (1955–60), by Paul Pascoe. The English Modernist training Pascoe had received in London during the 1930s served him well here. The building, with its horizontal concave elevation, gabled canopy, and slim vertical control tower topped with an octagonal control room, shows how adept he was at manipulating a variety of shapes into a unified whole.

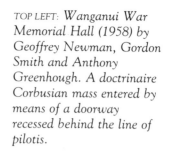

Again, the pilotis make their appearance, this time providing an entry forecourt in front of a set-back ground-floor vestibule, with stairs leading to an assembly hall and concert chamber. Standing in the large square in front of the building, the viewer sees only the huge, white-painted supported wall with a slightly off-centre division of pierced and solid concrete blocks. Like Donald Hosie's Sarjeant Gallery on the hill above (see page 104), it has a flattened appearance with just a hint of a dome, although in the case of the hall, the dome is placed off-centre. The structure has significant affinities with Le Corbusier's Villa Savoie, particularly in the way its solid white mass floats above the square and in the use of a dramatic cut-out stairway on its eastern elevation.

All Saints' Church (1959), Ponsonby, Auckland, by Richard Toy. The architect deliberately alluded to the whare in designing the porch of this church.

Interior of All Saints' Church. The interior is elaborately decorated using abstract patterned motifs which recall those of the traditional Maori crafts.

In church architecture a more innovative approach was beginning to be felt. Plischke had led the way with his 1951 Roman Catholic Church of St Mary at Taihape, where he adopted an appropriately basilican plan for an imposing concrete church. In 1956, Paul Pascoe designed an Interdenominational Chapel at Arthur's Pass, which combined the tent-like forms of a mountain hut with those of the Maori meeting-house. The use of the distinctive Maori wide-gabled porch was even more spectacularly evident in Richard Toy's 1959 All Saints', Ponsonby, Auckland. While deliberately working against the Gothicisms of traditional church architecture, Toy alluded to the Selwyn style by using the double-pitched roof of the Selwyn Library, Parnell (see page 27) and simulating its board-and-batten construction in vertical grooves

LEFT: Church of St Mary (1951) Taihape, by Ernst Plischke. This Modernist basilica has a forbidding appearance despite its rounded windows and glass-walled bell tower.

BOTTOM LEFT: Interior of Church of St Mary. Plischke believed that the appearance of the exterior should be subordinated to the interior. The interior is, typically, almost devoid of applied ornamentation, although Plischke did design the plaster and gold-leaf reredos behind the altar.

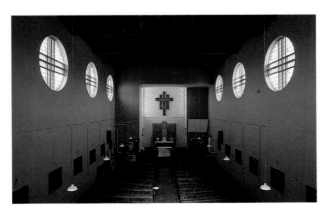

153

*Dilworth School Chapel
(1959), Auckland, by
Abbott, Hole & Annabell.
The steeply pitched roofs of
the Selwyn churches are
imitated in this attempt to
discover a local vernacular
architectural style.*

*Second House (1950),
Northboro Road, Belmont,
Auckland, by the Group
Construction Company.
Called, jokingly, the
Pakeha House by the young
architects who designed and
built it, this house took its
verandah shape from the
whare.*
AUCKLAND UNIVERSITY
SCHOOL OF ARCHITECTURE
LIBRARY.

incised in the new church's concrete walls. Inside,
the urge to break away from conventional forms
of church decoration without, like Plischke,
producing something almost forbidding in its
simplicity, led to over-decoration. In the same
year, Abbott, Hole & Annabell's Dilworth
School Chapel also followed the Selwyn
tradition, with its steeply pitched roof and open-
beam ceilings. This tendency and the
appropriation of Maori forms were symptomatic
of the desire of many Pakeha architects and
artists to find a means of expression which could
properly be called a New Zealand vernacular style.

It was one of the strongest motivating factors
behind the activities of Group Architects, an
association of young graduates of the Auckland
School who, taught by Vernon Brown,
attempted a fascinating synthesis of the principles
of Modernism with New Zealand social, technical
and architectural resources. They looked at the
domestic architecture of Japan and Scandinavia,
and read about Wurster in San Francisco in Ford
and Creighton's *The American House Today*, but
they took the barn and the whare rather than
the Villa Savoie as their starting point.

First formed as the Architectural Group in
1946, while its members were still at university,
the organisation produced a magazine, *Planning*,
which included articles by Plischke and Vernon
Brown, a letter from Richard Neutra in Los

Angeles praising their constitution, and a witty
but trenchant criticism of Cecil Wood's design for
Wellington Cathedral. Among its members were
Marilyn Reynolds and Barbara Parker, the first
women to become prominent in what, no reader
can have failed to realise, had been an entirely
male profession.

*Interior of First House
(1950), Belmont, by the
Group Construction
Company. There being no
client to accommodate, the
architects drastically
simplified the plan,
subordinating everything to
the need to be open to the
sunny climate. The mural is
by Anthony Treadwell.*
AUCKLAND UNIVERSITY
SCHOOL OF ARCHITECTURE
LIBRARY.

Upon graduation in 1950 the renamed Group
Construction Company consisted of Bill Wilson,
James Hackshaw, Ivan Juriss, Bruce Rotherham,
Bret Penman, Campbell Craig and Allan Wild.
They first produced two speculative houses for
average-income owners in the Auckland suburb
of Belmont. Using a low-pitched corrugated-iron
roof, creosoted vertical weatherboard walls, and
an open-planned, passageless interior with raked
ceilings and plywood walls, these were a radical
departure from the ubiquitous state house.
Following the two Belmont houses, the
Construction Company ceased building and
began to practise as Group Architects; by 1953
three members — Hackshaw, Juriss and Wilson —
were left, and the partnership split up finally in
1958.

During and after their period of association all
three produced some fine houses. Juriss's own
house at Stanley Point (1954) shows strong
Japanese influence while Hackshaw's Thom
House, in Mt Albert, designed in the same year,
is an atrium house planned around a central
courtyard, on to which sliding glass panels open.

*Plan of Thom House
(1953), Morningside, by
James Hackshaw. Behind a
characteristically
understated brick exterior is
a house planned around an
open courtyard, designed to
be planted with flowers
which would bleed colour
into the glass-fronted rooms
surrounding it.*
REPRODUCED IN *HOME AND
BUILDING,* MAY 1955.

*Malitte House (1954),
Milford, Auckland, by Bill
Wilson. Like other early
Group houses, this is a
simple rectangle planned to
a structural module. It is
possible to integrate
kitchen, dining room and
children's playroom.*
REPRODUCED IN *HOME AND
BUILDING,* NOVEMBER 1955.

In 1954 Bill Wilson designed his Malitte House at Milford, Auckland, with open-planned living areas and children's bedrooms separated from adults'. The use of a clerestory window to ensure that sunlight enters these back rooms became a much-emulated feature, as did Group Architects' use of exposed structure. In all their work exterior detailing was very much a secondary consideration; as James Hackshaw puts it, echoing Le Corbusier, 'if the planning is right, the whole will be right'.

By the end of the 1950s Modernism was a firmly if belatedly established architectural precept. An increasing number of New Zealand architects were to use its functionalist principles, in their search for that quintessential 'New Zealandness' so long deemed desirable, particularly in domestic architecture. Group Architects, widely regarded as having found the formula, even managed, after some persuasion, to get the State Advances Corporation to accept three open-planned designs as suitable for state housing loans. By the time James Hackshaw designed his 1959 house for the potter Len Castle, *Home and Building,* too, had got the message: 'Towards an Indigenous Architecture' proclaimed its headline.[16]

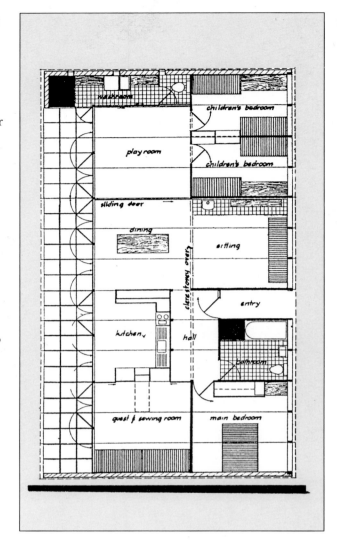

CHAPTER NINE
Architecture as Individualism

Futuna Chapel
(page 177)

The quiet revolution in domestic architecture initiated by Vernon Brown at the Auckland University School of Architecture during the 1940s and 1950s was to have important implications throughout the following decades as those who had been taught by him became some of the country's significant architects. Although the majority of New Zealand's population continued to live in suburban houses which most resembled the familiar state houses of the first Labour Government, gradually people other than the wealthy aspired to domestic surroundings that bore little resemblance to the state housing areas, which were becoming increasingly drab. Parents realised the advantage of open planning in welding together a family unit; wives in particular welcomed it as an end to slavery in a distant kitchen which had little physical relationship with other areas of the more traditional house. By 1960 a sizable number of architects were able to make a living designing family houses which were innovative in both planning and the economical use of local materials, particularly wood. They attracted clients more willing to experiment; the architectural profession now began to award those of its peers who produced unconventional designs.

It is obvious to anyone who has glanced at contemporary books on Scandinavian domestic architecture that the work of Vernon Brown and of the members of Group Architects was indebted to such sources. In Wellington, Anthony Treadwell, S. W. Toomath and Charles Fearnley had the same influences and designed timber houses which look very like Vernon Brown's. The 1964 Yock House in Ngapuhi Road, Remuera, by Lillian Chrystall (b. 1926), employed many of the architectural features also observable in the early houses by Group Architects.

Peter Middleton was, like Vernon Brown, an Englishman who taught at the Auckland School of Architecture. An energetic teacher, writer and practising architect, his ideas accorded well with the Auckland School's prevailing housing ideology. Having arrived in New Zealand in 1950, he first attracted attention when his small Latch House won the 1955 N.Z.I.A. Bronze Medal. This was in favour of Bill Wilson's Malitte House (see page 156), which was regarded as being too much for the jury. 'A House in the Classical Manner' was the way *Home and Building* described the Latch House, praising it for its 'balance, palpable order, repose, restraint, clarity, impersonality and a respect for tradition'.[1]

Middleton, obviously writing his own copy for the magazine, credited his building with the qualities of an English country gentleman demonstrated in his own physical appearance, to the discomfort of his more nationalistically inclined academic contemporaries.

But one did not necessarily need to have attended the Auckland School to know about post-and-beam construction, sarked timber ceilings, cork-tiled floors, clerestory lighting or rough-sawn stained weatherboards. In 1963 in the Christchurch suburb of Riccarton, Don Donnithorne (b. 1926) added bedrooms and a living room extension to a timber-framed and timber-roofed house he had built for himself in 1952, using brick walls and brick-paved floors. If his original inspiration for the house has come from the work of the same American timber architects who had influenced Group Architects, his later extension shows a familiarity with the work of Danish architects who favoured wooden ceilings, sliding walls of glass and the integration of contrasting materials.

Donnithorne had trained at the Christchurch Architectural Association's Student Atelier and later worked with Humphrey Hall and Paul Pascoe, for whom Modernism had always been an important factor. By 1958, when Donnithorne set up his own office, Scandinavian trends in domestic architecture were a growing force. Less obviously severe than German Modernist ideas, they were to have a ready appeal for many New Zealand architects. Writing in 1974 he recalled that 'one other important influencing factor was the constant reminder of a tradition of fine work carried out by such early practitioners as Mountfort, Hurst Seager, Cecil Wood and others'.[2] It is interesting to note that Christchurch architects frequently call on such a pedigree as a means of explaining the existence of a so-called 'Christchurch School', yet the work of architects in New Zealand's other main cities has never been distinctly different from that of Christchurch. Certainly there is often to be found a lineage stemming from employment in successive practices (such as the one which allows a direct line of succession to be drawn from Mountfort to Seager to Cecil Wood and thence to Miles Warren), but despite this, New Zealand's architecture history is more notable for the number of individualists it has produced than the existence of separate schools or traditions, attractive though such a notion may be.

Bilingual Danish/English books such as *Moderne danske hjem* (*Modern Danish Homes*) and *Enfamiliehuset af idag* (*Family Houses of Today*), both published in 1959 in Copenhagen, illustrated with plans, elevations and fine black and white photographs of furnished interiors, were eagerly consulted by younger architects during the late 1950s and early 1960s. They immediately saw the relevance of the low-cost timber houses of Denmark and Finland to New Zealand conditions; they were keen to exploit the opportunities such plans offered to break away from the traditionally fixed four-walled room by extending walls out into the garden, merging rooms imperceptibly with nature or, as architects tend to say, 'bringing the outside in', by utilising large expanses of glass. Such devices were particularly appropriate to Auckland, where rapidly growing suburbs along the Waitemata Harbour offered extensive sea views, or Titirangi, in the Waitakere Ranges, where sites were ideal for the integration of houses with the surrounding native bush.

House (1957) at Kohimarama, Auckland, by Rigby, Mullan. The whole house is embraced by a low-pitched roof with the gable over the long side of the rectangle. To the uninitiated this gave it the appearance of a woolshed rather than a home.

In 1959 the English *Decorative Art Studio Yearbook* illustrated a long, low house which ran east–west along a cliff edge above the Waitemata Harbour at Kohimarama. The work of Auckland architects Rigby, Mullan, it is a fine example of the successful adaptation of contemporary Scandinavian architectural ideas for New Zealand conditions. The whole house is covered by a single flattened gable roof, not entirely coincidentally reminiscent of Group Architects' 'Pakeha' house (see page 154). A paved terrace is shaded by the deep overhang of the sloping eaves and bounded by scoria rock walls. The timber-framed walls of the house sit on a concrete base. The sitting room, which looks out across the

harbour, has a wall of sliding glass panels; other fixed glass panels continue in a band along the eaves line. Interior wall surfaces and items of built-in furniture are of pale gold Finnish birch; other walls are of ribbed mahogany or are painted blue-grey or white. The use of contrasting textures is heightened at one end of the sitting room by a large, free-standing fireplace of red volcanic scoria, which also functions as a wall separating the main living area from the bedrooms.

Ivan Juriss's admiration for the work of the great Finnish architect Alvar Aalto can be seen in his 1960 Mann House at Violet St, Mt Albert, Auckland. Juriss had always differed from his partners at Group Architects in his approach to both style and matters of finish. He was not a strong advocate for the creation of a vernacular style and after the members of the Group went their separate ways he came, like Jim Hackshaw, to regard the Group's early work as over-rationalised in its modular regularity. Despite the fact that it was one of the first houses of unpainted concrete block construction built in Auckland and at the time seemed uncompromisingly modern to its bewildered neighbours, his Mann House has a refinement of finish which was characteristic of its architect. Juriss, who had also rejected the idea of the glass wall, lit the interior of the house carefully so as to avoid dullness. The problem was solved by designing windows at unexpected heights in a variety of shapes and sizes and by the use of a

Mann House (1960), Mt Albert, Auckland, by Ivan Juriss. The dominant slope of the roof disguises the fact that the house is made up of cell-like spatial units which flow from one to the next. The architect's use of unpainted concrete block was regarded as unusual at the time.

clerestory. A polyurethaned matai floor contrasts effectively with the grey concrete, giving an impression of considerable visual warmth.

In 1953 the young Christchurch architect Miles Warren (b. 1929) had travelled to England, where he worked with the London County Council on the Roehampton Estate. He had begun architectural work in 1946, when at the age of sixteen he entered Cecil Wood's office; this was followed by a period of study at the Auckland University School of Architecture, from which he graduated in 1950. In London he was, in his own words, 'extraordinarily fortunate to be sitting right in the middle of the birth of Brutalism'[3] and had the unique experience of being shown over the Hunstanton School (1954), Norfolk, by its young architects, Peter and Alison Smithson. Scandinavian influences were prominent at the London County Council's Department of Architecture at the time, and the Roehampton Estate was, as Nikolaus Pevsner observed, Swedish in inspiration.

first such building was the sequence of eight Dorset Street Flats (1956–57), which the architect has described as 'simply a box of concrete block walls — with two full-height openings to the north and slots to the rear, and other solid boxes for the bathroom and wardrobe'.[4] The block walls stop at door height and support fair-faced concrete beams; door and window detailing shows the depth of the concrete block; roofs are low pitched, timber framed and covered with corrugated iron, their eaves and verges set back to reveal the thickness of the walls.

The Christchurch City Council engineers, unfamiliar with concrete block load-bearing walls, insisted on a frame of reinforced-concrete columns for the Dorset Street Flats, but later acknowledged that this was not necessary. The Christchurch public was as bemused by these flats as the Aucklanders who had dismissed the Group's houses as barns or chicken coops. The first occupants had no difficulty in adapting to their compact and solidly built surroundings in which varnished rimu board ceilings contrasted warmly with the painted blocks, and foliage quickly softened the enclosing garden walls.

LEFT: Dorset Street Flats (1956–57), Merivale, Christchurch, by Miles Warren. Instead of having the usual timber frame or the steel-reinforced frame with masonry in-fill, these flats are merely concrete-block boxes. Initially they were regarded as fortress-like, yet today their structural method is widely used.
SIR MILES WARREN.

RIGHT: M. B. Warren House (1960), Christchurch, by Miles Warren. The placement of the window is typical of the carefully contrived relationship between solid and void which characterised the work of Scandinavian architects.
SIR MILES WARREN.

Miles Warren travelled to Denmark and saw the work of the architect Finn Juhl, whose 1941–42 house at Ordrup had been widely illustrated in periodicals of the day. This house and other small-scale houses, provided the New Zealand architect with a model for the early Christchurch houses he built after coming back to New Zealand 'brimful of ideas and determined to force them on an unsuspecting public'. He quickly realised that Group-style timber housing was unsuitable in the cooler Canterbury climate and so began to design flats and houses which had walls of white-painted concrete block. The

In 1960 Miles Warren used similar techniques when designing a house for his parents. He arranged the rooms, each as wide as the gable, in three wings of bedrooms, living rooms and garage. Mr and Mrs Warren were used to living in a Cecil Wood house, so their architect son repeated its steeply pitched 40° roof and coved ceilings. The architect writes that the roof forms of this house and others like it led to their being quickly dubbed 'pixie' houses, but in fact they harkened back to the early New Zealand cottage with its separate roof over each room.

Few of those architects who designed houses influenced by contemporary Scandinavian architecture earned large fees from such jobs. While Miles Warren's Christchurch clients were almost invariably wealthier than the Group's in Auckland, the clients of both practices understood that it made economic sense to employ an architect who knew how to use· perhaps unconventional materials efficiently. The shocked resident of Mt Albert who observed to Mr Mann that his year-old Ivan Juriss house (see page 159) would be nice when it was finished was expressing the kind of architectural conservatism which had allowed the 1930s state house to hold the New Zealand suburban landscape in a kind of tyranny. In the public mind, concrete block was regarded as a material unsuited for domestic building but so, ironically, was timber.

The worst that the conservative observer could say about any modern house was that it looked like a farm building. Group Architects and other vernacularists may have delighted in the barn- or shed-like qualities of their indigenous houses, but it was this that made them unacceptable to the public. The State Advances Corporation, which granted loans for house building, agreed; it was extremely difficult to get a loan for anything other than a standard, conventionally planned brick-and-tile house. Wood was regarded as flimsy and unreliable, but bricks looked strong; the timber-framed house must be brick clad. The much-consulted *Carpentry in New Zealand*, first put out by the Department of Education Technical Correspondence School in 1958, illustrated exactly how the brick veneer wall should be attached to a timber frame on a

concrete foundation, using a 1½-inch (4-centimetre) cavity between the brick work and the timber framing in order to prevent dampness.

In 1950 the returned serviceman who was the client for the Group Construction Company's first house managed to obtain a State Advances Loan only because the architects stood their ground and argued for construction in wood. Ivan Juriss recalled:

> They weren't implacably opposed to timber, but they put all sorts of restriction on its use. Exterior vertical board and batten construction for instance was forbidden because it was regarded as likely to let in water, however, the first Group House *was* clad with vertical ship-lapped boards . . . it all depended on the individual building inspector.

There was also official disapproval of plans which had kitchens opening out on to living areas. Sometimes it was necessary to produce two sets of drawings, one for the client showing an open-plan concept, the other showing a separate kitchen in order to satisfy a council official. To guarantee a good resale value the home owner was well advised to avoid exposed rafters, weatherboards and anything other than a concrete base. Body carpet covered fine matai floors, gibraltar board lined the walls, and ceilings were plastered over at considerable expense. In kitchens wood was banished in favour of formica, sometimes with an imprint that mimicked a timber or tiled surface. The patio, as opposed to

Architecture as Individualism

BOTTOM LEFT: *A typical brick-and-tile house built at Avondale, Auckland, during the early 1960s. There is no wood visible, and the wrought-iron patio railing is a characteristic feature. The Venetian blinds would invariably have remained closed all day to prevent fading of the carpet.*

Figure from Carpentry in New Zealand, *showing how brick walls should be attached to timber frames.*

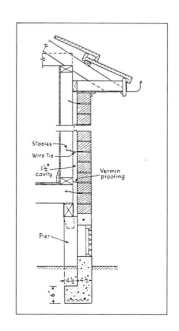

NEW ZEALAND ARCHITECTURE

'Springfield Mark 2' (1966), by Lockwood Homes. Although exterior timber was covered in aluminium sheathing painted white, the interior walls were of knotty radiata pine. The two-car family was increasingly common in the prosperous 1960s so the double car port proved an added attraction for buyers.

the deck, was concreted and given wrought-iron railings. Wooden decking reminded people of the slatted shearing-shed flooring available in central North Island timber yards, designed conveniently to allow sheep droppings to fall through. The battle against wood was won when the introduction of aluminium joinery meant that no wood at all need be visible on the exterior of the brick-and-tile house. All over New Zealand, in both rural and urban locations, brick-and-tile residences went up. Small wonder, then, that Group Architects, who stripped all these coverings away to reveal not a home but a bach, met with such resistance.

invention when, in order to counter the public's and the State Advances Corporation's objections to timber as well as a problem of gum seepage, La Grouw hit upon the solution of covering the pine with an aluminium sheathing. During the 1960s new home buyers gradually came to like the Lockwood show houses, realising that timber was an excellent building material and that there was no need to wallpaper their attractive all-wood walls.

During the 1950s and 1960s both National and Labour governments encouraged private, low-cost housing schemes by providing access to cheap loan money from the State Advances Corporation. Under the Group Building Scheme housing companies such as Neil Housing or Universal Homes, for instance, would purchase land, usually in the peripheral suburbs of a city, subdivide it and then build houses on it using their own civil engineers, surveyors and architects. The companies operated on a low-risk basis under a guarantee from the Government that it would buy back any houses the company could not sell. Under the Insurance Leasehold Scheme the purchaser could pay off the house loan with an Insurance Endowment Policy which in effect saw the house leased to the insurance company, which was then paid over a fifteen-year period.

One of the country's most successful group housing entrepreneurs was Ron Neil, a young toolmaker who in 1951 gathered a group of friends and relatives as his first employees and built a series of small, low-cost houses in the Auckland suburb of Blockhouse Bay. He was one of the first builders to see the advantages of the Government's buyback scheme and he was able to persuade the A.N.Z. Bank to finance his plans for company expansion. By 1960 Neil Housing had built up a large land bank and developed considerable expertise in the creation of successful subdivisions.

The recipe for success in a business with such high profit per unit was to respect the public's conservatism in architectural matters. It is not surprising that the first Neil houses in Margate Street, Blockhouse Bay, were almost indistinguishable from that familiar image of the past, the 1930s state houses. By the early 1960s, however, a wider variety of exteriors had been introduced and open-plan ideas had begun to influence the way the semi-public, dining/living/kitchen areas were designed. There was also a choice of sheathing materials, roof types and materials, windows and steps. It was thus possible for the housing company to satisfy the client's

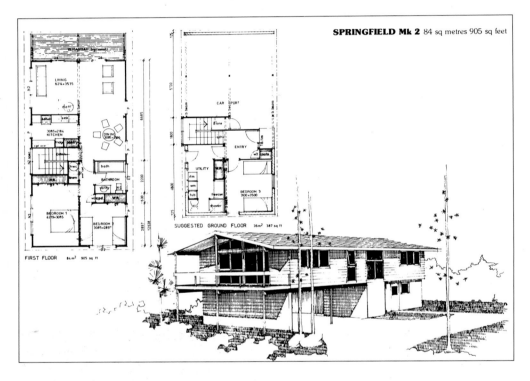

SPRINGFIELD Mk 2 84 sq metres 905 sq feet

The achievement of Johannes La Grouw, an Amsterdam-born architect who settled in Rotorua in 1953, is, then, all the more extraordinary. Arriving in New Zealand in 1951 he first imported from Holland steel-framed houses clad with Fibrolite panel walls which had a core of sugarcane chipboard. A number of these were erected by the Wellington City Council in the suburb of Island Bay. After moving to Rotorua, La Grouw started building houses of New Zealand-grown Oregon pine using a Norwegian wooden log-cabin system of construction but, not surprisingly, the houses were resisted by the public, who regarded them as too cottage-like and disliked the extensive use of wood. Finally La Grouw introduced the highly successful Lockwood house, constructed in *Pinus radiata*. Necessity became the mother of demand for some element of individual display without being too dangerously innovative. The more affluent and socially confident house buyer who wanted to display signs of architectural flair avoided such group housing schemes, but for a great many young married people they offered an early opportunity for home ownership. Gradually Neil Housing was able to persuade its clients to accept lowered roof pitches, split levels, car ports, ranch-slider doors, aluminium joinery and touches of colonial detailing — all of them architectural phenomena first exploited in the so-called 'architect-designed', higher end of the market.

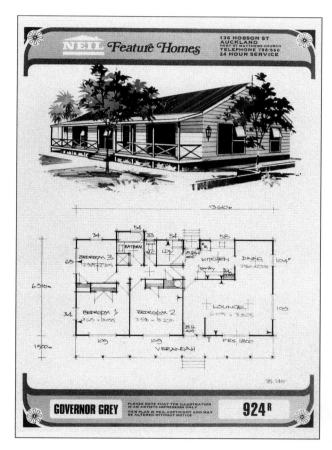

During this period a small number of New Zealand architects designed houses reflecting a more international emphasis. They preferred to ally themselves less with Scandinavian trends than with a type of domestic architectural Modernism which has as its ancestor Mies Van der Rohe's German Pavilion for the International Exposition at Barcelona in 1929. Open, pavilion-style houses had been further developed in California by Richard Neutra and Craig Ellwood, both of whom designed structures which appeared to float above the ground. They made use of continuous glazed walls through which interior spaces were sometimes projected by

means of outriggers or 'spider-legs'. In Neutra's houses, particularly, these often ended in a shallow pool. Sometimes the slab roofs were given deep overhangs by means of daring cantilevers which created an illusion of a lack of support. Such virtuoso tricks were made possible only by the advent of steel-reinforced concrete, which allowed architects to use large suspended structures.

There had been intimations in the pages of *Home and Building* of the emergence of a 'Pacific style' as early as 1950. One house illustrated in the magazine was by Auckland architects Massey, Beatson, Rix-Trott & Carter. Its integration of indoor/outdoor relationships, informality of plan, exposed and contrasting use of natural materials as well as its wide overhangs prompted the writer to speculate 'whether there is not at least a possibility of the development of a unifying "Pacific style"'.[5] On the evidence of the design, its architects were hardly familiar with the work of Californian architects. However, in the work of two young Auckland architects Peter Mark Brown (1929–78) and Alan Fairhead (b. 1926) an interest in Californian trends, particularly in Richard Neutra's work, is clearly reflected. They had also met Harry Seidler, the Viennese-born Sydney architect who had worked with such important Modernists as Marcel Breuer in New York and Oscar Niemeyer in Rio de Janiero and who had come as guest speaker to an architectural convention held in Auckland in 1957.

RIGHT: *Brake House (1976),
Titirangi, Auckland, by
Ron Sang. Vertically laid,
wide cedar weatherboards,
now moss-covered, form
severe, geometrically
abstract shapes against the
background of native bush.
Glass walls on two sides
make it possible to see right
through the house. This
house was not designed to
fit unobtrusively into its
natural environment. Its
rectangular rigidity forms
the strongest possible
contrast to it, yet it appears
to be engulfed by nature.*

*Sargent House (1973)
Remuera, Auckland, by
Ron Sang of Fairhead, Sang
& Carnachan. The
architect deliberately
exploited the aggressive
potential of concrete by
pouring it into corrugated
boxing, and the sharp edges
were then roughly knocked
off and left unpainted.*

Like Seidler in Australia, Mark Brown &
Fairhead attracted a clientèle very different from
that of Group Architects. At the Auckland
School of Architecture they had not been overly
impressed with Vernon Brown's eloquent pleas in
favour of a vernacular timber architecture. They
encouraged their wealthier clients to allow the
incorporation of mirrors, glass and ceramics into
their houses; they imported marble and granite
from Italy and ceramic tiles from Ifoverkin in
Finland; they began to include shaped swimming
pools in gardens. Some of their most impressive
houses were designed for bush settings in
Titirangi. The Pacific image was reinforced in
Home and Building, which headlined one of these
'A House for the Sub-Tropics'.

The now drastically altered Winter House
(1962), called Redwoods, at Kohimarama
included a reflecting pool in the Neutra manner;
the open plan was able to be manipulated by
means of a free-standing wall and curtains or
folding doors. In 1965 Mark Brown & Fairhead's
Orr-Walker House, consisting of two glazed
pavilions linked by an entry hall and also sited
amid the Titirangi bush, won the N.Z.I.A.
Bronze Medal. In size and planning it differs
significantly from the much simpler and plainer
'vernacular' houses. Its tawa ceilings are covered
with a clear varnish to give them a sheen, off the
dining room there is an ornamental pool, and
through the glass walls of the hall a rock garden
is visible.

In 1969 Mark Brown & Fairhead were joined
by Ron Sang (b. 1938), a Fiji-born graduate of the
Auckland School who shared their enthusiasm
for Neutra and had long admired their work.
Although Sang and his partners had a
complementary sense of design he was to
elaborate further on their Californian influences
in designing houses that were in many cases
architectural display pieces for extremely wealthy
clients. The Sargent House (1973) was Sang's
response to a brief which stipulated a house built
entirely of concrete for a client who owned a
major construction company. Its pre-cast concrete
panels, flying beams and perilously cantilevered
balconies were novel at a time when timber was
becoming increasingly popular as a material for
building houses.

*Brake House. A watergarden fills a part of the valley
over which the house is built.*

In 1976 Sang created another virtuoso work for
photographer Brian Brake, whose house spans a
kauri- and manuka-filled gully in the Titirangi
hills. A long floor plan ensures that every room
faces the sun; the one area given a significant
height is the glass stairwell, which has been
extended upwards to catch the full colour of a

liquidambar tree outside. One of the most distinctive (and also most troublesome) features is a roof which, viewed from the road above, looks like a mirror reflecting the surrounding trees. It is, in fact, a pond five centimetres deep. Sang continued to pursue an architectural approach which by 1976 had taken him into realms of display which were a direct antithesis of the ideas propagated by Vernon Brown; Brown's influence had already waned in Auckland by the time Sang arrived in New Zealand in 1957. One can only speculate what Brown would have made of Sang's Hooper House (1976), which overlooks the Waitemata on Paritai Drive and utilises the extensive views by means of walls of darkened mitred glass without mullions. Cedar boards and plastered concrete blocks are painted white and the plan wraps around a swimming pool sheltered from the street.

Similarly adventurous to contemporary eyes were the Auckland houses of Prague-trained Vladimir Cacala (b. 1926), whose allegiance to the Miesian 'less is more' was obvious the moment he arrived from Czechoslovakia in 1952. At first a member of Brenner Associates with Steve Jelicich and the painter Milan Mrkusich, Cacala established his own practice in 1959 and in 1960 had the singular distinction of seeing his 1957 Blumenthal House at St Heliers, called, significantly, Mondrian, illustrated in two international periodicals, *Arts and Architecture* (published in Los Angeles and including Neutra, Walter Gropius and Marcel Breuer on its editorial board) and *Domus*, published in Milan. Cacala's Kay House (1960) in Victoria Avenue, Remuera, is a typical, if small-scale, example of his work. Here again are the vertical white-painted cedar boards deliberately used to form a smart contrast with surrounding trees. Glass is used extensively, even on the long verandah balustrade.

During the 1970s Cacala and his partner Walter Leu were to be responsible for many blocks of flats, most of them constructed out of Winstone Vibradec concrete blocks, which lent themselves to rapid construction at low cost. With interiors devoid of architraves, cornices, beadings or skirtings, they presented a convincingly 'modern' look to their inhabitants. Much use was made of textured wall finishes, including hessian, exposed aggregate and a variety of sprayed-on surface finishes which could be highly effective if used sparingly. Cacala, employing a musical analogy, advocated a certain amount of repetition of motifs in order to produce a unified effect in matters of form, texture and colour.

Architecture as Individualism

Blumenthal House (1957), Auckland, by Vladimir Cacala. Auckland photographer Ted Mahieu provided these illustrations of the house, called Mondrian, for the Italian architectural periodical Domus *in June 1960. While admiring the use of glass and metal to create a 'vigorous simplicity', the magazine made much of the size of the banana palm, planted as a screen for the staircase which leads from the front door to the upper living area.*
VLADIMIR CACALA.

In 1974 the American architectural historian William Allin Storrer visited New Zealand. According to his analysis published in the *N.Z.I.A. Journal*, New Zealand had failed to find an architecture of its own because of its over-reliance on British models as the result of its colonial past and because of a later adherence to a faceless International style as a means of rejecting that colonial past. This perceived

Kay House (1960), Remuera, Auckland, by Vladimir Cacala. The concrete-framed upper storey is cantilevered out, and a wide roof overhang gives protection from the sun.

reliance on borrowed forms had led to middle-
and low-income housing 'uniformly depressing in
its undistinguished character', the Government
receiving the blame for the construction of
housing which was an insult to the citizens.
Storrer proposed a solution: the use of
contemporary New Zealand materials in a
manner natural to the New Zealand
environment. His call for a domestic architecture
which was original and organically related to the
surrounding landforms was to find a ready
response in a group of Wellington architects who
wished, like Storrer, 'to bring about houses which
were designed individually to the site, the climate
and the client's lifestyle'.[6] Prevailing Auckland
notions of architectural suitability were
superseded as the Wellington trail-blazers Ian
Athfield (b. 1940) and Roger Walker (b. 1942)
attempted to create a new vernacular by means
quite at variance with those of the Auckland
Group architects.

Walker and Athfield were flamboyant
characters; unlike their professional predecessors
and many of their contemporaries they delighted
in architectural debate and frequently adopted a
deliberately disrespectful tone. Athfield enjoyed
telling people that he had worked in Warren &
Mahoney's Christchurch office for a mere three
months, at the time when the Scandinavian-
influenced 'pixie' houses were being designed. It
has been suggested that it was here that both
Walker and Athfield became interested in the
compartmentalised and fragmented domestic
spaces with which they were to dot the
vertiginous hills of Wellington. In their work the
ordered horizontality of the Auckland architects
was banished; now the emphasis was to be
vertical. Structural elements, instead of being
treated with self-effacing restraint, were treated
decoratively.

Miles Warren himself, in an important and
controversial article published in *New Zealand
Architect* in 1978, described what he called the
'A. & W. style' as exhibiting 'massive exaggerated
timber posts and beams and diagonal struts and
ties galore [which] horse about in strange places,
plumb through the middle of the room and bang
over the face of the windows'. Common to the
houses of both Walker and Athfield were very
steeply pitched roofs which did not embrace the
whole building in the Group manner but rather
each individual room; the result was a 'collection
of gables, half gables and slices . . . juxtaposed
together to produce complex sculptural shapes,
sometimes looking like a wilful uncontrolled
collision'. It is not difficult to detect a tone of

disapproval in Warren's statement that in these
Wellington houses 'no functional requirement
can justify the complex exotic roof forms'.[7]

In 1966, having worked for Miles Warren for
three months and Stephenson & Turner for six
weeks, and having been dismissed as a partner
from the Structon Group after four years, Ian
Athfield began to build his own extraordinary
house on a steep hillside above Wellington
Harbour. Built with the aid of very few drawings,
the house is made up of rooms which have the
potential to change their function. Its
continuous, hand-shaped exterior is of concrete
with a white-painted plaster finish. There are
port-holes (into one of which Ernst Plischke was
photographed peering sceptically during his 1975
visit to New Zealand), balustrades, and caves
created from concrete piping. All are smoothly
plastered so as to create a building which seems
to flow down the hill instead of sitting erect.

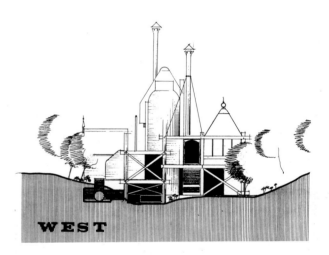

WEST

In his 1969 Fraser House, Queenstown, Athfield
tried to relate his work to New Zealand's colonial
past by using finials, steeply pitched roofs, dormer
windows and double-hung sashes rescued from a
demolition site. Amazingly, the house was
financed by a State Advances Loan, despite its
weatherboard construction and multi-levelled
design. This venture into historical allusion was
continued with the McIntyre House at Karehana
Bay, designed in 1969 and completed in 1972.
References to New Zealand's architectural past
continued with an open trussed roof and, on the
cottage level, a criss-crossed verandah. Athfield's
conservation ethic was again evident from his use
of demolition brick work to create an entry
staircase tower; roofing was corrugated iron,
telephone poles were used for frames and
concrete pipes formed the entries into the
children's bedrooms.

In these and other houses Athfield deliberately exploited randomness. A fierce opponent of the uniformity of state housing, he emphasised an individualistic approach to architecture, working closely with his clients, whose involvement in the construction process was a condition of the contract. Ten years later, his Buck House at Havelock North (see page 192) indicated that Athfield, in creating a dwelling that is a veritable sculpture, was still developing ideas which had their origin in his own house of 1966.

Roger Walker's Wellington houses were different but scarcely less shocking. Like Athfield, he was appalled at 'the sameness and degrading monotony of our suburban areas', but equally he despised the 'applied veneers and temporary titillations of the consumer housing brochures'.[8] He believed that there was an increasing demand for houses that reflected the variety of people themselves: rooms should be conceived as spaces rather than compartments, and these spaces should flow into and hang over one another, with different roof shapes and heights reflected internally (compare this with the Group's belief that if the planning was right the exterior would be too), and much stronger colours used.

Walker's 1973 Wood House, originally built as a speculative venture, used rustic weatherboards; its cottage-like form with double gables sported finials and a colonial verandah. Undoubtedly his 'domestic *cause célèbre*' was the large Britten house (1972–74) at Seatoun Heights, which Gerald Melling described as 'a village-house'.[9] The house is distributed over no fewer than ten levels, the top-most one a turret-like capsule which functions as a retreat above the main bedroom and allows the inhabitants to be completely isolated from the rest of the house and from the neighbours. The house is a series of small spaces independently roofed but with larger kitchen and living spaces opening onto a brick-paved courtyard. With its round windows set in huge drain pipes, soaring metal flues, cross braces across windows, and sliced-off gables which terminate in a horizontal roof or a square wooden box, the Britten House exemplifies Walker's distinctive architectural wit. The building won for its architect a national award in 1977 and, like Athfield's own house, attracted attention far beyond Wellington. Unlikely though it may seem, both Athfield and Walker also designed blocks of flats. David Mitchell has commented that Park Mews (1974) 'was a pop assemblage of Colonial peaks and Walker circles . . . the last thing Walker would let any building of his design say was "this is a block of flats" . . . so Park Mews looks like a huge Walker house (though a Walker house looks like a string of minute flats to some)'.[10]

Architecture as Individualism

LEFT: *Britten House (1972–74), Seatoun, Wellington, by Roger Walker. 'Imagination is stalking the streets,' wrote Roger Walker early in his career. This house shows just how far he was prepared to go in designing houses which bore as little relationship as possible to anything in New Zealand's architectural history.*

Park Mews (1974), Wellington, by Roger Walker. The architect was able to adapt his highly individualistic architectural style to the problem of designing inner-city apartments.

Wong House (1965–67), Remuera, Auckland, by Claude Megson. Although this house, like many of Athfield's and Walker's, is made up of small cell-like units, the architect avoided the colouristic exuberance and formal exhibitionism of his Wellington contemporaries.

In 1974 Roger Walker, determined to do something about the drab uniformity of the average New Zealand suburb, launched his 'Vintage Homes'. These were based upon simple early Colonial building styles and were designed to find a market somewhere between the architect-designed home and the builder's house. The concept of a modular construction system permitted the use of a variety of materials and alternative layouts. By now the colonial look had great appeal and Walker was able to set up franchise builders around the country to construct the homes he had designed. Within two years Vintage homes sprouting cut bargeboards, finials, brick chimneys, the ubiquitous port-hole window and exposed beams were appearing in many New Zealand towns and cities. The battle for timber had been well and truly won.

The Auckland architect and teacher Claude Megson (b. 1936) was also in favour of exuberance and fancy as an antidote to the growing uniformity of mass-produced housing and its marketing of standard products with standard variables. The jury which awarded his Wong House (1965–67) an N.Z.I.A. Bronze Medal in 1969 was so worried at the increasing monotony of developer housing that it took the opportunity while praising Megson's design to call upon architects to contribute to the improvement of mass-produced houses. The Wong House was awarded the Bronze Medal almost apologetically, because the jury believed that there was still room for the carefully crafted house.

Despite the serious message the jury wanted to get across to the profession and to the public, it was the Wong House's exceptionally daring formalism which made it significant. Timber framed, it was clad with brown-stained cedar weatherboards, its many floor levels cascading down the edges of a steep, wooded valley on the slopes of Mt Hobson. The numerous interior spaces, cell-like construction and formal elevational treatment were clearly a reaction to open-planned Modernism in the same way that many of Athfield's and Walker's houses were. Although the jury criticised the bewilderingly complex and occasionally diminutive interior, they described the Wong House as inescapably expressive of the late 1960s.

An architect who seemed to summarise many of the convictions, styles and influences of his time was the Hawke's Bay architect John Scott. Born in Haumoana in 1924 of Arawa, Scottish, Irish and English ancestry, Scott was lectured by Vernon Brown at the Auckland School of Architecture from 1946 to 1950. He was for a time associated with Group Architects and particularly with Bill Wilson, then worked for a parallel practice, Structural Developments, before returning to Haumoana. Scott's earliest houses were distinctly Group-ish.

In 1966 Scott designed The Brow for the Pattison family at Waipawa, a large farm-house which sits on the top of a hill and has a strongly angular design based no longer on the low-verandah Group houses, although it does have a clerestory. The exterior makes much of the contrast between whitewashed concrete block and dark-stained wood and here there is a similarity to the Scandinavian-influenced angularity and relationships of solid and void in Miles Warren's Christchurch houses. Unlike Warren, Scott has never travelled overseas and has no intention of doing so; The Brow's entrance is indebted more to the porch of the whare than anything further afield.

Bringing the outside in was a major consideration of the design, so every room has a full-length glass door opening onto a terrace or, in the case of upper-floor rooms, onto a balcony. In fact it is possible to see from one side of the house to the other, through a series of glass doors which separate rooms along the axis. Scott took characteristic care to ensure an elegant finished appearance for the exposed structural members, such as the timber buttresses which support the main transversal beam in the sitting room.

Elements of the Group style persisted in the houses James Hackshaw designed during the later 1960s and 1970s, particularly one for his own family in Brilliant Street, in St Heliers, Auckland, in 1970. Here, the architect maintained his earlier allegiance to post-and-beam construction and a variety of other techniques pioneered in the Group's low-cost housing over a decade earlier. The scale is enlarged, the planning less severely rationalised, and the surfaces deliberately given a more finished appearance.

appropriated the angled roof made famous by the South American architect Oscar Niemeyer, it was functional. The roof rises to its greatest height at the diving end of the pool and reduces towards the shallow end; the sharper rise towards the street entry accommodates the two-levelled dressing rooms, coffee lounge and club room. A solid concrete wall faces the sometimes battering sea; the two side elevations are of glass, while the Oriental Parade facade is decorated with small glass port-holes, which let in light during the day but at night provide an attractive pattern of sparking lights.

Interior of Hackshaw House (1970), St Heliers, Auckland, by James Hackshaw. Such a thing as an evening room, as shown here, would have been unthinkable in a Group house. The unadorned plainness and open-planned over-rationalisation of the Group's early work is replaced by respect for domestic privacy. JAMES HACKSHAW.

New public buildings of this period were to offer many people in New Zealand their first experience of truly contemporary architecture. Up-to-date homes in Titirangi, Khandallah or Waipawa were relatively inaccessible, but office blocks in Queen Street, Lambton Quay, or Manchester Street were there for all to see. When in 1960 Mark Brown & Fairhead's unashamedly modern Auckland office for Pan American Airlines filled the small space between the Edwardian Baroque South British Insurance and the City Club Hotel (all three now demolished) the shock in Shortland Street must have been something like that felt in Vienna when in 1908 Adolf Loos's American Bar appeared in the tiny thoroughfare off Karntnerstrasse.

On Wellington's Oriental Parade the Freyberg Pool appeared, designed by King & Dawson in 1960 and completed in 1964 on the site of the old Te Aro Baths. Although the architects

In Wellington, Stephenson & Turner's fourteen-storey Shell House, designed by Plischke's former partner Cedric Firth and completed in 1960, made extensive use of prefabrication. It has a steel frame and a reinforced-concrete core for seismic loading, but its most noticeable feature is its curtain wall of glass. In Queen Street, Jack Manning's A.M.P. Building (1962) was built while the architect was with Thorpe, Cutter, Pickmere & Douglas. It too has a concrete frame, sheathed with a curtain wall consisting of aluminium frames clad with shiny stainless steel, and glazed with units of heat-absorbing glass and green opaque glass spandrels. The ground-floor columns are clad with black ebony granite. As David Mitchell has written, 'A.M.P. was a scaled-down Kiwi version of the glass skyscraper of America', and he quotes the architect's own words: 'Every architect working on office buildings at that time was in

Freyberg Pool (1960), Oriental Bay, Wellington, by King & Dawson. The butterfly roof, a popular design feature of the time, has a structural purpose. Light floods the pool from the two glazed side elevations.

LEFT: *A.M.P. Building
(1958–62), by Thorpe,
Cutter, Pickmere &
Douglas. The glass curtain
wall looks as smart today as
it did in 1962. The design
architect, Jack Manning,
used polished stainless steel
to frame the glass panels
which cover the building's
entire upper surface.*

RIGHT: *Auckland City
Council Administration
Centre (1954–66), Aotea
Square, Auckland, by Tibor
K. Donner, Auckland City
Council Architect. This was
to be one of a series of long
slab buildings surrounding
the square, but for reasons
of prestige a tower block
was built instead. The
curtain walls are made up
of anodised aluminium and
a variety of differently
textured and coloured glass
panels.*

love with glass boxes.'[11] Most pre-war public office buildings had been wall-bearing, 'hole-in-the-wall' structures like the 1925 Dilworth Building (see page 112). All were very heavy and constructed of reinforced concrete poured *in situ*. Windows were usually small, but were gradually enlarged as wall-bearing construction gave way to the skeleton frame. This in turn was replaced by the internal frame, or core, of the kind used in the 1939 Miller's Building (see page 137), which required only a light framework of mullions and glass. In the 1960s an external envelope of metal and glass detached from the structural form was possible and the curtain wall was all the rage.

By 1965 so many glass boxes had been built that the Government Architect, F. G. F. Sheppard, uttered words of warning in the *N.Z.I.A. Journal*. In his opinion, 'a dozen glass boxes in a line can play havoc with an urban environment'.[12] In addition he regarded them as difficult to handle aesthetically and, because of their indeterminacy in size, in danger of losing the human scale. Gordon Wilson's Bowen State Building, completed in 1961, had been an early example (see page 151). A later government building, the Vogel Building (1966), broke up the

curtain wall of glass with protruding floor slabs and strong vertical rhythms, a pattern followed in the Fergusson and Freyberg Buildings, of 1976 and 1979 respectively. Because the client for the Manchester Unity Building (1966) would under no circumstances permit a glass front, Structon Group Architects decided on a honeycomb motif in pre-cast concrete panels.

In Auckland, like the Aotea Centre of the following decade, the city's Administration Centre was already old-fashioned when it opened in 1966. This was hardly the fault of the City Architect, Tibor K. Donner, who some ten years earlier had designed a building which was in the forefront of modern trends. In the event, funding difficulties saw its erection preceded by seven years by its near neighbour the Bledisloe Building. Rather unfairly, the Administration Centre was likened to a stack of egg crates, and increasing familiarity did not endear it to the public of Auckland. Extensive publicity about its being the tallest building in the country at the time of its *design*, pioneering in its search for lightness and advanced in the amount of prefabrication of its parts did not disguise the fact that it had been superseded in all these respects some years before its completion.

If the *enfants terribles* of the 1950s had mainly been Aucklanders, by the mid-1960s the situation had changed significantly. Unlike his near contemporary Miles Warren, who spent only his final two years there, Christchurch-born Peter Beaven (b. 1925) received all his architectural education at the Auckland school, listening to Vernon Brown. Beaven and Warren both had their secondary schooling at Christ's College; Warren fitted into the environment well, but Beaven's lifelong suspicion of the establishment probably has its origins in this period of his life. It is surprising, therefore, to discover in Beaven one of the strongest advocates for a Christchurch architectural tradition. Combined with this respect for traditionalism is more than a streak of individualism which, with the addition of a natural gift for polemic, has made Beaven one of New Zealand architecture's most colourful figures.

Peter Beaven has always preferred to work outside the confines of an established architectural practice, finding his inspiration in Mountfort's Christchurch buildings and in a belief that progress can only come out of an understanding of tradition. The architectural climate of New Zealand's other cities appalled him. Auckland he dismissed as 'money and pressure', while Wellington seemed to him to have 'a bloody awful oppressive atmosphere, occasionally tempered by hard winds . . . and there's a clever-clever imported flavour about it — whole conversations shipped into Wellington. Bugger it.' Like Athfield and Walker he was shocked by the appearance of the New Zealand suburb. He believed, as Chapman-Taylor did, that buildings shape people's lives: 'A building is one of the most durable things of our society. Whatever iniquities it may contain will sooner or later penetrate the most disinterested mind, the dullest soul.'[13]

According to Beaven, responsibility for the 'bloody little incubator runs' in which children were brought up lay with central government decision-making and with an authoritarian approach to town planning. In 1970 he told *Building Progress* that 'the New Zealand house has become cleverly standardised; most people have no chance of building any of the glamorous ideas in the overseas magazines or of living in unusual suburbs'.[14] By 1974 his disillusionment with the attempt to achieve imaginative solutions to the problems he had diagnosed was complete, and Peter Beaven was to spend the following decade living in England.

Architecture
as Individualism

Canterbury Arcade (1965), Auckland, by Peter Beaven. In a characteristic attempt to counteract the bland uniformity of the curtain wall, Beaven enlivened this facade with features designed to give depth and visual interest.

Beaven's Canterbury Building Society (1959–60) and Manchester Unity Building (1965) in Christchurch had already shown what a dash of imagination could do for high-rise office buildings. The shape of things to come was evident in 1965–67, when Beaven adapted qualities he had admired in the streetscapes of European cities when remodelling the Canterbury Arcade in Auckland. In what David Mitchell called 'a virtuoso display of planning skills',[15] he created an arcade from Queen Street and provided the slim High Street facade with a set of offices with a frontage which exhibited the balconies, verandahs, French windows and attics one might expect to see in the centre of Paris but certainly not in Auckland.

Still more unconventional is Beaven's Lyttelton Road Tunnel Authority Building, which was opened in 1964. Modernist in terms of the way in which function determined form, the structure has an added symbolic dimension. The architect described it as a boat moored to a wharf; its site is actually the place at which early pioneers began their journey back over the Port Hills to Lyttelton, where their ships lay at anchor. Its structure consists of a concrete frame on columns and double beams resting on bulb piles and pads,

*Lyttelton Road Tunnel
Authority Building
(1962–65), Heathcote
Valley, Christchurch, by
Peter Beaven. Intricate in
detail, imaginative in its
symbolism, and sculpturally
daring in form, this building
was ahead of its time.*

*Whakatane Airport (1971)
by Roger Walker. A shock
for both tourists and
travelling New Zealanders,
the building's practical
limitations are outweighed
by its fancifulness. The
exposed timber roof
structure, tunnels, perilous
circular stair and cottage-
like rooms firmly contradict
passengers' expectation of
what an airport should be.*

supporting a tub-shaped, cantilevered top floor.
The colour scheme and all furniture were
designed by the architect, who in 1965 won an
N.Z.I.A. Gold Medal for his striking creation.

Beaven's 1971 Banks Peninsula Cruising Club
at Lyttelton is much more intimate in scale than
the monumental Tunnel Authority building;
with its lighthouse-derived verticality,
proliferation of nautical detail, use of bright
colour and yacht-like nooks and crannies, it has
something of the wit and exuberance of Roger
Walker's Wellington houses. Unlike Walker, who
managed to get his outrageous Whakatane
Airport (1971) approved by the Ministry of
Works, Beaven's innovative spirit was controlled
and not overtly theatrical, because it was based
on a respect for tradition.

When he designed the playful Chateau
Commodore Hotel in Christchurch in 1972–73,
Beaven blatantly advertised his debt to
Mountfort and the earlier Canterbury architect's
medieval antecedents. Here is a monument to
pleasure which alludes to the baronial halls of
England. An oriel window supported with
brackets refers to Stokesay Castle, Shropshire,
built in 1285, and the dining room, with its
struts, beams and trusses, refers to a thirteenth-
century barn at Cherwill, Wiltshire. There are
even turrets and moats in this rural building,
which is sited at the edge of Hagley Park in
Christchurch.

Peter Beaven did not, however, neglect New
Zealand's colonial heritage. He had long been an
advocate of mews-type housing developments as
the solution to New Zealand's high-density city
living problems. He believed that linked-row
housing in cottage-like clusters with social
amenities nearby would eventually supplant the
traditional quarter-acre subdivision for at least
half of New Zealand's population. In 1969 his
highly innovative student village proposal for
Canterbury University came to nothing when the
Professorial Board, alarmed at reports of student
rioting in Europe, scrapped the scheme because
they were persuaded to believe that it could be
too easily barricaded. The following year Beaven's
Habitat, now called Pitarua Court, was built in a
quiet cul-de-sac in Wellington's Tinakori Hills,
but neither the Riccarton Mews proposal, a true
neighbourhood centre comprising thirty-seven
houses, a paved area with trees, a licensed
restaurant, a pub, a swimming pool and an
artificial stream, nor the elaborate colonially
detailed scheme for twenty-four apartments next
to Pompallier House in the Bay of Islands went
ahead.

By contrast, Miles Warren's career during the
1960s and 1970s, when he designed some of the
country's most noticeable and widely publicised
buildings, was quickly to bring the practice of
Warren & Mahoney, founded in 1958, to
national eminence. Warren's Constructivist
leanings were apparent as early as 1962, when the
Harewood Crematorium, which took full
advantage of an absolutely flat site, provided the
country's architectural magazines with some of
the most dazzling vistas they had ever illustrated.
Every detail of construction was clearly exposed,
including the now familiar white-painted concrete
blocks and the dark-stained trusses and purlins of
the V-shaped chapel roof. The New Zealand
Institute of Architects awarded the building a
Gold Medal in 1964.

*Christchurch College
(1964), Christchurch, by
Warren & Mahoney.
The domestic scale of the
buildings around the
quadrangle of this
University of Canterbury
hall of residence is achieved
by the use of trabeated
concrete beams contrasted
with white-painted
concrete-block walls, a
technique developed in
Warren's earlier work.*

In 1964 Warren began work on the designs for
Christchurch College, which he described as 'an
ideal brief for architects working in the brutalist
phase of the modern movement'.[16] Based on the
English residential university college, Warren &
Mahoney's 120 bedroom/studies, dining hall,
common rooms, chapel and library are tightly
grouped on either side of a grass quadrangle. The
dining hall closes one end and the library the
other, while the chapel projects across the
broadwalk, all three having double height
volumes and distinctive M-shaped roofs.
Although David Mitchell criticised Christchurch
College for the insistence of its constructivist
ethic, its uncomfortableness and the 'endless
clarification of elements',[17] there can be no doubt
of its grandeur, a quality it shares with much of
Warren & Mahoney's later work. For the superb
Chapel of the Upper Room, added in 1966,
Warren drew directly on Cecil Wood's dining hall
at Christ's College; the design relationships
between the two are clear at a glance, both
having plain walls and a richly detailed timber
roof. The chapel is a one-room space not divided
into nave, transept and sanctuary, and
appropriately approached by means of a stairway
from ground level; embracing each set of inward-
facing pews are tall windows which admit sharply
geometric shafts of light into the space; the altar
is free-standing and dramatically silhouetted; the

*Chapel of the Upper Room
(1966), Christchurch
College, by Warren &
Mahoney. Every detail of
the structure is exposed in a
manner designed to make a
virtue of the conjunction of
hard surfaces.*

*The Dining Hall (1925),
Christ's College,
Christchurch, by Cecil
Wood. This was an obvious
and appropriate model for
the Chapel of the Upper
Room, and the architect
acknowledged the influence
of his former teacher's work
with pride.*

floor is paved with red-brown tile bricks. Every
detail of the structure is exposed in a manner
designed to make a positive virtue of the
conjunction of hard surfaces.

173

NEW ZEALAND ARCHITECTURE

Between 1964 and 1973 Warren & Mahoney designed the Student Union buildings at Canterbury, Auckland and Massey Universities. Massey University still awaits the Great Hall originally designed for it; the Auckland building increasingly seems cramped in its tight location and severe in its brutalist insistence; only the Christchurch Student Union, a similarly designed structure in which every single junction is displayed both inside and out, fulfils its purpose. But the building which brought Warren & Mahoney most credit during this period was the massive Christchurch Town Hall (1966–72), built following a national competition, for which Peter Beaven also produced a notable though ultimately unsuccessful submission.

The design of Christchurch Town Hall is essentially Modernist in that, again, form is determined by function. The height of the auditorium and its oval roof are determined primarily by acoustical considerations. The thick walls required for the isolation of the various performance areas meant that a structural frame with infill panels was unsuitable, and consequently the forms tend to be simpler and less dominated by exposed structural elements than some of the partnership's earlier buildings. A unifying design motif featuring paired columns is found throughout the building and creates a sense of unity despite the juxtaposition of many contrasting shapes. Inside, the Brutalist/Constructivist ethic still dominates promenade areas and staircases and the effect is harsh, particularly because of the vast amount of brightly coloured carpet used. The oval-shaped auditorium with its audience-embracing sound reflectors is, however, impressive from every vantage point.

Wellington's Michael Fowler Centre, designed by Mahoney in 1975 and completed in 1983 has obvious similarities to the oval Christchurch Town Hall; both auditoriums have a seating capacity of around 2500, but Wellington's has a raked stalls area, allowing a better view of the stage. The acoustics, like those designed for Christchurch by Professor Harold Marshall, require the use of reflectors, which hang from the side walls in a continuous curve rather than an angular form; the effect is much calmer on the eye than at Christchurch. The foyer areas are less harsh and their textures are further softened by hanging banners made by the Wellington artist Gordon Crook.

Christchurch Town Hall (1966–72) by Warren & Mahoney. Modernist in the way in which its functions determined the forms used, this hall is restrained in its exhibition of exterior structure. The height and shape of the oval auditorium were determined by acoustics.

Michael Fowler Centre (1975–83), Wellington, by Warren & Mahoney. This is similar to the practice's Christchurch hall in capacity, plan and appearance.

*The Beehive (1964–82),
Wellington, concept by Sir
Basil Spence, completed by
the Government Architect.*

Wellington's most noticeable building is the Beehive, as the 1965 addition to Parliament Buildings has become generally known. John Campbell and Claude Paton's building (see page 67) was left incomplete in 1918; its facilities became more and more inadequate and eventually many dingy rooms behind the General Assembly Library had to be pressed into service as members' offices. By the 1960s it was evident that there were three possibilities available: to complete John Campbell's building, to retain the existing Parliament Building and construct a modern building beside it, or to demolish all the existing buildings and start again.

In 1964 the eminent British architect Sir Basil Spence visited New Zealand, mainly to talk about his newly opened Coventry Cathedral. When he was introduced to Keith Holyoake, the Prime Minister casually asked Spence what kind of building he would recommend for the site. According to the Government Architect, F. G. F. Sheppard, Spence replied that on the following Monday morning he would have something ready for Holyoake's consideration. The result of that weekend's thought was a circular conception which, like a ziggurat, diminished in size as it increased in height. It was this design suggestion which was eventually adopted, despite objections from parliamentarians in favour of the completion of the existing Parliament Buildings,

and from members of the architectural profession who believed that the centre of government in the capital city should be designed by a New Zealand architect. The Government Architect and the Ministry of Works prepared working drawings, sometimes consulting Spence, who had by then returned to England. There was never any suggestion that Spence be formally engaged to design the beehive-shaped building he had sketched and his association with the building soon ended.

The Beehive stands on a solid rectangular podium; above it a circular drum contains the main reception rooms; above again there are five floors of ministerial suites, surmounted by the Prime Minister's suite and the Cabinet Room at the very top. The circular floors, decreasing in diameter, are supported on a circular core which extends from the foundations to the roof deck. Under the core a raft foundation is tied to the perimeter columns to provide seismic strengthening. Horizontal forces on the building are resisted by the circular perforated core. All the floors were pre-cast.

The circular design was approved not only because of its distinctive appearance, but also because of its functional efficiency in permitting a high percentage of usable space. This has proved to be somewhat less practical than originally envisaged and, indeed, by the mid-1980s the

RIGHT: *West Plaza
(1970–74), Auckland, by
Price, Adams, Dodd.
Sitting with slim elegance
on its narrow site, this
building is typical of the
work done by a practice
whose interest in sculptural
architectural forms was
paramount.*

*Meteorological Office
(1962–68), Wellington, by
the Ministry of Works.
Detail of exterior showing
the concrete fins which not
only provide shade but also
enliven what would
otherwise have been another
concrete monolith.*

building became overcrowded, and some members of the country's executive had to be accommodated outside its structure. Those who have worked in the building have found its circular design disconcerting and difficult to manage, despite daily encounters with its complex layout. On the exterior, care was taken to ensure that the scale of the Beehive's main reception area related visually to the scale of the existing Parliament Buildings by means of a similar spacing of columns, and balance of light and shade. Concrete fins shield the administrative offices from the sun and give rhythmical emphasis to the exterior. A copper roof over the Prime Ministerial and Cabinet floors gives the building an appropriately defined crown.

Some of the same techniques were used in the Meteorological Office, Wellington, designed in 1962 and completed in 1968. It is the work of the Architectural Division of the Ministry of Works, led by F. G. F. Sheppard, with William Alington as design architect. Constructed of reinforced concrete, it has a central core which bears the lateral load. The rhythms created by bands of pre-cast concrete fins rescue the building from a forbidding appearance, as well as restricting the amount of direct sunlight allowed into the interior. The form of the building is very largely determined by the various meteorological functions it houses: its lower floors accommodate the departmental head office, the cantilevered fourth floor houses the forecasting centre, and the roof functions as observation platform and as the location of the radar aerial.

Of the many public buildings erected during the 1970s three stand out because of the variety of surface treatments and consequently the face each presents to the street spectator. In Wellington, the National Library, designed in 1974 but not completed until 1986, is as forbidding a fortress as any in New Zealand. Its debt to McKinnell & Knowles's 1964–69 Boston City Hall is obvious — almost as obvious as the debt Price, Adams, Dodd's 1970–74 aerofoil-shaped West Plaza in Fanshawe Street, Auckland, owes to the 1955 Pirelli Building, Milan, by Ponti, Roselli, Valtolina & Dell'Orto. The fins on the curving facade of West Plaza serve an even more strongly sculptural purpose in addition to the obvious practical one.

West
Plaza

Graydon Miskimmin, the Government Architect from 1975 to 1984, had worked on both the Beehive and the National Library before designing the Wanganui Departmental Building in 1979. Although cited in the A.A.A. Monier Design Awards for that year as 'reflecting the particular use and requirements of a government building dealing with a broad cross-section of the public',[18] the diagonally braced cell-like box forms seem to hint at something far more impersonally

METEOROLOGICAL OFFICE

bureaucratic. Imi Porsolt, giving a 'Critical Glance' over the awards for 1979 referred to 'wholes of deadly regularity' and doubted whether its cell-like construction would cater for greatly varying space sizes and shapes.[19] The 1970s ended with a challenge for architects of public buildings to produce designs which did not sacrifice utilitarian, even humane considerations for structural ones.

The 1960s saw unprecedented growth in the number of churches built in New Zealand, and some of them are outstanding buildings. Initially, church builders showed resistance to the reductive forms of the Modern Movement, but following changes in the Roman Catholic liturgy after the Second Vatican Council (1962–64), church design began to reflect the increasing democratisation of the relationship between congregation and clergy and the *shared* nature of worship. The people were brought closer to the altar, buildings used for social activities began to be integrated within the confines of the church itself, expensive stained-glass windows were replaced by panes of coloured glass arranged in abstract patterns, and exteriors of churches often took on the domestic quality of their neighbours. New materials such as steel and concrete, formerly regarded as inappropriate, were increasingly used with expressive skill.

The most admired church of the period was undoubtedly John Scott's Futuna Chapel (1960) in the Wellington suburb of Karori, which has since been the subject of a book-length study. Futuna, in its planning actually anticipating the Vatican II changes, alludes to the whare, the woolshed, New Zealand's timber Gothic architecture and the domestic roofs of Karori. Scott's Havelock North Church of Our Lady of Lourdes (1960) is scarcely less accomplished.

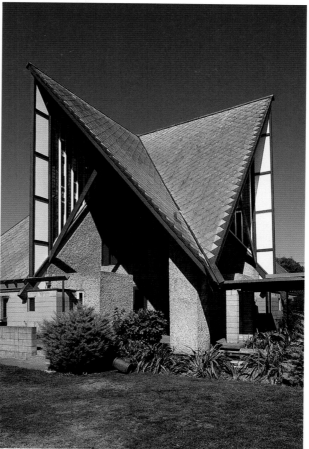

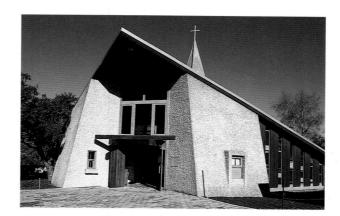

LEFT: *Wanganui Departmental Building (1979) by the Government Architect. Almost as if the architect wished to reinforce the view of the government departments housed within it as unapproachable bureaucracies, the notion of exposed structure is taken to an unacceptable extreme.*

TOP RIGHT: *Futuna Chapel (1958–60), Karori, Wellington, by John Scott. Boldly experimental and highly regarded, the chapel is rather self-conscious in its manipulation of sharply angled forms.*

Church of Our Lady of Lourdes (1960), Havelock North, by John Scott. The architect's debt to Le Corbusier's Notre Dame du Haut at Ronchamp (1950–55) is evident in the bold angularity of the facade, the projecting roof line and diminutive but carefully placed windows.

Interior of Church of Our Lady of Lourdes. The insistence on wood is inevitably reminiscent of the ceilings of such churches as All Saints', Howick. Again the architect has introduced light above the altar by means of a lantern.

James Hackshaw's 1964 Chapel, part of the House of Studies he designed for the Sisters of the Mission in Upland Road, Auckland, has been greatly altered from its initial highly original form. Positioned at the centre of the complex, the chapel was entered from a balcony reached by a corridor where the twenty postulants' bedrooms were located. The architect stressed simplicity of form in order that his chapel should contrast as sharply as possible with the overly detailed churches being built at the time. The flat roof was pushed up above the main roof line to form a surrounding clerestory, the windows of which were designed by Colin McCahon, a frequent collaborator in Hackshaw's ecclesiastical buildings. Altar furniture, instead of being imported from Italy or Australia, was designed by the architect. Nothing was permitted to disturb the calm atmosphere created by white walls, a warm, wooden ceiling and a rimu parquet floor.

Hackshaw said that when he had to design a church he would spend some time in Mountfort's St Mary's Procathedral (see page 32) and the Chapel of St John's College (see page 26) to absorb the intensity of their colour and light. His later churches drew on a variety of sources: the 1977 Liston College Chapel is in fact a lean-to shed in the best Group tradition; the Church of St Ignatius (1978) at St Heliers is domestically scaled to fit neatly within its suburban bungalow environment; St Francis's at Browns Bay (1978) is a large concrete-block church which includes many traditional features and is notable for its uncluttered breadth.

Other architects chose to design more elaborate structures. F. John Bowering, in association with Abbott, Hole & Annabell, designed the Whiteley Methodist Church, New Plymouth, in 1963 as the replacement for a historic church destroyed by fire in 1959. Characterised by a very steeply pitched roof, it is typical of many churches built in New Zealand during the 1960s. A wide entrance porch leads to a narrower vestibule, which then opens out to the main body of the church. The steeply pitched roof, the use of steel joists and laminated wood members, and the exploitation of dramatic lighting effects were familiar to New Zealand's church architects from the variety of American churches illustrated in books published by the *Architectural Record*. Their most elaborate expression is to be seen in R. H. Toy's 1966 and 1978 designs for the completion of the long-delayed Holy Trinity Cathedral, Parnell, in Auckland.

By the late 1970s it was apparent that many New Zealand architects were pursuing individualistic and often widely differing paths. Some of the most notable of them became household names as the result of press exposure of the new architecture and the controversies it occasioned. People now realised that architecture was a subject for lively debate and that there was much in the New Zealand built environment which could do with rethinking. During the 1980s, the most exciting in the country's history in terms of new developments, these tendencies were to develop still further.

CHAPTER TEN
Experiment, Debate and Demolition

Fay, Richwhite Building
(page 183)

*The view up Grafton Gully
towards Symonds Street
gives an indication of the
types of high rise building
which became such a
familiar sight in Auckland
during the 1980s.*

Ironically, architectural awareness in the wider community increased as a boom economy during the 1980s encouraged the demolition of a great many older buildings in New Zealand's larger cities. As the result of people's growing resentment at the way their surroundings were being changed so rapidly and, it appeared, thoughtlessly, architectural *causes célèbres* were taken up in the popular press as well as in such professional magazines as *Architecture New Zealand* and *Home and Building.* By the time the nation's Sesquicentenary arrived in 1990 it was clear that New Zealanders had a highly ambiguous attitude to many aspects of their country's past, including its architectural history. The controversies concerning architecture during the decade led many towards a new respect for New Zealand's built environment, just as threats to the natural environment heightened awareness of the need to conserve natural resources.

By 1980 the avant-garde architects of the late 1960s and early 1970s were the country's senior practitioners, the best of them continuing to assimilate new styles and influences. A younger group of architects, many of them only recently released from the schools, were to adapt traditional ideological differences among the country's architects to the new pluralism of approach offered by Post-modernism. The result was an architecture characterised by variety,

display, intellectual rigour and humour. It was frequently informed, too, by an understanding of what had preceded the buildings of the present.

Sadly, many dull public buildings were also erected. Typical of those which aroused strong feelings of disapproval was the State Insurance Building on the corner of Waring Taylor Street and Lambton Quay, Wellington, built as a replacement for the uniquely Lutyensesque 1919 State Fire Insurance Building by Hoggard, Prouse & Gummer. It was completed in 1984 to a design by the firm of Hoadley, Budge & Partners, who originally envisaged two identical glass towers. The second tower, still unbuilt, was to replace Gummer & Ford's State Insurance Building of 1940 (see page 138), the survival of which in 1990 remains a subject of controversy. Claire Benge criticised the Hoadley, Budge building for the lack of a clear relationship between its white Kairuru marble podium and its black glass tower. The podium does delineate the site boundary but, she says, 'sits heavily on the street, a bland and unrelenting three-storey band'.[1] A comparison between this building and its predecessor leads to the inescapable conclusion that change is not necessarily progress.

The year 1990 saw the completion of the Glossop, Chan Partnership's large National Bank Centre, which necessitated the demolition of an entire central Auckland block in favour of a

podium topped by twin towers clad in banded dark blue and green double glazing. With their smoothed corners and slanting roof lines these glass towers are evidence of the extent to which architects have moved away from the glass box Modernism originated by Mies Van der Rohe's Seagram Building (1958).

Nearby in Albert Street is the A.S.B. Bank Centre, designed in 1987 by Peddle, Thorp & Aitken and based on a concept by Australian architect Paul Tavuzzi. The building's thirty-five storeys were completed using a new top-down construction technique that allowed the basement, car-parking levels and tower to be worked on simultaneously, thus reducing construction time. The 115-metre tower was temporarily supported by a diaphragm retaining-wall and the contractors used a self-climbing form to erect the tower's core. This building has the largest floor plate of any high-rise commercial office structure in New Zealand.

New Zealand's most controversially received glass box was the Bank of New Zealand Building in Willis Street, Wellington. The building was designed by Stephenson & Turner in the late 1960s, but work on the site did not begin until 1973. The movement-resisting steel box frame was the subject of many prolonged industrial disputes, so that the bank was not finally occupied until 1984. Although its designers imagined its polished surface of prefabricated glass and black granite panels would give shimmering and subtle light effects, the building attracted many uncomplimentary epithets indicating that observers found sinister associations in its dark form.

The architect Roger Walker described the B.N.Z. Building as one generally liked by architects, particularly for the way in which its superlative materials were put together, but as a member of the public he said that he found it 'expressionless, unwelcoming and sullen'.

Experiment, Debate and Demolition

TOP LEFT: *National Bank Centre (1987), Auckland, by Glossop, Chan Partnership. These smart, shapely twin towers offer a welcome change from the all-pervasive box shape.*

Interior of A.S.B. Bank Centre. The glistening Fior di Pesco marble, plate glass and brass detailing of the extensive public access area project an architectural image of grandeur and security.

BOTTOM LEFT: *A.S.B. Bank Centre (completed 1991), Auckland, by Peddle, Thorp & Aitken in association with Peddle, Thorp & Harvey Pty Ltd. Spanish white granite and Italian mahogany granite spandrels give this 35-storey glass tower, more than many other high-rise buildings designed in the 1980s, a sense of permanence.*

181

It is not, despite its technical dexterity, a confident building. Its ground relationships with neighbouring buildings and streets are tentative. Its height does not soar. It is authoritarian rather than authoritative. It does not express the richness of its function nor the diversity of its tenants.[2]

He described as 'heroic' the attempt to control the vertical gales which habitually play about its main entrance by means of a pyramidal glass-roofed walkway.[2]

For Sir Miles Warren, on the other hand, the B.N.Z. Building was 'the most convincing example in New Zealand of American up-market office buildings of the 60s'. He regarded it as unfortunate that it arrived

in all its big black starkness a decade late to become the whipping boy of the architectural anti-establishment. The bank is the opposite of 'small is beautiful' and the fashion to dismember buildings into the maximum number of conflicting forms. It is monochrome, wicked black, not bright and multi-coloured. It is faced with imported opulent granite not genuine Kiwi corrugated iron or carpentry bravura, not even concrete.[3]

Bank of New Zealand Building (1973–84), Wellington, by Stephenson & Turner.

Many architects aligned themselves with equal eloquence either for or against the B.N.Z. in the spirited manner characteristic of architectural debate during the 1980s, a significant and welcome change from the anti-intellectualism of earlier decades. Typical also of the times is the ambivalence about the real significance of New Zealand's architectural past, so that the fate of Thomas Turnbull's 1899–1901 former Bank of New Zealand Head Office on the corner opposite remains undecided in 1990.

The New Zealand building that suffered most from delays in commissioning and construction was the long-awaited Aotea Centre, the opening of which in 1990 was greeted with understandable disappointment by both architects and public, despite their recognition of the fact that Auckland badly needed a large performing arts venue to replace the small, though acoustically excellent, Town Hall.

The Aotea Centre has its origins in a Centennial Hall designed in 1976 by the City Architect, Ewan Wainscott, in unimaginative homage to Aalto's Finlandia Hall (1971). It was not warmly received by the Auckland City Council of the day or by architects. In 1985, however, despite mounting criticism of the designs and submission of a rival scheme by students and teachers at the Auckland School of Architecture, the building of the slightly altered Wainscott plans was fast-tracked. The dull result was defended by those who supervised the job as being a building deliberately designed to provide a neutral background to the events which would take place inside it. Few people were persuaded that such a description was anything more than an excuse to cover a very real failure of inspiration. No less an authority than the American architect Joseph Esherick described the building's appearance as one of 'abject neutrality'.

Many Aucklanders focused their discontent about the rapid change in the central city on the mirror-glass facade of the Mid-City Centre, built to designs by the Sinclair Group in 1981. This practice, founded in 1971, is typical of a number which maintain offices in both Auckland and Wellington and have staffs numbering over fifty people. Using computer-aided design methods they are able to produce a large volume of work for both domestic and commercial markets, although the latter tends to dominate. Like the Structon Group, another large practice based in Wellington but maintaining offices in both Auckland and Palmerston North, the Sinclair Group offers clients advice on matters as diverse as town planning and interior decoration.

The Mid-City Centre is a cinema and shopping complex which extends from Queen Street through to Elliott Street. Although the Queen Street facade in part takes cues from the surrounding buildings, its combination of a mullionless mirror-glass wall, granite portal and stainless-steel and neon detailing represents an unashamed attempt on the part of the architects to enliven what was at the time one of the dreariest parts of Auckland's main street. The building's Elliott Street brick facade refers to the

brewery which once occupied the site. It will eventually be joined by a bridge to the 32-storey Mid-City II, the building of which started in 1990.

The city's most admired glass building is the New Zealand Insurance / Fay, Richwhite

Building at 151 Queen Street. It is the work of Peddle, Thorp & Aitken, an Australian practice, founded in 1889, which extended its operations to New Zealand during the 1960s building boom. The concept design architect was Dino Burratini, whose association with Peddle, Thorp & Aitken ran from 1984, when sketch plans were first presented, to 1988 and the building's completion.

Visible from all parts of the central city, the Fay, Richwhite Building is clad in Dutch glass and Argentinian granite, intriguingly staggered so that the conformity of colour actually enhances rather than detracts from the overall appearance. The top floors of the rectangular tower are stepped down and faceted so that, from the east or the west, the building appears to be not one but three towers. The surfaces of the north and south elevations are modelled in a more restrained manner which managed to avoid the extreme blandness of the clichéd curtain wall.

LEFT: *Mid-City Centre (1981), Auckland, by Sinclair Group. Mirror glass blurs the distinction between wall and sky and reflects the building's neighbours.*

RIGHT: *Fay, Richwhite Building (1984–88), Auckland, by Dino Burratini with Peddle, Thorp & Aitken. The building's staggered and faceted glass forms are interesting from every vantage point.*

The Fay, Richwhite Building is notable for the care which went into all aspects of its design and construction. As the result of extensive wind tests, the podium of the building was moved back to enable it to deflect the wind upward from the street. Cars parked within the building are rendered invisible by means of granite-clad pre-cast concrete panels, which cover the car-parking floors. The foyer is most dramatic, rising 18 metres above the street, its stepped forms echoing those at the top of the building.

Karangahape Road. The complex incorporates a fale, shopping arcade and offices, and makes extensive use of materials and colours with which people from Western Samoa may identify. The fale resembles the traditional Samoan house in both form and construction, its timber pole-and-beam roof structure supporting an elongated domed roof. Doubtless the successful marrying of European and Polynesian architectural traditions both here and at the Waikato Museum of Art and History (1987) in Hamilton was a significant factor in the choice in 1990 of this practice, having expanded following a merger with Bossley, Cheshire Architects, to build the Museum of New Zealand on the shoreline at Wellington.

It is appropriate that the world's largest Polynesian city should be the site for a building which consciously echoes the forms of non-Maori Polynesian architecture. Noteworthy buildings by the Auckland JASMaD Group, formed in 1963, have been built throughout the country as well as in the Pacific Islands, Malaysia and Saudi Arabia. JASMaD led the way when in 1977 it built Maota Samoa, Samoa House, in Auckland's

The Auckland University Recreation Centre (1973) and Arts and Commerce Faculty (1979–84) are similarly inventive; they soften the prevailing Brutalist aggression of the campus's other buildings by employing such domestically associated features as hipped roofs, verandahs and overhanging eaves. Manning Mitchell's School of Music (1980) also represents a departure from the Brutalist norm, although in a completely different style.

JASMaD's prevailing style is owed in large part to principal partner Ivan Mercep's familiarity with post-war domestic architecture in Auckland. Similarly, Ted McCoy's respect for the Victorian forms of Dunedin's architectural tradition informs his blending of old with new buildings. In 1979, McCoy & Wixon designed the Hocken Building in Dunedin. Unfortunately, its form was determined more by the university's need to conserve space than by its proximity to Maxwell Bury's Otago University (see page 34). Pitched, rather than flat, roofs and a studied avoidance of a regular grid treatment of windows do not alleviate the impression of the academically forbidding, although David Mitchell finds in this

*Otago Boys' High School
Extension (1982), Dunedin,
by McCoy & Wixon. The
architects made no attempt
to emulate the soaring spires
of Lawson's original school
buildings, instead producing
a large, carefully detailed
structure which alludes
more to the shapes of
Dunedin's domestic
architecture.*

very large building an unexpected reference to
Dunedin's Victorian terraced houses. In 1982
McCoy added a classroom block behind Lawson's
imposing main building at Otago Boys' High
School. The block is partly faced with crushed
Oamaru stone rather than the blocks used by
Lawson, and, instead of creating a rival
monolith, McCoy has fragmented his classrooms
into a variety of refined Modernist shapes which
allude to the steeply pitched roofs of Dunedin's
domestic architecture.

Regionalist influences are less obviously present
on the unusual Auckland Harbour Board
Building (1980–83), which was built at the city
end of Princes Wharf by an architectural
collective made up of Dodd, Paterson Architects
with Newman, Pearce. Lifted high above the
water on concrete piers, the building was
designed to be a gateway between the city and
the harbour; its distinctive shape derives from the
highly sculptured Bean Rock Lighthouse, situated
in the middle of the Waitemata Harbour,
between Mission Bay and Rangitoto. The
Harbour Board building was designed as a
counterfoil to Wiseman's Ferry Building (see page
70); in terms of proportion they have many
similarities, although these are by no means clear.
Like the Ferry Building, the Harbour Board is
entered from beneath, but instead of the older
building's arcaded openings the entrance foyer,
placed in the centre of a sunlit plaza, is of glass

*Auckland Harbour Board
Building (1980–83), by
Dodd, Paterson Architects
in association with
Newman, Pearce.
Regionalist visual links are
so understated here as to
deny the building the
symbolic value its architects
hoped for. The 'legs'
supporting daring
cantilevers reinforce a
crustacean analogy.*

supported by steel fingers which call to mind the
derricks on container ships. The nautical
metaphor is continued above, where utility
functions are housed in a mirror-glassed box
whose facets are shaped like sails.

In an attempt to create visually interesting
buildings a number of New Zealand architects,
following overseas trends, have emphasised
formal architectural qualities by making
structural features ornamental. One of the first
such buildings was Warren & Mahoney's Union
House (1980–84), also to be found on Auckland's
Quay Street. Instead of constructing a
conventional concrete-framed office building, the
architects, in close consultation with engineers
Holmes, Wood, Poole & Johnstone, used an
exposed frame of columns and beams braced with
a system of external pre-cast concrete diagonal

*LEFT: Union House
(1980–84), Auckland, by
Warren & Mahoney.
Exposed structure is here
used ornamentally;
connection joints are
designed to be compatible
with nautical shapes but
they also perform a vital
structural role.*

*TOP RIGHT: A.S.B. Stadium
(1988), Auckland, by
Dodd, Paterson Architects
demonstrates the fashion for
enlivening what are
otherwise rather plain
buildings with brightly
painted exposed structural
details.*

*BOTTOM RIGHT: Clocktower
House (1985), Queenstown,
by John Blair. Alpine
verticality is echoed in this
fanciful structure.*

building is basically a huge industrial shed, its
structural detailing gives it spatial qualities which
Paul Walker described as 'a disorder of
accretions'.[4] There is, however, no denying the
vibrancy of its colourful and shiny surfaces.

members. In this way the lateral wind and
earthquake forces are transmitted to the base of
the building. The superstructure is braced and
connected to the basement by a system of steel
plates and thin connecting rods; its ground-level
structure relies on base isolation for earthquake
resistance. The architects claim this was the first
time the principle was ever used in a commercial
building.

The year 1988 saw the completion of a huge
development, known as Chase Plaza, by the
Chase Corporation in the heart of Auckland.
Chase used the services of a number of
architectural firms, including the Walker Co-
partnership, which was responsible for the
Brandon, Brookfield building on Victoria Street
and for the structure behind the historic Scott's
Building, designed by Mason & Wales in 1882,
the facade of which was kept. A notable feature
of the plaza is a space-frame ceiling canopy made
of Plexiglass sheets imported from Germany,
supported on a frame of anodised aluminium.
Similar decorative exposed structures were used
on the Chase Stadium, now the A.S.B. Stadium,
which was completed to designs by Dodd,
Paterson Architects in 1988 in readiness for the
Commonwealth Games in 1990. Although the

During the 1980s a building boom in the tourist
resort of Queenstown gave architects the
opportunity to display individual styles in an
environment unique to its grandeur. One of the
most prolific architects in Queenstown has been
John Blair (b. 1942), whose professional
association with the town began when he acted
as supervising architect on Warren & Mahoney's
Travelodge Hotel in 1972–73. Like Roger Walker
and Ian Athfield, with whom he attended the
Auckland School of Architecture during the
mid-1960s, Blair was prepared to surprise, even
shock, by challenging existing traditions.
Queenstown, looking for a distinctive
architectural image, gave him ample opportunity
to do so.

In 1983 Blair's Base Amenities Building at
Coronet Peak (destroyed by fire three years later),
while clearly owing much to Canadian architects
Righter, Rose & Lankin's Pavillon Soixante-Dix,
established him as one of the country's foremost
architects even though he had deliberately
chosen to work outside the main centres. His

shingled Clocktower House (1985) provided Queenstown with an appropriately scaled if slightly over-inventive building on an important corner site. O'Connell's Pavilion (1987), a four-storeyed shopping complex arranged around a glass-roofed atrium, has dynamic street elevations achieved with overhangs and canopies.

The 1988 Queenstown Tourist Hotel Corporation Hotel by Roger Walker Interact, a company formed in 1981, gave the holiday resort another virtuoso exercise in contemporary architecture, one which won a special N.Z.I.A. award for environmental response. Walker designed the hotel around a courtyard which opens towards Lake Wakatipu in much the same way as the town's narrow streets. A matrix of aluminium grilles echoes the verticality of the surrounding mountain peaks, while dining and lounge areas sparkle with the sheen of marble flooring, stainless steel and glass.

Neither a creative regionalism nor varieties of spatial formalism were to offer many attractions to Ian Athfield, who had lost none of his daring despite the passage of time. Post-modernists were eager to restore ornament, metaphorical meaning, historical allusion and symbolic association to an

architecture of large public buildings which by the end of the 1970s had seemed in need of a rejuvenatory shot. But the New Zealand public, although tired of the severities of Government-inspired architecture in particular, were thoroughly bemused by many of Ian Athfield's exercises in architectural imagination.

In 1983 his First Church of Christ Scientist in Wellington's Willis Street was completed. Given a brief which encouraged him to experiment rather than conform to traditional theological determinants, Athfield produced a building dominated by a smooth rounded form familiar from his own house but supported on two columns, one erect, the other buckled precariously and both with bright pink pottery capitals. James Walker's round stained-glass window looks like an eye to some, yet the real point is that the whole building has as many readings as it has observers. Its glazed verandahs and round-topped shuttered windows hint at both Colonial and Hispanic conventions; inside, distorting mirrors on the ceiling play havoc with space.

Ian Athfield's Moore Wilson Warehouse, completed in 1984, makes as much use of humour as SITE's 1976–77 Notch Project in Sacramento, or the Tilt Showroom (1976–78) at Tucson, Arizona. Athfield retained the balconied wall of the original Victorian warehouse but juxtaposed it with a tilted concrete-block wall, split in half by a large axe-head which remains embedded in the fabric. At the far end of the building a

Experiment, Debate and Demolition

LEFT: *T.H.C. Hotel (1988), Queenstown, by Roger Walker. Extensive glass walls with structural supporting frame help to blur the distinction between the courtyard garden and the marble walkway.*

RIGHT: *First Church of Christ Scientist (1983), Wellington, by Athfield Architects. Its unusual shapes have encouraged a whole range of interpretations, few of them religious. Like much Post-modernist architecture, this building resists a single interpretative line, encouraging a multiplicity of meanings.*

LEFT: *Moore Wilson Warehouse (1984), Wellington, by Athfield Architects.*

RIGHT: *Telecom House (1988), Wellington, by Athfield Architects. Wellington's most colourful high rise building, its folded facade surely owes something to Gummer & Ford's State Insurance.*

precariously tilted glass box, which looks like a fallen section from one of the city's many curtain-walled buildings, houses a staircase. In a city as prone to earthquakes as Wellington, Athfield's humorous pursuit of references to destruction borders on the black. Certainly passers-by have mixed responses to the joke, which was, no doubt, the intention. Athfield's Cable Restaurant (1984), with its anthropomorphic latticed octopus-head form is equally disturbing.

In 1987 Athfield Architects linked three older Wellington buildings belonging to Hannahs with a new building which borrowed elements from the existing fabric, to create the Robert Hannah Centre. Other architectural practices which entered the competition to rationalise the dispersed Hannahs complex of buildings favoured the corporate tower; Athfield's scheme allowed not only the retention of the familiar older buildings but also the addition of some unexpected military imagery, including corbelled battlements, a lift tower like a fortified turret, and steel gates within an arcaded entry. Richard Wright referred to 'the Euro-Kiwian romantic cocktail so cleverly mixed by Athfield and Co.'.[5]

Some people are determined to find lavatorial metaphors in the practice's 1988 Telecom House in Manners Street, Wellington, whose fourteen floors are distinctively faced in bright green tiles; it has possibly escaped their attention that the building makes clear reference to the undulating facade of Gummer's 1940 State Insurance Building. The roof colonnade is also a reminder that Athfield is not immune to the Post-modern free Classicism which had been increasingly adopted as a public building style in New Zealand during the 1980s.

It is ironic that such historical reference should have come into fashion during what has been an era of demolition, although it must be said that architects have, with a few notable exceptions, been vociferous in defence of older buildings

whose demolition might have brought them lucrative briefs. Throughout New Zealand cities, new buildings began to sprout an ill-assorted array of Classical pediments, cornices and columns in an attempt to keep abreast of the times. Few have managed to achieve the stylistic grandeur which usually characterised the work of Warren & Mahoney as the practice continued to receive many of the country's major large-scale commissions.

If Athfield is content merely to allude wittily to a Classical precedent, Warren & Mahoney prefer to shape an entire building according to such principles of design in a thoroughly serious manner. In 1985, Roger Walker's Wellington Club (1972), on the Terrace, was demolished because its limited floor area was said to render it cost-ineffective. It was replaced by a very much larger, Classically inspired structure by Warren & Mahoney, which Rob Ansell described as being 'as radical as the one it replaced but unlike Walker's its urban language is familiar'.[6] It now consists of a club building on the Terrace and a much larger eighteen-storey tower block behind. Neo-classicism was considered appropriate for a gentlemen's club, so the building displays round-headed windows, curved cornices and paired columns. In the case of the pretentious Lyttelton Harbour Board Building (1985–86), the allusion is, inexplicably, to a grand English Neo-classical house, and the building certainly achieves the required sense of authority but is scarcely in sympathy with the nineteenth-century character of Lyttelton, as was intended.

Imposing architecture may be more successful in a larger urban context. The 1987–89 Citibank Centre in Auckland's Customs Street has a three-storey colonnade, overhanging cornice, miniature tower with hipped roof, and an arched and rusticated entry, acknowledging both Queen's Arcade and Gummer & Ford's Dilworth Building. The Neo-classical grandeur of Warren & Mahoney's 1986–89 building at 49 Boulcott Street, Wellington, is similarly appropriate to its context, but the podium of its near neighbour, the Mercer Tower (1988–89) is an example of poorly handled Classical reference. Consisting of semi-elliptical arches with keystones, it manages to look both flimsy and crushing.

Citibank Centre (1987–89), Auckland, by Warren & Mahoney. Although massively scaled, it integrates with its surroundings, particularly the corner-sited Dilworth Building.

49 Boulcott Street (1986–89), Wellington, by Warren & Mahoney. The practice's penchant for Post-modern Classicism is evident in this brightly coloured entry with double height Doric columns supporting a flattened segmental arched pediment.

Mercer Tower (1988–89), Wellington, by Warren & Mahoney. Although the podium treatment of an arch with keystone device has been flatteringly compared to Piranesi, this is a grim structure from all vantage points.

Parkroyal (1984–88), Christchurch, by Warren & Mahoney. The hotel's 45° angled plan was determined by the site relationship to a transformed Victoria Square.

Television New Zealand Centre (1985–89), Auckland, by Warren & Mahoney. Playful shapes and bands of glass windows ensure that the mysterious but alluring processes which entertain the nation remain obscure.

details, including the furniture. The two bedroom wings extend along the street frontages and have a stepped profile which, on the side nearest the Town Hall, moves respectfully to its lowest point. A glass atrium encloses the space between the two wings and a glazed lift tower gives views of Victoria Square to the Port Hills. The partially complete Television New Zealand Centre (1985–89) in Auckland is a similarly grandiose structure, with greater design flair than the Christchurch hotel.

Warren & Mahoney have also indulged in the regrettable practice of facadism, a method of saving a historic building by incorporating the strengthened facade within the new building. Rarely entirely successful, facadism does allow those imaginative souls who pass them at street level the flickering illusion that buildings such as the Bank of New Zealand in Queen Street, Auckland, Christchurch's Clarendon Hotel or Kirkcaldie's in Wellington are still there. In the case of the hopelessly vulgarised Queen's Head Hotel in Auckland not even that illusion is possible. Those responsible for such acts of pseudo-conservation do not hesitate to inform a dubious public that it is lucky to have the facades at all.

More formalist concerns were to the forefront when Warren & Mahoney designed the Parkroyal Christchurch in 1984. Attempts were made to link it visually with the same practice's Christchurch Town Hall, its immediate neighbour; the buildings are physically linked and together form a conference centre. The corner-sited hotel building took its plan from the diagonal axis of Victoria Street and the plan became a design determinant for many of the

*Tower blocks rear up
behind familiar but
vulgarised historic facades.
Leonard Terry's Bank of
New Zealand, Auckland, is
now reduced to a thin shell
as is the old Queen's Head
Hotel further up Queen
Street. Warren &
Mahoney's transformation
of the Clarendon Hotel in
Christchurch is scarcely
more successful than these
two abject failures.*

The economic boom of the 1980s allowed
architects to persuade wealthy clients to
experiment with a whole array of hitherto
unconceived-of domestic architectural styles. At
the middle and lower ends of the market, housing
companies promoted a wide variety of
prefabricated homes, most of them favouring
timber construction, aluminium joinery and
corrugated-iron roofing in styles which seldom
departed from a neo-colonial vocabulary except
where a 'modern dream home' was required.
Then the stylistic imagery burgeoned to include a
whole range of historical references jumbled
together in displays of expensive pretentiousness.
Like Chatswood on Auckland's North Shore,
whole suburbs became showplaces for such
homes.

*Houses at Chatswood, a
North Shore suburb of
Auckland, where many
houses display the fashion
for Mock Tudor, Colonial
and Spanish-Pueblo styles
rendered in modern
materials.*

State housing, apparently doomed to an endless repetition of old designs, had begun to change by the 1960s as governments encouraged private companies such as Neil Housing and Beazley Homes to house the people. It was not until the 1980s that the state was to return to its former role as commissioner of designs from up-and-coming architects. In 1985 architects Manning Mitchell and Rewi Thompson began projects for the Housing Corporation at Manukau City. Like the original state houses of the 1930s, these new ones made serious attempts to individualise the details of each house within the framework of a series of similar designs. Significantly different, however, is the fact that while the 1930s houses are mostly in the familar English Cottage style, the houses of David Mitchell and Rewi Thompson are both innovative and challenging.

Mitchell designed seven Fibrolite-clad house types for Rata Vine Drive. Their gabled rectangles certainly owe something to the state house tradition, but the way these forms are stepped, recessed, indented, decorated and embellished with bright contrasting colours is startlingly new. Rewi Thompson at Laurelia Place adopted a quite different approach. Instead of good humouredly parodying the state house as

Mitchell had done, he related his designs to the gentle slope of the land on which they sit. Semi-detached units with silver ribbed-metal walls occupy the top sites; at lower levels individual bach-like houses rest on poles, and their curved mono-pitch roofs echo the undulating curves of the roofs of the units above, creating a highly sophisticated formalist visual unity. That this effect should be created out of such unprepossessing materials as plywood, corrugated iron, Fibrolite and exposed tanalised timber is testimony as much to the architect's design skill as to his admiration for the work of the Auckland Group Architects during the 1950s. Both Thompson and Mitchell in their different ways have looked back into New Zealand's architectural history in order to help it to move forward.

Of the so-called 'architect-designed' houses familiar from the advertising copy of real-estate agents, one of the most widely acclaimed is Ian Athfield's Buck House (1980), outside Havelock North in Hawke's Bay. Once again Athfield's studied asymmetries and use of white plastered forms smoothed over dormers, gables and chimneys are evident. It is interesting to note that some other white houses, notably Anscombe's Washpool (1935), in Spanish idiom, and Gummer's Arden (1926) and Tauroa (1916) are in the area yet the Buck House remains an outlandish architectural object positioned quite naturally within the context of its gently sloping site. The house is further proof of this architect's combination of inventiveness and respect for tradition.

If the verandahs and dormers of the Buck House give a passing nod in the direction of New Zealand vernacular architecture, David Mitchell's Gibbs House (1984) in Parnell, Auckland, gives none whatever. Athfield's house was a culmination, Mitchell's an inauguration.

*Gibbs House (1984),
Auckland, by David
Mitchell. Although the play
of many structural shapes
and textures may well have
had a functional origin, the
architect has ensured that
they go far beyond that.*

Mitchell's timberless house has its origins in the International style. Its geometric skews, virtuoso combination of surfaces, and exploitation of risk at the expense of conventional ideas of domestic comfort, look forward to the work of younger architects whose Auckland houses deliberately flouted the hard-won principles of the indigenous tradition, causing them to be labelled in some quarters as Internationalists and therefore traitors.

Two Auckland architects, Pete Bòssley and Pip Cheshire, achieved the remarkable feat of contriving to shock the bourgeoisie while housing them. Bossley and Cheshire were both born in 1950, in Nelson and Christchurch respectively, and neither had initially planned an architectural career. Bossley studied law before enrolling at the Auckland School of Architecture; Cheshire graduated in political science and ran a successful fibreglass business before following the same path. They were taught at the Auckland school by disaffected, classically trained Modernists who had limited historic consciousness, but who encouraged their students' interest in the work of French sociological theorists. The emphasis on a pluralistic approach to meaning which they found in the writings of Robert Venturi provided Bossley and Cheshire with a personal anti-manifesto. They were freed from the hegemony of Modernism, with its ideal of a single, universal meaning to architecture, and gained the intellectual ammunition needed to challenge some of their country's architectural orthodoxies. Neither was afraid to put pen to paper in defence of his ideas and lively debate was the inevitable result.

At first Pip Cheshire built in wood, influenced by the 1966 edition of G.A. *Houses* devoted to Moore, Turnbull, Whitaker, Lyndon's Sea Ranch on the California coast. The steep mono-pitch roof and wood cladding connected easily with the New Zealand indigenous school, yet had a new spatial enthusiasm which Cheshire was to exploit in his Turner House (1981). This was a New Zealand farm-house with a lean-to roof, built in a suburban setting. While basically cruciform, its planning deliberately involved elements of puzzle through the generation of unexpectedly interacting spaces suitable for a tightly knit family with a shared interest in music. Later in the decade, influenced by the work of painters Stephen Bambury, Philippa Blair and Patrick Hanly, and the vibrance of his city's Polynesian culture, Cheshire developed an interest in colour and the clash of materials, and this was reflected in his Vernon Town House (1985). Here Corbusian cubist boxes became the vehicles for a decorative display based as much on Mondrianish abstraction as on Polynesian pattern making.

outside and inside. Rational planning was supplanted by spatial games and comfort by a sense of daring. Modest plainness was abandoned in favour of the conscious pursuit of cool elegance. Such houses could be quickly dismissed as playthings for the nouveau riche by those who conveniently forgot that some of the finest New Zealand domestic architecture had been produced in exactly the same way.

Pip Cheshire's work first attracted wide public attention with his white houses, which related to both the Neo-modernism of the New York Five architects and New Zealand's tradition of white 1930s Moderne houses. Nothing, however, could have been further from the country's wood tradition, and houses such as his Markus House (1988) at Milford, Noel Lane's pink Moor House at Stanmore Bay (1987), and Pete Bossley's Heatley House at Achilles Point (1984–86), aroused ire in the neo-vernacularists, who regarded them as rip-offs and were prepared to supply a roll call of the American architects who had been plagiarised. Given such accusations in a profession as frankly mimetic as architecture, it is appropriate to recall Oscar Wilde's remark that plagiarism is the privilege of the appreciative man.

While the Markus, Moor and Heatley houses certainly owed not a little to Michael Graves and Richard Meier, the Amercian designers of what Charles Jencks memorably named 'ideal pavilions of private life',[7] their real importance for New Zealand architecture lay in their flagrant denial of principles already in danger of becoming fixed. These houses demonstrated that no longer was there a need for a clear relationship between

One of the most expensive houses built during the 1980s exploited the Post-modernist fervour for historical allusion. Pete Bossley's enormous act of homage to Frank Lloyd Wright, the Barnes House (1986) at Herne Bay, Auckland, was to be

looked at, the architect suggested with witty understatement, 'as an alternative to how we normally build in New Zealand'. Bossley provided an 830-m² house which acknowledged details in many of Wright's prairie houses from the period 1900–10, about which his clients were enthusiastic. The stone and exposed timber of the Wrightian organic house are inventively combined; the extreme angularity of decoration, the discreet open planning, the wide eaves, the overhanging portico entrance are all present in the Barnes House. The architect unshamefacedly acknowledged the excessive nature of its detailing and explained that he had deliberately left the ends of the house open and frayed by means of intricate pergolas because 'it can't go on forever'.[8]

Multiple historicist references from what Nikolaus Pevsner regarded as the period of the birth of Modernism abounded on Stephen Smythe's Pervan House (1981) at Epsom. Pete Bossley contrasted it with the practice's 1979 Gregory House, which he described as 'a happy jumble of forms detailed in a relatively "straight" New Zealand modernist-via-the-Group dialect'. The Pervan House arose out of 'an entirely different spoonful dipped in the alphabet soup of history' and Bossley extolled its 'incorporation of potentially unsympathetic or unrelated elements to suggest new possibilities while still evoking half-remembered memories or dreams'. Bossley was the right person to describe a house which alluded to Lethaby, Lutyens, Voysey, Webb, Mackintosh and Binney and whose architects, like Bossley, regarded history as 'a relatively value-fluid storehouse, a grab bag which can be selectively raided to suit the immediate purpose — expression of the present'.[9]

In Queenstown, John Blair had the opportunity to experiment with houses built for wealthy clients, sometimes as holiday cribs. Their interest in having an unusual second home matched the

architect's desire to design forms which, instead of trying vainly to blend with the alpine landscape's huge natural forms, played against them to create what he calls 'a balance of strengths'. The strong diagonal forms of his 1985 Anderson House may in some way mirror those of the distant peaks and its emphatic horizontals the surface of Wakatipu, but the Fibrolite cladding, painted in two-tone blue and gold, creates an abstract composition which owes more to Modernist architecture than to a desire that the building should blend into its context. There is a similar tension in his 1986 cedar and schist Boult House, but it is less evident in the 1990 Swain House. The Swain House, a very large white house with unmistakable echoes of Peter Eisenman's late Modernism, is situated on the shore of the lake at Frankton Arm and, in its constructivist ethic, forms the greatest possible contrast to its surroundings, including houses nearby.

On the gentler hills around Arrowtown, architects have responded to different challenges, all of them related in some way to the surroundings. Blair's 1980 Tennant House hugs the ground in sympathy with the rolling hills, but the angles of its roof line pick up those of the

LEFT: *Pervan House (1981), Epsom, Auckland, by Evans, Smythe. Here the allusions are to English, Scottish and New Zealand architects from the turn of the century.*

Anderson House (1985), Queenstown, by John Blair. The house exploits a tension between elements that blend in with their spectacular alpine surroundings and those that contradict it.

Swain House (1990), Queenstown, by John Blair. A complex display of Corbusian gestures places this lakeside house firmly in the Late-Modernist camp.

NEW ZEALAND ARCHITECTURE

TOP RIGHT: *Jackson House (1988), Arrowtown; by Peter Beaven. The architect's medievalising tendencies are here given full rein.*

House (1988) at Arrowtown by Ian Athfield. Another of the architect's white houses which, instead of exploiting the smooth shapes of his own or the Buck House, refers instead to those of the Central Otago cottage.

BOTTOM RIGHT: *Kelly House (1987), Paraparaumu, by Nigel Cook. Looking like a cross between a woolshed and a glass-house, this house has an electronic control system to regulate temperatures in its centrally placed conservatory.*

mountain peaks seen in the distance. In his 1969 Spary House I, Peter Beaven had done much the same thing, giving his clients a large house with verandahs which opened out to the landscape. In 1988 Beaven won a national award for Spary House II, in which the construction materials exactly pick up the range of colours in the natural environment, to the point where even the strong ridge parapet reflects the snow-covered mountains above. Again verandahs surround the house, and they are detailed to continue the slope of the roof line without interrruption. Solidly regionalist too is a house designed by Ian Athfield in 1988 to reflect Central Otago's cottage architecture, but assembled so that the atmosphere of an early settlers' town is recreated.

In sharp contrast to this exercise in creative regionalism is Beaven's massive Jackson House, which was completed in 1988. Here the client had a strong interest in medieval art and architecture; who better than Beaven, with his Christchurch medievalising tendencies so clearly evident, to design the house? Using stone quarried close by, builders and sculptors erected a house dominated by a medieval great hall and approached by means of an arched portal which leads into an enclosed yard surrounded by a stone wall. Above the portal a two-storeyed tower contains bedrooms and a studio. The balconies and verandahs are detailed in modern materials with great concern for historical accuracy, yet the architect has said that despite considerable study of Mountfort and the work of the Welsh architect

William Burgess, 'the elevations simply grew from the plan and a sketched balancing of solids and voids went on continuously throughout the work'.[10]

Such attempts in the 1980s at a new architectural regionalism differ considerably from the neo-vernacularism advocated by architects who preferred to develop what Vernon Brown and the Group Architects started when they allied aspects of modern Scandinavian architecture with the forms and materials of New Zealand's rural buildings. In an important article in 1988,[11] Auckland architect Nigel Cook wrote critically of Walker and Athfield, who had used forms which were closely connected to the New Zealand landscape and to our own distant and approved past, but whose work did not constitute a permanent source. Some Auckland architects he observed as having moved in the direction of a 'Mediterranean/academic' style, a charge which brought a swift rejoinder from Pete Bossley.

Bossley rejected Cook's thesis, claiming it reflected a belief 'that architecture should concern itself *primarily* with the production of nice spaces to inhabit', a belief which, according to Bossley, 'has dominated (if not throttled) New Zealand domestic architecture for the last fifty years'.[12]

In describing his Kelly House (1987) at Paraparaumu, Nigel Cook wrote of 'a structure that would use our uniqueness and find meaning in these islands that is post colonial rather than post modern'.[13] The Kelly House makes strong visual reference to a red-painted corrugated iron woolshed on the property (and found all over New Zealand) and to the glass-house. In a semi-rural environment such a house blends in; it is modestly without a formal entrance, yet its central core is a conservatory with a roof vent controlled by electronic sensors monitoring sun movement and temperature.

Other architects like Nick Stanish (b. 1942) have refused to commit themselves to regionalism, internationalism, or neo-vernacularism, preferring to take elements from each. His subdued brown and green 1981 Evans House at Titirangi, designed with Briar Green, owes much to the Group tradition, even referring to the Japanese influence seen years earlier on Ivan Juriss's own 1954 house. Stanish's Clark House (1986) at North Kaipara proves that for him the examination of a multiplicity of architectural issues is the right way to go about designing a house.

Similarly eclectic in approach are Cook, Hitchcock & Sargisson, a prolific Auckland practice which has provided the city with some of its liveliest domestic architecture. It was founded by Terence Hitchcock (b. 1935), an architect who trained at the Auckland school and worked in architectural offices in Napier and Tauranga, then travelled to Scandinavia in 1959–60. In the early 1960s he produced houses in Tauranga, including one for the writer Sylvia Ashton-Warner, which rivalled the Scandinavian-inspired

designs of Miles Warren. Following the establishment of Cook, Hitchcock & Sargisson in 1970, Hitchcock and Marshall Cook (b. 1940), once an apprentice at Group Architects, developed their enthusiasm for Voysey, Baillie-Scott and Lutyens, and their New Zealand counterparts Binney, Sholto Smith and Gerald Jones, to the point where David Mitchell could use the term 'neo-Arts and Crafts' to describe their house style.[14] Cook's Napier Street Townhouses (1982) at Freemans Bay, Auckland, with their discreet use of Georgian shutters, Post-modern Classical columns and pergolas, have become influential. Local colour and variety are emphasised, reflecting their designer's conviction that houses should belong within their distinctive suburban settings. His own prizewinning house in the suburb of Parnell transformed the conventional entry hall into a indoor street, on to which all the other rooms can be opened or closed.

Terry Hitchcock's interest in the American shingle style is demonstrated in the 1986 Burton House, in Portland Road, Remuera. Incorporated within the house is a survivor of a group of shingled summer-houses formerly on the site and once situated in the garden of a house nearby, designed by C. R. Ford. Hitchcock's house is divided into two wings and five distinct levels. An open flow of internal space is provided by a long high-ceilinged hall, which links the two wings. Its playful skews and diagonals, studied

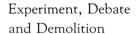

LEFT: *Clark House (1986), North Kaipara, by Nick Stanish. Its pergola-surrounded exterior is deliberately unspectacular, quite belying the sophistication of its interiors.*

Cook House (1987), Parnell, Auckland, by Marshall Cook. A variety of rooms face on to the central hall, which also serves as dining area.

197

imbalances of solid and void, and immaculate detailing are typical of its architect's sophisticated approach to design. His 1990 Cullum House is as much an exercise in self-reference as it is homage to Scandinavian architecture, to the work of Vernon Brown, Group Architects and the Lutyens generation of Auckland architects.

TOP: *Burton House (1986), Remuera, Auckland, by Terry Hitchcock. Shingled all over, this house fits naturally on its steep site, surrounded by green foliage. By contrast, interiors are airy and open with white plaster walls and kauri ceilings.*

BOTTOM: *Cullum House (1990), Auckland, by Terry Hitchcock. The house was planned around a large pohutukawa, and the dark, rear elevations with their flattened gables and symmetrically placed white-trimmed windows refer back to the architect's earlier interest in Scandinavian domestic architecture.*

While New Zealand architects too numerous to mention continue to design with sophistication, awareness of social issues and attention to client need, there are those for whom such considerations are of little importance. Yet it is buildings that help to give New Zealand its specific identity. Initially it was thought that our architecture should reflect England's, and the result was a proliferation of scaled-down versions of English buildings. Some architects, however, had maintained from a much earlier date than is usually recognised that the creation of an

indigenous New Zealand architecture was a priority. At different times in our history, architectural influences from many countries have been called upon to play a role in the creation of architecture which was considered peculiar to these islands. In both cases, the best architects were those familiar with the history of their discipline and thoroughly informed about the work of their contemporaries.

Today, despite fine work by architects dedicated to the design of buildings that are pleasing both aesthetically and in terms of function, one cannot help but be seriously concerned at the increasing subdivision of New Zealand into small plots of land, upon which houses of a frightening dullness and similarity are hastily and thoughtlessly erected. With public buildings, too, the expedient solution has won out all too often, with the result that many buildings look as though they are supposed to last for a few years rather than for a generation or more. Too many of New Zealand's fine historic buildings have, despite protests, been demolished by people ignorant of our architectural history in order to make way for some kind of ill-defined future.

In years to come, New Zealanders may regret that they continued to transform their cities into non-residential, characterless workplaces from which it is a pleasure to escape, instead of learning from those in other countries who understood the damaging effects of wholesale destruction of urban heritage.

There are, however, hopeful signs. Conservation architecture is a growing discipline and the New Zealand Historic Places Trust is helping to update the woefully inadequate legislation that protects buildings. The public appetite for information about our architecture has grown enormously. Architects are increasingly finding that their clients are not merely people who sign cheques but are architecturally literate and expect to be able to discuss sophisticated issues with the professionals they have consulted.

This book has been almost entirely devoted to New Zealand's surviving noteworthy buildings. An equally lengthy volume could have been written about New Zealand's lost buildings and no doubt will be, as people begin to understand the importance of our architectural history. This country *does* have an architectural history, and it shapes our perceptions of what is distinctive about New Zealand.

1: Raupo, Timber and Stone

1   Isabel Ollivier, Early New Zealand Eyewitness Accounts of Maori Life, vol. 2, Alexander Turnbull Library Endowment Trust with Indo-Suez N.Z. Ltd, Wellington, p. 133.
2   Ollivier, Eyewitness accounts, vol. 4, p. 133.
3   Ollivier, Eyewitness accounts, vol. 2, pp. 32–3.
4   E. M. Story, 'Our Fathers Have Told Us', Alexander Turnbull Library, Wellington, MS 1926, p. 192.
5   Charles Hursthouse Jnr, An Account of the Settlement of New Plymouth (Capper Press, Christchurch, 1975).
6   Nancy M. Taylor (ed.), The Journal of Ensign Best (Turnbull Library Monograph, Wellington, 1966), p. 226.
7   Jeremy Salmond, Old New Zealand Houses 1800–1940 (Reed Methuen, Auckland, 1986), p. 60.
8   Philip Cox and Clive Lucas, Australian Colonial Architecture (Lansdowne, Sydney, 1978), p. 158.
9   Fergus Clunie, 'The Pompallier Project: Progress report and recommendations', 1989, New Zealand Historic Places Trust.
10   W. H. Oliver (ed.), The Oxford History of New Zealand (Clarendon Press, Oxford / Oxford University Press, Wellington, 1981), p. 107.
11   P. Wilson, 'The Architecture of Samuel Charles Farr, 1827–1918', University of Canterbury M.A. thesis, 1982, p. 48.
12   John Stacpoole, Colonial Architecture in New Zealand (A. H. & A. W. Reed, Wellington, 1976), pp. 16–17.
13   Patricia Burns, Te Rauparaha: A New Perspective (A. H. & A. W. Reed, Auckland, 1980), p. 290.

2: The Birth of Antipodean Gothic

1   Margaret H. Alington, Frederick Thatcher and St Paul's: An Ecclesiological Study (New Zealand Historic Places Trust / Government Printer, Wellington, 1965), p. 22.
2   Jonathan Mané-Wheoki, 'Selwyn Gothic: The Formative Years', in Art New Zealand 54, Autumn 1990, pp. 76–81.
3   R. M. Ross, 'Bishop's Auckland', in Frances Porter (ed.), Historic Buildings of New Zealand: North Island (Cassell, Auckland, 1979), p. 83.
4   Alington, Frederick Thatcher, p. 22.
5   Alington, Frederick Thatcher, p. 26.
6   Ian J. Lochhead, 'Antipodean Gothic: Gilbert Scott, Benjamin Mountfort and the Medieval Vision in New Zealand', unpublished paper delivered before the Comité International d'Histoire de l'Art, XXVIIe Congrès International, Strasbourg, 1989.
7   Stacpoole, Colonial architecture, p. 55.
8   Lochhead, Antipodean Gothic.
9   John Stacpoole, William Mason: The First Colonial Architect (Auckland University Press / Oxford University Press, Auckland, 1971), p. 60.

3: Cottages, Villas and Country Houses

1   Robert Furneaux Jordan, Victorian Architecture (Penguin, London, 1966), p. 199.
2   Salmond, Old New Zealand houses, p. 112.
3   Salmond, Old New Zealand houses, p. 188.
4   Barbara Fill, Seddon's State Houses (New Zealand Historic Places Trust Monograph, Wellington, 1984), p. 16.
5   W. J. Phillipps, 'The Te Kuiti House', in Art New Zealand, December 1938, p. 87.
6   W. J. Phillipps, Carved Maori Houses of the Western and Northern Areas of New Zealand (Dominion Museum / Government Printer, Wellington, 1955), p 140.

4: The Architecture of Prosperity

1   Stacpoole, Colonial Architecture, p. 104.
2   J. Mordaunt Crook, The Greek Revival (John Murray, London, 1972), p. 17.
3   P. C. McCarthy, 'Victorian Oamaru: The Architecture of Forrester and Lemon', University of Canterbury M.A. thesis, 1986, pp. 15–16.
4   McCarthy, Victorian Oamaru, p. 70.
5   J. W. F. Cattell, 'Domestic Architecture in Christchurch and District 1850–1938', University of Canterbury M.A. thesis, 1981, p. 39.
6   Peter Richardson, 'An Architect of Empire: The Government Buildings of John Campbell in New Zealand', University of Canterbury M.A. thesis, 1988, p. 32.
7   Ian Rockel, Taking the Waters: Early Spas in New Zealand (Government Printer, Wellington, 1986), p. 30.
8   Ann McEwan, 'Alfred and Sidney Luttrell: Early Commercial Architecture in Canterbury', in Art New Zealand 51, Winter 1989, p. 96.
9   Diane Wynn-Williams, 'The Basilicas of F. W. Petre', University of Canterbury M.A. thesis, 1983, p. 43.
10   George Bernard Shaw, What I Said in New Zealand (Commercial Print, Wellington, 1934), p. 23.

11 Wynn-Williams, *F. W. Petre*, p. 97.
12 John Stacpoole and Peter Beaven, *Architecture 1820–1970* (A. H. & A. W. Reed, Wellington, 1972), p. 51.

5: Changing Influences in Domestic Architecture

1 J. W. Chapman-Taylor, 'Plas Mawr', in *New Zealand Building Progress*, February 1914, p. 895.
2 J. W. Chapman-Taylor, 'Bradshaw Housebook', 1953, Auckland University School of Architecture Library.
3 Chapman-Taylor, *New Zealand Building Progress*, February 1914, p. 895.
4 J. W. Chapman-Taylor, 'Simple Homes', in *Progress*, March 1910, p. 170.
5 Judy Siers, 'J. W. Chapman-Taylor, Architect, 1878–1958', in *N.Z.I.A. Journal*, 20 April 1968, p. 111.
6 Chapman-Taylor, *Progress*, March 1910, p. 170.
7 Samuel Hurst Seager, 'Architectural Art in New Zealand', in *Journal of the Royal Institute of British Architects*, 29 September 1900, p. 481.
8 F. de J. Clere, 'Domestic Architecture in New Zealand', in *Studio: Yearbook of Decorative Art 1916*, p. 121.
9 Ian J. Lochhead, 'The Architectural Art of Samuel Hurst Seager', in *Art New Zealand 44*, Spring 1987, p. 95.
10 *Progress*, May 1906, p. 166.
11 Gerald Jones, 'How Houses May Be Improved', in *Progress*, June 1912, p. 1133.
12 R. K. Binney, 'The English Tradition in New Zealand', in *Architectural Review*, May 1927, pp. 172–6.
13 Daniel O'Neill, *Sir Edwin Lutyens' Country Houses* (Lund Humphries, London, 1980), p. 108.
14 Robert Esau, 'Helmore and Cotterill: The Formative Years', University of Canterbury M.A. thesis, 1988, p. 39.
15 Basil Ward, Curriculum Vitae, Auckland University School of Architecture Library.
16 Binney, *English tradition*, p. 173.
17 *Progress*, September 1913, p. 653.

6: The Conservative Solution

1 *N.Z.I.A Journal*, July 1926, p. 72.
2 Karen Weitze, *California's Mission Revival* (Hennessey & Ingalls, Santa Monica, 1984), p. 71.
3 David Kernohan, *Wellington's New Buildings* (Victoria University Press, Wellington, 1989), p. 152.

4 Chris Cochran, 'A Plea for the Twenties and Thirties', in *New Zealand Architect 3*, 1980, p. 22.
5 Wayne Nelson, 'Restored with Grace', in *Historic Places in New Zealand 20*, March 1988, p. 24.
6 *Building*, 12 August 1921, p. 101.
7 Rob Ansell, *Past Tense: An Exhibition of Furniture, Applied Arts and Architectural Drawings at Vogel House*, (Wellington, 1986), p. 34.
8 Stacpoole and Beaven, *Architecture 1820–1970*, p. 74.

7: Modern, Moderne and Deco

1 *N.Z.I.A. Journal*, February 1932, p. 121.
2 *N.Z.I.A. Journal*, February 1935, pp. 73–7.
3 *N.Z.I.A. Journal*, December 1933, p. 65.
4 Ian J. Lochhead, 'New Zealand Architecture in the Thirties: The Impact of Modernism', in *Landfall 152*, vol. 38, no. 4, December 1984, p. 467.
5 Ansell, *Past tense*, p. 39.
6 *Building Today*, vol. 1, no. 1, October 1936, p. 19.
7 *Home and Building*, May 1938, p. 13.
8 *Home and Building*, August 1938, p. 24.
9 Michael King, 'A Place to Stand: A History of Turangawaewae Marae', University of Waikato Centre for Maori Studies research paper, 1981.
10 King, *Place to stand*, p. 27.
11 Wendy Fitzpatrick, 'Government Sponsored Housing in New Zealand', University of Auckland B.Arch. thesis, 1987, p. 92.
12 I. V. Porsolt, 'Broadcasting House, Durham St, Auckland, and My Share in its Design', Auckland University School of Architecture Library.
13 William Toomath, submission of New Zealand Historic Places Trust before the Town Planning Hearings Committee of the Wellington City Council, 22 March 1988.

8: The Search for the Vernacular

1 Kenneth J. Davis, 'A Liberal Turn of Mind: The Architectural Work of Gordon Wilson, 1936–1959', University of Auckland B. Arch thesis, 1987, p. 21.
2 Davis, *Gordon Wilson*, p. 28.
3 Linda Tyler, 'The Architecture of E. A. Plischke in New Zealand, 1939–1962', University of Canterbury M.A. thesis, 1986, p. 31.
4 F. H. Newman, 'New Zealand Housing in an Expanding Society', in *N.Z.I.A. Journal*, September 1959, p. 220.
5 *Building Progress*, 1 November 1947, p. 7.

6   Fred Beckett, Biographical sketch of Vernon Brown, University of Auckland School of Architecture Library.

7   Richard C. Peters, 'William Wilson Wurster: An Architect of Houses', in Sally Woodbridge, *Bay Area Houses* (Oxford University Press, New York, 1976), p. 121.

8   Paul Pascoe and Humphrey Hall, 'The Modern House', in *Landfall*, vol. 1, no. 1, 1947, p. 121.

9   Robyn Ussher, 'The Modern Movement in Canterbury: The Architecture of Paul Pascoe', University of Canterbury M.A. thesis, 1986, p. 63.

10   Tyler, *E. A. Plischke*, p. 114.

11   I. V. Porsolt, 'Henry Kulka: Architect', in *Landfall 49*, September 1971, p. 290.

12   *Home and Building*, February/March 1951, p. 36.

13   Nikolaus Pevsner, 'New Architecture and New Art', in New Zealand *Listener*, 26 December 1958, p. 4.

14   Ussher, *Modern Movement*, p. 135.

15   David Mitchell and Gillian Chaplin, *The Elegant Shed: New Zealand Architecture since 1945* (Oxford University Press, Auckland, 1984), p. 64.

16   *Home and Building*, September 1960, p. 50.

9: Architecture as Individualism

1   *Home and Building*, 1 September 1955, p. 22.

2   *N.Z.I.A. Journal*, August 1974, p. 158.

3   Miles Warren, 'Style in New Zealand Architecture', in *New Zealand Architect 3*, 1978, p. 4.

4   *Warren & Mahoney Architects* (Warren & Mahoney, Christchurch, 1989), p. 2.

5   *Home and Building*, April/May 1950, p. 21.

6   *N.Z.I.A. Journal*, October 1974, p. 205.

7   Warren, *New Zealand Architect 3*, 1978, p. 10.

8   *Dominion*, 24 April 1970.

9   Gerald Melling, *Positively Architecture!* (Square One Press, Dunedin, 1985), p. 52.

10   Mitchell and Chaplin, *Elegant shed*, p. 70.

11   Mitchell and Chaplin, *Elegant shed*, p. 40.

12   *N.Z.I.A. Journal*, vol. 32, no. 9, p. 313.

13   Keith Cronshaw, 'Peter Beaven: Turrets All Over Town', in New Zealand *Listener*, 9 March 1974, p. 15.

14   *Building Progress*, March 1970, p. 34.

15   Mitchell and Chaplin, *Elegant shed*, p. 55.

16   *Warren & Mahoney*, p. 13.

17   Mitchell and Chaplin, *Elegant shed*, p. 52.

18   *Auckland Architectural Association Journal 2*, December 1979, p. 9.

19   *A.A.A. Journal 2*, December 1979, p. 10.

10: Experiment, Debate and Demolition

1   Kernohan, *Wellington's new buildings*, p. 66.

2   *New Zealand Architect 5*, 1986, p. 25.

3   Kernohan, *Wellington's new buildings*, p. 26.

4   *Architecture NZ*, March/April 1988, p. 38.

5   *Architecture NZ*, November/December 1989, p. 38.

6   Rob Ansell, 'Classicism in Wellington', in *Architecture NZ*, July/August 1989, p. 64.

7   Charles Jencks, *Architecture Now* (Harry N. Abrams, New York, 1988), p. 74.

8   *New Home Trends*, vol. 5, no. 2, p. 36.

9   Pete Bossley, 'Pervan House: A Familiar Image?', in *New Zealand Architect 1*, 1986, p. 7.

10   *Architecture NZ*, September/October 1989, p. 35.

11   Nigel Cook, 'The Language of Housing', in *Architecture NZ*, November/December 1988, p. 40.

12   *Architecture NZ*, March/April 1989, p. 20.

13   *Architecture NZ*, May/June 1988, p. 53.

14   Mitchell and Chaplin, *Elegant shed*, p. 100.

ABUTMENT   a masonry mass which receives the thrust of an arch, vault or strut.

ACROTERION   originally a pedestal for a statue at the apex of a pediment of a Greek temple; the term also refers to both the pedestal and the ornament (frequently the scalloped acanthus leaf) that surmounts it.

AEDICULE   the framing of a door or window with two columns, piers or pilasters supporting an entablature and pediment.

AMBULATORY   literally a 'place for walking in', specifically, a processional aisle behind the high altar. Usually found in large, aisled churches.

AMO   the upright supports of the lower ends of the maihi on the front gable of a whare.

APSE   the semicircular or polygonal space at the end of the chancel, which houses the altar.

ARCADE   a line of arches raised on columns or piers, either free standing or blind.

ARCHITRAVE   the moulded frame surrounding a door or window. In Classical architecture, the lowest part of the entablature. See ORDER.

ART DECO   the decorative style that takes its name from the Exposition Internationale des Arts Decoratifs et Industriels Modernes, held at Paris in 1925. Widely used in the architecture of the 1930s, it is characterised by angular or zigzag surface forms or ornaments.

ART NOUVEAU   a style of decoration in architecture and the applied arts developed principally in France and Belgium in the 1890s. Characterised by organic, dynamic forms and long, sinuous lines, it was popular in Great Britain and the U.S.A. See JUGENDSTIL.

ARTS AND CRAFTS   An English movement in the applied arts and architecture during the second half of the nineteenth century. It emphasised the importance of craftsmanship in the face of increasing industrialisation.

ATRIUM   the main inner court of a Roman house, open to the sky.

BALUSTER   a short post or pillar in a series, supporting a rail and thus forming a balustrade.

BALUSTRADE   a railing system found along the edge of a balcony.

BARGEBOARD   a (frequently decorated) board that hangs from the projecting end of a roof and hides the horizontal roof timbers.

BARREL VAULT   a continuous semicircular arch or tunnel of brick, stone or concrete. Also known as a TUNNEL VAULT.

BAS RELIEF   see RELIEF.

BASILICA   a church divided into a central high nave, lit by a clerestory, and two or more aisles along its sides. It often has a vestibule.

BAY WINDOW   see WINDOW.

BEADING   a narrow, moulded wooden strip that ornaments a surface. Often used as a framing device and found, for example, on the edge of a pane of glass or at the point against which a door or window sash closes.

BEARER   any horizontal beam, joist or member that supports a load.

BLIND PANEL   a screen to obstruct vision or keep out light.

BOARD-AND-BATTEN CONSTRUCTION   a type of wall cladding consisting of closely spaced boards, the joints of which are covered by narrow wooden strips (battens).

BRACE   see ROOF.

BRACKET   a small piece of stone or wood designed to carry a projecting weight (e.g., a cornice).

BRACKETED CORNICE   see CORNICE.

BROKEN GABLE   see GABLE.

BRUTALISM   a movement in modern architecture that emphasises stark forms and raw surfaces, particularly of concrete. The term was coined in England in 1954.

BULB PILE   a cast-in-place pile, constructed so that some concrete is forced out at the bottom of the casing, forming a pedestal or bulb shape at the foot of the pile. Also known as a pedestal pile.

BUNGALOW   a one-storey, frame house, often provided with verandahs.

BUTTRESS   a mass of masonry or brick work, projecting from or built against a wall to give added strength. The FLYING BUTTRESS is a feature characteristic of Gothic architecture, in which lateral thrusts of a roof or vault are taken up by a straight bar of masonry carried on an arch, and a solid pier or buttress sufficient to receive the thrust.

CAMPANARIO   the bell tower on a Spanish Mission building.

CAMPANILE   a bell tower, often free standing.

CANTILEVER   a beam, girder, truss or other structural member that projects beyond its supporting wall.

CAPITAL   the head or crowning feature, usually decorated, of a column or pilaster. See ORDER.

CARPENTER GOTHIC   a style, first popular in the U.S.A. during the mid-nineteenth century, characterised by the application of elaborate Gothic motifs in wood.

CARTOUCHE   a carved or painted ornamental panel resembling a sheet of paper with its edges turned over.

CASEMENT WINDOW   see WINDOW.

CASTELLATION   a form of ornamentation in which a house is given crenellated battlements like those of a fortified castle.

CHAMFER   an angle or edge cut off diagonally.

CHANCEL   the eastern end of a church, reserved for the clergy. Often raised a few steps from the nave and separated from it by a screen, the chancel is also known as the SANCTUARY.

CHINOISERIE   a French term referring to the appropriation of Chinese designs for furniture or architectural ornament.

CLADDING   the finish covering of the exterior wall of a frame building.

CLASSICAL ARCHITECTURE   the architecture of Hellenic Greece and Imperial Rome, on which that of the Italian Renaissance and many subsequent styles, such as the Baroque and Greek Revival, were based. See ORDER.

CLASSICISM   architecture that gives emphasis to the correct use of Greek, Roman or Italian Renaissance principles.

CLERE VOIR   a semicircular slatted panel designed to break up a solid verandah wall.

CLERESTORY   the upper zone of a wall, pierced by windows that admit light into a church or room.

COB   a mixture of clay, water, grasses and animal manure, compressed into layers to form walls.

COFFERED CEILING   one which has deeply recessed square or polygonal panels, often highly decorated.

COLLAR BEAM   see ROOF.

COLONNADE   a row of columns supporting an entablature, arches or a roof.

COLUMN   in Classical architecture, a cylindrical support consisting of base, shaft and capital. See ORDER.

COLUMN-AND-BEAM CONSTRUCTION a structural method based on a vertical column supporting a horizontal beam.

COMPOSITE PILASTER   a pilaster the capital of which is decorated with a Roman elaboration of the Greek Corinthian order, which combines its distinctive acanthus leaves with the Ionic order's volutes.

CONSOLE   a decorative bracket in the form of a vertical scroll that projects from a wall to support a cornice, or a door or window head.

CONSTRUCTIVISM   the Russian art movement that flourished between 1913 and 1921 and that at first concentrated on abstractly conceived relief constructions made in wire, glass and sheet metal, but later embraced both architectural and engineering schemes.

COPING   a protective cap at the top of a wall, parapet, or chimney. It may be flat, sloping or curved and is designed to protect the masonry from water penetration.

CORBEL   a projection or stepped series of projections, used to support an overhanging member.

CORDOVA TILE   a curved, terracotta-coloured tile much used in Spanish Mission style architecture.

CORINTHIAN ORDER   the slenderest and most ornate of the three Greek orders, characterised by a bell-shaped capital with two rows of sculptured acanthus leaves and an elaborate cornice. See ORDER.

CORNICE   a moulded projection crowning a building, wall or arch. In Classical architecture the term refers specifically to the top, projecting section of an entablature. The weight of a BRACKETED CORNICE is supported by projecting members. See ORDER.

COVED CEILING   one that has a concave moulding produced by the sloped or arched junction of wall and ceiling.

CRENELLATION   the crenels of a fortified parapet are the open indentations which alternate with the solid portions, called merlons.

CRESTING   decoration along the ridges of a roof, often with perforated tiles.

CROW-STEPPED GABLE   see GABLE.

CUPOLA   a domed roof on a circular base, often set on the ridge of a roof.

CYMA RECTA   a moulding with a double curvature that is concave at the outer edge and convex at the inner edge.

CYMA REVERSA   a moulding with a double curvature that is convex at the outer edge and concave at the inner edge.

DADO   a protective ornamental panelling applied to the lower walls of a room.

DECORATED GOTHIC   the second of three phases of English Gothic architecture, from c. 1280 to c. 1350, it was preceded by Early English and followed by Perpendicular Gothic. It was characterised by rich decoration and tracery.

DENTIL   one of a band of small, square, tooth-like blocks that form part of the characteristic ornamentation of cornices on Greek and Roman buildings. A frequently used decorative feature, they can often be found on the cornices of wooden villas in New Zealand. See ORDER.

DORIC ORDER   the plainest and sturdiest of the three orders, the Doric has a fluted column with a simple capital. See ORDER.

DORMER WINDOW   see WINDOW.

DOUBLE-HUNG SASH WINDOW   see WINDOW.

DRIPSTONE   a stone or wood moulding that projects over and around the head of a doorway or window and throws off rainwater.

DRUM   a circular, square or polygonal wall supporting a dome.

DUTCH GABLE   see GABLE.

EARLY ENGLISH GOTHIC   the first of the three English phases of Gothic architecture, from c. 1180 to c. 1280, based on Norman antecedents and succeeded by the Decorated style.

EAVES   the part of a roof that projects beyond the wall.

EDWARDIAN BAROQUE   an early twentieth-century movement roughly corresponding to the reign of Edward VII (1902–10) in England, which looked back to the buildings of the English Renaissance of the sixteenth and seventeenth centuries, particularly the work of Wren and Hawksmoor. The style was popular in New Zealand public building because of its associations with English imperial grandeur.

ENGAGED COLUMN   a column partially built into a wall, not free standing.

ENGLISH DOMESTIC REVIVAL   a movement in the second half of the nineteenth century. It was closely linked to the Arts and Crafts movement and encouraged interest in English medieval and Tudor domestic architecture.

ENTABLATURE   In Classical architecture, the elaborated beam carried by columns, and divided horizontally into architrave frieze and cornice. See ORDER.

EPA   posts at the ends of a whare, between the poupou and pou tahu.

FACADE   the exterior face or front of a building.

FACING   the finish applied to the outer surface of a building.

FAIR-FACE   a smooth surface, usually brick or concrete.

FALE   a Samoan house, traditionally open-sided and constructed on an elliptical base.

FANLIGHT   a small window opening over a larger casement or sash window.

FASCIA   a plain, horizontal band, often under the eaves of a roof or under an architrave. See ORDER.

FENESTRATION   the arrangement of windows on a facade.

FESTOON   see SWAG.

FINIAL   a tall, thin ornament placed at the apex of a gable.

FLYING BUTTRESS   see BUTTRESS.

FOLIATED WINDOW   see WINDOW.

FRENCH WINDOW   see WINDOW.

FRETWORK   open or interlaced work in relief, often elaborately ornamental and contrasting dark patterning against light.

FRIEZE   The middle division of an entablature, between the architrave and the cornice. Also a decorated band immediately below the cornice of an interior wall. See ORDER.

GABLE   a vertical, triangular-shaped wall at the end of a ridged roof, reaching from eaves level to apex. A BROKEN GABLE is split at the centre, and the gap may be filled with an urn or other ornament. A CROW-STEPPED or DUTCH GABLE has a stepped coping.

GEORGIAN ARCHITECTURE   British architecture during the period of George I to George IV (1714–1820). Its earlier phase is called Palladian and its later phase is called Regency, but it always followed Classical tradition.

GIANT ORDER   see ORDER.

GIRDER   a horizontal supporting beam.

GOTHIC   the architectural style which prevailed in Western Europe from c. 1200 to the beginning of the renaissance of Classical architecture that began in Italy in the fifteeenth century and spread north during the sixteenth century. Its most distinctive feature was the pointed arch.

GOTHIC REVIVAL   the late eighteenth-century revival of the Gothic style. It lasted for almost a century and was concurrent with the Greek Revival.

GREEK REVIVAL   an architectural style that had its origins in archaeological research done in Greece in the late eighteenth century. Its major figures were the Germans Schinkel and Klenze, Charles 'Athenian' Stuart in England and William Playfair and Thomas Hamilton, who transformed Edinburgh into the 'Athens of the North'.

HALF TIMBERING   a method of construction in which the walls have a timber framework with spaces filled with plaster or brick.

HAMMER BEAM   see ROOF.

HEKE   a rafter.

HEXASTYLE   having six columns, for example, at one end of a portico.

HIGH RELIEF   see RELIEF.

HIGH RENAISSANCE   the short period lasting from c. 1500 to c. 1527, during which the ideal balance between form and technique is generally held to have occurred, particularly in the work of Leonardo da Vinci, Raphael and Michelangelo.

HIPPED ROOF   a roof which slopes upward from all four sides of a building.

HOOD   a cover placed above an opening or an object as a means of sheltering it.

IN ANTIS   a term used of columns set within a portico, or of the portico itself.

INGLENOOK   the space on either side of a fireplace or within the fireplace opening, often provided with seating.

INTERNATIONAL STYLE   often used synonymously with the term Modernism to refer to the functional architecture created by such figures as Le Corbusier and Walter Gropius in Western Europe and the United States and applied throughout the world. It was characterised by white-rendered cubic shapes, the absence of mouldings, and large windows arranged in bands.

IONIC ORDER   a column characterised by a capital with large volutes. See ORDER.

JAMB   the straight, vertical side of a door or window frame.

JOIST   horizontal timber, concrete or steel beams laid parallel to each other to support floor or ceiling loads.

JUGENDSTIL   literally 'youth style': the German term for Art Nouveau.

KAHO   a batten laid horizontally on the rafters of a whare to support the various layers of roof thatch.

KAINGA   an unfortified place of residence.

KING POST   see ROOF.

KNEE BRACE   a corner brace placed diagonally to strengthen the connection between two joined members.

KORURU   a figure placed at the apex of the gable of a whare.

KOWHAIWHAI   a patterned form of painted ornamentation.

LANCET WINDOW   a narrow window with a sharply pointed arch, characteristic of Early English Gothic architecture.

LANTERN   a windowed superstructure crowning a roof or dome.

LATH   a strip of wood, fixed to a frame, that serves as a base for plastering.

LIGHT   any aperture through which daylight is admitted. A pane of glass is often referred to as a light.

LINTEL   a beam bridging an opening.

MAIHI   facing boards on the gable of a whare, the extending lower ends of which are usually carved.

MATCHLINING   thin boards that have a tongue along one edge and a groove along the other, so that they can fit together and hold securely.

METOPE   the flat panel between the triglyphs on the Doric frieze of an entablature, often carved. See ORDER.

MINSTRELS' GALLERY   a small balcony inside a church or house, usually over the entrance.

MITRED GLASS   when two pieces of glass are positioned edge to edge and the oblique surface of each forms a right angle, allowing them to fit securely together.

MODERNE   a style characterised by the application of Art Deco ornamentation and often used synonymously with that term. It also refers, with a slightly derogatory overtone, to the work of those architects who decorated cubic Modernist forms with Art Deco motifs in order to appear less avant-garde.

MODERNISM   see INTERNATIONAL STYLE.

MODILLION   a horizontal bracket, often in the form of a carved scroll, supporting a cornice or eaves.

MOULDING   continuous lines ornamentally grooved (concave) or projected (convex).

MULLION   a vertical bar of wood or stone dividing a window opening into lights.

NAVE   the main body of a church, intended primarily for the laity and distinct from the chancel.

NEO-CLASSICISM   the last phase of European Classicism in the late eighteenth and nineteenth centuries. Characterised by monumentality, strict use of the orders and sparing application of ornament.

NEO-GEORGIAN   this term refers to the revival of Georgian architectural style. It was encouraged by Sir Edwin Lutyens in the years immediately preceding the First World War and was taken up again in the 1920s and 1930s, when architects and clients resistant to Modernism found in the characteristic restraint and balance of Georgian architecture a happy compromise.

NOGGING   the practice of tightly fixing short pieces of framing timber between studs, to which lining materials can then be applied.

OGEE TOWER   a tower which has a double curvature, both concave and convex.

OPEN-BED PEDIMENT   see PEDIMENT.

ORDER   a column with base, shaft, capital and entablature. In Classical architecture there were five orders: the Greek Doric, Ionic and Corinthian order, and the Roman Tuscan and Composite orders. A GIANT ORDER is more than one storey in height.

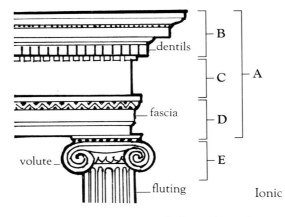

A entablature; **B** cornice; **C** frieze; **D** architrave; **E** capital.

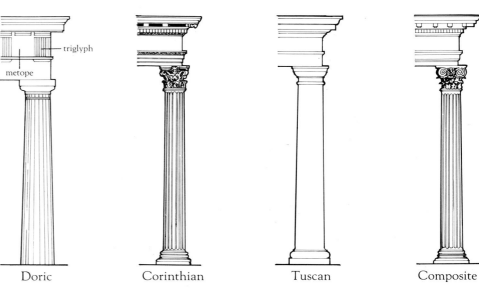

Doric   Corinthian   Tuscan   Composite

ORIEL WINDOW   see WINDOW.

PA   a fortified place.

PALISADE   a series of stout poles, pointed on top and driven into the earth, used as a fence or fortification.

PALLADIAN WINDOW   see WINDOW.

PAPAKA   slabs placed horizontally between the uprights of walls and forming a skirting board inside a whare.

PARAPET   a low wall at any point of a sudden drop, as at the edge of a terrace, roof, battlement or balcony.

PATAKA   a food storehouse raised on posts.

PEDENTIVE   one of a set of curved wall surfaces that form a transition between a dome, or its drum, and the supporting masonry.

PEDESTAL PILE   see BULB PILE.

PEDIMENT   in Classical architecture, the triangular gable at the end of a roof; now a surface used ornamentally over doors or windows, usually triangular but occasionally curved. An OPEN-BED PEDIMENT has a gap in the base moulding. A SEGMENTAL PEDIMENT is in the shape of an arc. See ORDER.

PELMET   a cornice built into the head of a window to conceal drapery fittings.

PENDANT   an ornamental terminal, elongated so that it hangs downwards.

PERGOLA   a covered walk in a garden or attached to a house. It is usually formed by a double row of trellis work or posts with joists and covered with climbing plants.

PERISTYLE   a row of columns around a building or courtyard.

PERPENDICULAR GOTHIC   the last of the three English phases of Gothic architecture, from c. 1330 to c. 1550. It was characterised by vertical emphasis and elaborate fan vaulting.

PIER   a solid masonry support.

PILASTER   a shallow pier or rectangular column that projects slightly from a wall and may be decorated with one of the Classical orders.

PILOTIS   the pillars that support a building in such a way as to raise it to first-floor level, leaving the ground floor open.

PINNACLE   an ornamental, pyramidal or conical termination, crowning spires, buttresses or the angles of parapets.

PISE   a mixture of earth, gravel and water, rammed into some form of casing with a special tool called a pisoir.

POLYCHROMY   the practice of decorating architectural elements in a variety of colours. It was particularly fashionable on Victorian Gothic buildings but was largely ignored by English Greek Revivalists, despite the revelation that ancient Greek architecture was brightly, even gaudily, painted.

PORTAL   an impressive or monumental entrance gate or door to a building, often decorated.

PORTE COCHERE   a porch large enough to let a vehicle pass through it.

PORTICO   a roofed space, either open or partially enclosed, which forms the entrance and centrepiece of the facade of a house, temple or church.

POST-MODERNISM   a style established during the 1970s and 1980s as a reaction to the bland brick or concrete architecture that was the eventual heritage of Modernism. The title of the Philadelphia architect Robert Venturi's 1966 book *Complexity and Contradiction in Architecture* sums up the essence of Post-modernism, which was to encourage historical allusiveness, wit and craftsmanship.

POU   an upright supporting the ridgepole of a whare. The POU TAHU is the main post in the centre of the front wall, the POU TOKOMANAWA supports the middle portion of the ridgepole, and the POU TUARONGO is the main post in the middle of the back wall.

POU RAHUI   a post raised to warn people against infringing a tapu.

POUPOU   the upright parts of a solid wall framework of a whare.

PURLIN   see ROOF.

QUEEN ANNE STYLE   English Renaissance domestic architecture of Queen Anne's reign (1702–14). A revival of the style took place in the later years of the nineteenth century, its prime mover being Richard Norman Shaw.

QUEEN POSTS   see ROOF.

QUOIN   either the external angle of a building or wall, or the large corner stones used at the angle. These are usually either dressed or, in New Zealand, are of wood to imitate stone.

RAFTER   see ROOF.

RAPARAPA   the (frequently carved) projecting portion of the maihi, or bargeboards, of a whare.

RELIEF   a sculpture which is not free standing, but is carved either in HIGH RELIEF, i.e., is almost detached from its ground, or BAS RELIEF, which is much flatter.

RENAISSANCE CLASSICAL   the architectural style deriving from the revival of classical architectural forms during the fifteenth to seventeenth centuries.

RENDER   to apply a coat of plaster directly on to brick or stone work.

RENDERING   a shaded perspective or elevational drawing of an architectural project with the delineation of materials.

REREDOS   a wall or screen behind an altar, usually decorated.

REVEAL   the side of an opening for a door or window, between the frame and the outer surface of the wall.

RIDGEPOLE   the post that supports the ridge or horizontal line at the junction of the upper edges of two sloping roof surfaces of a whare.

ROOF

The COLLAR BEAM is a horizontal beam that ties together and stiffens two opposite rafters. The HAMMER BEAM is one of a pair of short horizontal members attached to the foot of a rafter and used in place of a tie beam. The KING POST stands on the tie or collar beam and supports the ridge. A PURLIN is a piece of timber laid horizontally on the principle rafters to support the commom rafters. The QUEEN POSTS are a pair of posts placed on a tie or collar beam, connecting it with the rafters. A RAFTER is a timber sloping up from the wall plate to the ridge. A STRUT is a timber connecting the king or queen post to the rafter. The TIE BEAM is a horizontal timber that connects two opposite rafters at their lower ends.

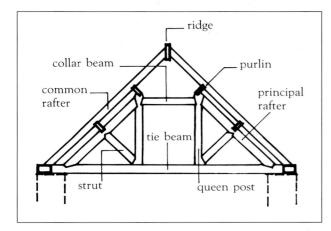

ROSE WINDOW   in Gothic architecture, a circular window filled with tracery to resemble a rose.

ROUGHCAST CONCRETE   an exterior finish formed by dashing crushed rock or pebbles into unset concrete.

RUSTICATION   originally, the working of external blocks of stone with a hammer to give a rough surface. A later meaning refers to smooth blocks which have recessed margins, accentuating the joins between blocks of stone.

SADDLEBACK ROOF   one which has two gables and one ridge, like a saddle.

SANCTUARY   see CHANCEL.

SARKING   thin boards used to line roofs.

SASH WINDOW   see WINDOW.

SCISSOR TRUSS   a type of truss used to support a pitched roof. The ties cross each other and are connected to the opposite rafters at an intermediate point along their length.

SCOTIA   a deep concave moulding.

SCRIBER   a thin batten with one edge cut to the shape of the wall-covering material and fixed to the edge of an architrave or boxed corner to exclude water.

SCRIM   a coarse, open-weave, mesh-like material such as heavy cloth, wire or fibreglass, used as a base for wallpaper, plaster or paint.

SCROLL   an ornament or moulding in the form of a scroll of paper.

SECESSION   see SEZESSION.

SEGMENTAL PEDIMENT   see PEDIMENT.

SEZESSION   the name given to a group of artists and architects in Berlin, Munich, Darmstadt and particularly Vienna who resigned from established academic institutions to encourage a number of modern movements. After 1900 the designs which Josef-Maria Olbrich applied to the severe forms of his Sezession Building in Vienna were imitated throughout the world. Also known as SECESSION.

SHUTTER   a movable screen used to cover an opening, especially a window.

SIDELIGHT   a framed area of fixed glass alongside a door or window opening.

SKILLION   a single-pitched (lean-to) roof attached to a building to enclose additional rooms.

SKIRTING   a timber board fixed around the edge of a room to cover the junction between wall and floor.

SOFFIT   the exposed under-surface of any overhead component, such as an arch, balcony, beam, cornice, lintel or vault.

SPANDREL   the triangular space between the sides of an arch and the horizontal and vertical on either side. On multi-storeyed buildings the term also refers to the wall panel which fills the space between the top of the window on one storey and the sill of the window in the storey above.

STEPPED GABLE   see GABLE.

STRAPWORK   a type of ornament consisting of a narrow fillet or band which is folded, crossed and interlaced.

STRING COURSE   a horizontal band of masonry extending across a facade. It may be flush or projecting; it can be flat-surfaced, moulded or carved.

STUD   an upright support, usually part of a series, that acts as support for a wall or partition.

STRUT   see ROOF.

SWAG   a carved ornament in the form of a garland of fruit or flowers and suspended at both ends in a loop. The term sometimes refers to a carved piece of cloth draped over two supports. Also known as a FESTOON.

TABERNACLE   an ornamented recess to contain holy relics or a free-standing canopy.

TAHU   the ridgepole of a whare.

TAPATU   the process of thatching the roof of a whare.

TEKOTEKO   the carved figure at the apex of the gable of a whare.

GLOSSARY

TERM   a pedestal merging at the top into a sculpted figure.

TERRAZZO   a flooring finish of marble chips mixed with cement mortar, its surface ground and polished.

TIE BEAM   see ROOF.

TOURELLE   a small tower characteristically corbelled from a corner.

TRABEATED   construction using beams and posts.

TRACERY   curvilinear openwork shapes of stone or wood, creating a pattern within the upper part of a Gothic window. Similar patterns can be applied to walls or panels.

TRANSEPT   the transverse portion of a church crossing the main axis at a right angle and producing a cruciform plan.

TRIGLYPHS   the blocks separating the metopes on a Doric frieze. See ORDER.

TRUSS   a rigid framework.

TUKUTUKU   ornamental lattice work on panels between the poupou in a whare.

TUNNEL VAULT   see BARREL VAULT.

VENETIAN GOTHIC   the Gothic architecture to be found in the city of Venice, particularly admired by John Ruskin (1819–1900), whose book *The Stones of Venice* (1851) gave great encouragement to the English Gothic Revival.

VERMICULATION   an ornamental imitation on stone facings of the tracks made by wood worm.

VESTIBULE   an entrance hall, antechamber or lobby.

VESTRY   a robing room in a church, in which vestments and sacred vessels are kept.

VILLA   in Roman times, a farm-house serving a country estate; in the Italian Renaissance, a country house surrounded by gardens; in nineteenth-century England, a detached suburban house; in late nineteenth- and early twentieth-century New Zealand, a medium-sized wooden house with a central corridor, often decorated with elaborately balustraded verandahs.

VOLUTE   the spiral scroll which forms the distinctive feature of the Ionic capital. See ORDER.

VOUSSOIR   one of the wedge-shaped stones of an arch.

WEATHERBOARD   a type of wood siding commonly used in New Zealand as an exterior covering. It consists of boards, each of which fits under an overlapping board.

WHAKAMAHAU   the porch of a whare.

WHARE   the generic Maori term for a house, hut, shed or habitation. There were many specific types of whare designated according to function.

WINDOW   There are many forms of window used in New Zealand architecture. A BAY WINDOW is a projection of a house, filled with windows; if the projection is curved it may be called a BOW WINDOW. A CASEMENT WINDOW is hung to a frame but hinges on its vertical side. A DORMER WINDOW projects from a sloping roof, and is placed in a gable. A FOLIATED WINDOW is adorned with leafage, as on Gothic tracery. A FRENCH WINDOW is a long, glazed door, opening in two leaves as a pair. A LANCET WINDOW is tall and narrow with an acutely pointed head, as used in Early English Gothic architecture. A LANTERN WINDOW is a windowed superstructure, crowning a roof or dome. A MULLIONED WINDOW has uprights dividing it into two or more lights. An ORIEL WINDOW projects from an upper storey and is supported by brackets or corbelling. A PALLADIAN WINDOW has three openings, the central one arched and wider than the other two. A ROSE WINDOW is circular and filled with tracery to resemble a rose. A SASH WINDOW is double-hung and slides vertically.

WUNDERLICH CEILING   an ornamented pressed-zinc or pressed-steel ceiling made in Australia by Ernest Wunderlich.

Alington, Margaret H., *Frederick Thatcher and St Paul's: An Ecclesiological Study*, New Zealand Historic Places Trust / Government Printer, Wellington, 1965.

Alington, Margaret H., *Goodly Stones and Timbers: A History of St Mary's Church, New Plymouth*, St Mary's Church, New Plymouth, 1988.

Andrews, Wayne (ed.), *Architecture in America: A Photographic History from the Colonial Period to the Present*, Atheneum Publishers, New York, 1960.

Angas, G. F., *The New Zealanders Illustrated*, Thomas McLean, London, 1846.

Architectural Heritage of Christchurch 3: McLean's Mansion, Christchurch City Council Town Planning Division, 1983.

Architectural Heritage of Christchurch 4: Cranmer Club, Christchurch City Council Town Planning Division, 1985.

Architectural Record Magazine (eds.), *Record Houses of 1970*, McGraw Hill, New York, 1970.

Architectural Record Magazine (eds.), *The Second Treasury of Contemporary Houses*, F. W. Dodge, New York, 1959.

Architecture of Denmark, The, Architectural Press, London, 1949.

Arnell, Peter and Bickford, Ted (eds.), *Charles Gwathmey and Robert Siegel Buildings and Projects 1964–1984*, Harper & Row, New York, 1984.

Banham, Rayner, *The New Brutalism*, Architectural Press, London, 1966.

Bovey, Des and McDonald, Kathleen, *Wanganui Buildings of Historic Interest*, John McIndoe, Dunedin, 1979.

Brocklebank, N. and Greenaway, R., *Oamaru*, John McIndoe, Dunedin, 1979.

Building Professionals of New Zealand 1988–1989, Images Pacific, 1989.

Burns, Patricia, *Te Rauparaha: A New Perspective*, A. H. & A. W. Reed, Auckland, 1980.

Burns, Ruth A., *Ivey Hall, Lincoln College: A Pictorial Comment*, Christchurch, 1977.

Carpentry in New Zealand, Government Printer, Wellington, 1958.

Coe, Peter and Reading, Malcolm, *Lubetkin and Tecton: Architecture and Social Commitment*, Arts Council of Great Britain, London, 1981.

Collins, R. and Entwisle, P., *Pavilioned in Splendour: George O'Brien's Vision of Colonial New Zealand*, Dunedin Public Art Gallery, Dunedin, 1986.

Cox, Philip and Lucas, Clive, *Australian Colonial Architecture*, Lansdowne, Sydney, 1978.

Crook, J. Mordaunt, *The Greek Revival*, John Murray, London, 1972.

Dansk Form: Saertryk af Arkitektur, Arkitektens Forlag, Copenhagen, 1958.

Davey, Peter, *Arts and Crafts Architecture: The Search for Earthly Paradise*, Architectural Press, London, 1980.

Docking, Gil, *200 Years of New Zealand Painting*, Lansdowne, Melbourne, 1971.

Dunster, David (ed.), *Architectural Monograph No. 5: Michael Graves*, Academy Editions, London, 1979.

Fearnley, Charles, Vintage Wellington, John McIndoe, Dunedin, 1979.

Firth, Cedric, *State Housing in New Zealand*, Ministry of Works, Wellington, 1949.

Fowler, Michael and Van de Voort, Robert, *The New Zealand House*, Lansdowne Press, Auckland, 1983.

Galer, Lois, *Bricks and Mortar*, Allied Press Dunedin, 1983.

Galer, Lois, *Houses and Homes*, Allied Press Dunedin, 1981.

Galer, Lois, *More Houses and Homes*, Allied Press Dunedin, 1981.

Geretsegger, Heinz and Peintner, Max, *Otto Wagner 1841–1918: The Expanding City*, Academy Editions, London, 1979.

Glancey, Jonathan, *New British Architecture*, Thames & Hudson, London, 1989.

Gray, A. Stuart, *Edwardian Architecture: A Biographical Dictionary*, Duckworth, London, 1985.

Griffiths, G. J., et al, *Otago Boys' High and Its Historic Neighbourhood*, Otago Heritage Books, Dunedin, 1983.

Gustavson, Barry, *From the Cradle to the Grave: A Biography of Michael Joseph Savage*, Reed Methuen, Auckland, 1986.

Gutheim, Frederick, *Alvar Aalto*, George Braziller, New York, 1960.

Hamilton, A., *Maori Art*, New Zealand Institute, Wellington, 1901.

Hammond, Janny, *Bush Carpenters: Pioneer Houses in New Zealand*, John McIndoe, Dunedin, 1979.

Hayward, Bruce W., *Granite and Marble: A Guide to Building Stones in New Zealand*, Geological Society of New Zealand, Wellington, 1987.

Hendry, J. A. and Mair, A. J., *Homes of the Pioneers*, Caxton Press, Christchurch, 1968.

Hendry, J. A. and Mair, A. J., *More Homes of the Pioneers*, Caxton Press, Christchurch, 1974.

Hodgson, Terence E. R., *Charles Tilleard Natusch: A Folio of Houses*, 1979.

A SELECT BIBLIOGRAPHY

Hodgson, Terence E. R., *Fire and Decay: The Destruction of the Large New Zealand House*, Alister Taylor, Martinborough, 1978.

Hodgson, Terence E. R., *Holly Lea 1899–1900*, 1976.

Hursthouse, Charles, Jnr, *An Account of the Settlement of New Plymouth*, Capper Press, Christchurch, 1975.

Jencks, Charles, *Architecture Now*, Harry N. Abrams, New York, 1988.

Jencks, Charles, *Current Architecture*, Academy Editions, London, 1982.

Jencks, Charles, *Modern Movements in Architecture*, Penguin, London, 1985.

Jencks, Charles, *The Language of Postmodern Architecture*, Rizzoli, New York, 1977.

Jordan, Robert Furneaux, *Victorian Architecture*, Penguin, London, 1966.

Kaplan, Wendy, *The Art That Is Life: The Arts and Crafts Movement in America 1875–1920*, Museum of Fine Arts, Boston, 1987.

Kemp, Jim, *American Vernacular: Regional Influences in Architecture and Interior Design*, Viking Penguin, New York, 1987.

Kernohan, David, *Wellington's New Buildings*, Victoria University Press, Wellington, 1989.

King, Michael, *Te Puea: A Biography*, Hodder & Stoughton, Auckland, 1977.

Klotz, Heinrich, *Twentieth Century Architecture*, Academy Editions, London, 1989.

Knight, C. R., *The Selwyn Churches of Auckland*, A. H. & A. W. Reed, Auckland, 1972.

Knox, Ray (ed.), *New Zealand's Heritage*, Paul Hamlyn / Whitcombe & Tombs, Wellington, 1972.

Koch, Alexander (ed.), *Neutra: World and Dwelling*, Alec Tiranti, London, 1962.

Kornwolf, James D. M. H., *Baillie Scott and the Arts and Crafts Movement*, John Hopkins Press, Baltimore and London, 1972.

Kulka, Heinrich, *Adolf Loos: Das Werk Architekten*, Verlag Von Anton Schroll, Vienna, 1931.

Living With the Past: Historical Buildings of the Waimari District, Waimari District Council.

Lochhead, Ian and Mané, Jonathan (eds.), *W. B. Armson: A Colonial Architect Re-discovered*, Robert McDougall Art Gallery, Christchurch, 1983.

Making New Zealand: Pictorial Surveys of a Century, Department of Internal Affairs, Wellington, 1940.

McArdle, Alma de C. and Bartlett, Deidre, *Carpenter Gothic: Nineteenth Century Ornamented Houses of New Jersey*, Whitney Library of Design / Watson Guptill Publications, New York, 1978.

McGregor, Miriam, *Early Stations of Hawke's Bay*, A. H. & A. W. Reed, Auckland, 1970.

Mee, Revd Peter R., *St Joseph's Cathedral, Dunedin, New Zealand: Centennial Year 1886–1986*, Tablet Printing Co., Dunedin, 1986.

Melling, Gerald, *Positively Architecture!*, Square One Press, Dunedin, 1985.

Mitchell, David and Chaplin, Gillian, *The Elegant Shed: New Zealand Architecture since 1945*, Oxford University Press, Auckland, 1984.

Modern Homes of New Zealanders by Architects of Standing, Keyes, Mann & Co., Auckland, 1917.

Morrison, Robin, *Images of a House*, Alister Taylor, Martinborough, 1978.

O'Neill, Daniel, *Sir Edwin Lutyens' Country Houses*, Lund Humphries, London, 1980.

Oliver, W. H. (ed.), *The Oxford History of New Zealand*, Clarendon Press, Oxford / Oxford University Press, Wellington, 1981.

Papadaki, Stamo, *The Work of Oscar Niemeyer*, Reinhold, New York, 1950.

Peters, Richard C., 'William Wurster: An Architect of Houses', in Sally Woodbridge (ed.), *Bay Area Houses*, Oxford University Press, New York, 1976.

Phillipps, W. J., *Carved Maori Houses of the Western and Northern Areas of New Zealand*. Dominion Museum / Government Printer, Wellington, 1955.

Pierson, William H., Jnr, *American Builders and their Architects: The Colonial and Neo-classical Styles*, Doubleday, New York, 1970.

schke, E. A., *Ein Leben mit Architektur*, Löcker, Vienna, 1989.

Plischke, E. A., *Design and Living*, Army Education Welfare Service, Wellington, 1947.

Plischke, E. A., *Vom Menschlichen im Neuen Bauen*, Verlag Kurt Wedl, Vienna, 1969.

Porter, Frances (ed.), *Historic Buildings of New Zealand: North Island*, Cassell, Auckland, 1979.

Porter, Frances (ed.), *Historic Buildings of New Zealand: South Island*, Methuen, Auckland, 1983.

Richards, J. M. (ed.), *New Buildings in the Commonwealth*, Architectural Press, London, 1961.

Richardson, Margaret, *Architects of the Arts and Crafts Movement*, Trefoil Books, London, 1983.

Rockel, Ian, *Taking the Waters: Early Spas in New Zealand*, Government Printer, Wellington, 1986.

Ross, R. M., *Melanesians at Mission Bay: A History of the Melanesian Mission in Auckland*, New Zealand Historic Places Trust, Wellington, 1983.

Saint, Andrew, *Richard Norman Shaw*, Yale University Press, New Haven, 1976.

Salmond, Arthur L., *First Church of Otago and How It Got There*, Otago Heritage Books, Dunedin, 1983.

Salmond, Jeremy, *Old New Zealand Houses 1800–1940*, Reed Methuen, Auckland, 1986.

Service, Alistair, *Edwardian Architecture*, Thames & Hudson, London, 1977.

Shaw, George Bernard, *What I Said in New Zealand*, Commercial Print, Wellington, 1934.

Shaw, Peter and Hallett, Peter, *Art Deco Napier: Styles of the Thirties*, Reed Methuen, Auckland, 1987.

Simpson, Duncan, *C. F. A. Voysey: An Architect of Originality*, Lund Humphries, London, 1979.

Spade, Rupert, *Oscar Niemeyer*, Thames & Hudson, London, 1971.

Spade, Rupert, *Richard Neutra*, Thames & Hudson, London, 1971.

Stacpoole, John, *Colonial Architecture in New Zealand*, A. H. and A. W. Reed, Wellington, 1976.

Stacpoole, John, *The Houses of the Merchant Princes*, Centre for the Study of Auckland History and Society, University of Auckland, Auckland, 1981.

Stacpoole, John, *William Mason: The First Colonial Architect*, Auckland University Press / Oxford University Press, Auckland, 1971.

Stacpoole, John, and Beaven, Peter, *Architecture 1820–1970*, A. H. & A. W Reed, Wellington, 1972.

Stern, Robert A. M., *American Architecture after Modernism*, A. & U., Tokyo, 1981.

Stern, Robert A. M., *Modern Classicism*, Thames & Hudson, London, 1988.

Taylor, Alan and Taylor, W. A., *The Maori Builds*, Whitcombe & Tombs, Wellington, 1966.

Taylor, Nancy M. (ed.), *The Journal of Ensign Best*, Turnbull Library Monograph, Wellington, 1966.

Te Rangi Hiroa, *The Coming of the Maori*, Maori Purposes Fund Board / Whitcombe & Tombs, Wellington, 1949.

Tempel, Egon, *New Finnish Architecture*, Architectural Press, London, 1968.

Troup, Gordon, *George Troup: Architect and Engineer*, Dunmore Press, Palmerston North, 1982.

Turner, Gwenda, *Akaroa*, John McIndoe, Dunedin, 1977.

Twombly, Robert, *Louis Sullivan: His Life and Work*, University of Chicago Press, Chicago, 1986.

Voysey, C. F. A., *Individuality*, Element Books, Shaftesbury, 1986.

Walden, Russell, *Voices of Silence: New Zealand's Chapel of Futuna*, Victoria University Press, Wellington, 1987.

Weitze, Karen, *California's Mission Revival*, Hennessey & Ingalls, Santa Monica, 1984.

Jeanie White, *Town Acre 456, Nelson, New Zealand: Historic South Street 1851–1988*, A.C.S. Publications, Nelson, 1988.

Wilson, John (ed.), *From the Beginning: The Archaeology of the Maori*, Penguin Books / New Zealand Historic Places Trust, Auckland, 1987.

Journal and Magazine Articles

Behalova, Vera J., 'Beitrag zu einer Kulka-Forschung: Der Raumplan', in *Bauforum 43*, 1974.

Blaschke, Anthony, 'Einhorn House', in *Architecture NZ*, September/October 1989.

Linzey, Mike, 'Te Kooti: Architect', in *Architecture NZ*, September/October 1989.

Lochhead, Ian J., 'St Bartholomew's Church, Kaiapoi: A Mountfort-Selwyn Connection', in *Bulletin of New Zealand Art History 9*, 1985.

Lochhead, Ian J., 'The Arts and Crafts Houses of Basil Hooper', in *Art New Zealand 39*, Winter 1985.

Mané, Jonathan, 'A Colonial Architect Re-discovered: William Barnett Armson 1834–1883', in *Historic Places in New Zealand 3*, 1983.

Mané, Jonathan, 'The Architecture of Ivey Hall', in *Historic Places in New Zealand 24*, 1989.

Mané-Wheoki, Jonathan, 'Selwyn Gothic: The Formative Years', in *Art New Zealand 54*, Autumn 1990.

Meyer, Bob, 'Ngaio's Railway Houses', in *Historic Places in New Zealand 22*, September 1988.

Prickett, Nigel, 'An Archaeologist's Guide to the Maori Dwelling', in *New Zealand Journal of Archaeology 4*, 1982.

Prickett, Nigel, 'Prehistoric Occupation in the Moikau Valley', in *National Museum Bulletin 21*, 1979.

Shaw, Peter, 'Louis Hay: Napier and the Chicago School', in *Art New Zealand 33*, Summer 1984.

Shaw, Peter, 'The Good Cottage: The Housebooks of J. W. Chapman-Taylor', in *Art New Zealand 36*, Spring 1985.

Shaw, Peter, 'The War Memorials of W. H. Gummer', in *Art New Zealand 48*, Spring 1988.

A SELECT BIBLIOGRAPHY

University Theses and Research Reports

Troup, Christina, 'The Vernon Brown Papers: An Inventory', *in Auckland University Library Bibliographical Bulletin 10*, 1978.

Armitage, J. H., 'Maori Housing in New Zealand: An Historical Overview', University of Auckland B.Arch. thesis, 1986.

Austin, M. R., 'Polynesian Architecture in New Zealand', University of Auckland Ph.D. thesis, 1976.

Bennett, P. R., 'Tudor Towers: The Rotorua Baths', Victoria University of Wellington B.Arch. thesis, 1984.

Bruce, M. A. 'R. A. Lippincott: The American Connection', University of Auckland B.Arch thesis, 1985.

Burns, G. F., 'Frederick de Jersey Clere: Man, Churchman, Architect', University of Auckland B.Arch. research report, 1979.

Cameron, C. F., 'State Housing and State Sponsored Housing in New Zealand', University of Auckland B.Arch thesis, 1970.

Cattell, J. W. F., 'Domestic Architecture in Christchurch and District 1850–1938', University of Canterbury M.A. thesis, 1981.

Davis, K. J., 'A Liberal Turn of Mind: The Architectural Work of Gordon Wilson, 1936–1959', Victoria University of Wellington research report (1987).

Esau, R. J., 'Helmore and Cotterill: The Formative Years', University of Canterbury M.A. thesis, 1988.

Falconer, S., 'J. T. Mair and First Presbyterian Church', University of Auckland School of Architecture research essay, 1986.

Fitzpatrick, W., 'Government Sponsored Housing in New Zealand', University of Auckland B.Arch. thesis, 1987.

Gardyne, S., 'Transition in Architectural Style from Beaux Arts to Bauhaus: Wellington Between the Wars', Victoria University of Wellington B.Arch. research report, 1981.

Goldie, C., 'Henry Kulka 1900–1971', University of Auckland B.Arch. thesis, 1986.

Hamilton, P., 'Francis Petre 1847–1918: An Investigation into New Zealand Architectural Biography', University of Auckland M.A. thesis, 1986.

Hogan, T., 'New Zealand Churches since 1900', Victoria University of Wellington research report, 1987.

King, M., 'A Place to Stand: A History of Turangawaewae Marae', University of Waikato Centre for Maori Studies research paper, 1981.

Lochhead, I. J., 'The Early Works of Benjamin Woolfield Mountfort 1850–1865', University of Auckland M.A. thesis, 1975.

Maingay, L. St J., 'Cecil Walter Wood, Architect of the Free Tradition', University of Auckland B.Arch. thesis, 1964.

Matthews, A. J., 'E. A. Plischke: The Connection between Theory and Form', University of Auckland B.Arch. thesis, 1986.

McCarthy, M., 'The Haughton Partnership: An Historical Overview', Victoria University of Wellington B.Arch. research report, 1982.

McCarthy, P. C., 'Victorian Oamaru: The Architecture of Forrester and Lemon', University of Canterbury M.A. thesis, 1986.

McCoy, E. J., 'Victorian Architecture in Otago', University of Auckland B.Arch. thesis, 1964.

Niven, S., 'J. W. Chapman-Taylor', University of Auckland B. Arch. thesis, 1974.

Pitts, G. L., 'A Review and Assessment of the Work of Group Architects', University of Auckland B.Arch. building report, 1968.

Richardson, P., 'An Architect of Empire: The Government Buildings of John Campbell in New Zealand', University of Canterbury M.A. thesis, 1988.

Shanahan, K. J., 'The Work of W. H. Gummer Architect' University of Auckland B.Arch thesis, 1983.

Starey, D., 'Auckland Architecture in the Twenties', University of Auckland B.Arch thesis, 1979.

Tyler, L., 'The Architecture of E. A. Plischke in New Zealand 1939–1962', University of Canterbury M.A. thesis, 1986.

Ullrich, R., 'The Railway House in Context', University of Auckland B.Arch. thesis, 1981.

Ussher, R. M., 'The Modern Movement in Canterbury: The Architecture of Paul Pascoe', University of Canterbery M.A. thesis, 1986.

Vorstermans, R. L. J., 'William Gray Young, Architect', Victoria University of Wellington B.Arch. research report, 1982.

Walden, H. R., 'New Zealand Anglican Church Architecture 1814–1963', University of Auckland M.Arch. thesis, 1964.

Wilkinson, A. K., 'The Neil House and the New Zealand Dream', University of Auckland B.Arch. thesis, 1981.

Wilson, P., 'The Architecture of Samuel Charles Farr 1827–1918', University of Canterbury M.A. thesis, 1982.

Wynn-Williams, D., 'The Basilicas of F. W. Petre', University of Canterbury M.A. thesis, 1983.

INDEX OF BUILDINGS
AND ARCHITECTS

214